J. G. STROSSMAYER

BISHOP
J. G. STROSSMAYER

NEW LIGHT ON VATICAN I

By Ivo Sivrić, o.f.m.

ZIRAL — Rome
Franciscan Herald Press — Chicago
1975

This book first published in 1975 by
ZIRAL – Zajednica Izdanja Ranjeni Labud, Via Merulana 124/B,
00185 Roma, Italy
and
Franciscan Herald Press, 1434 West 51st Street,
Chicago, Illinois 60609, U.S.A.

Bishop J. G. Strossmayer: New Light on Vatican I, by Ivo Sivrić
Copyright © 1975 by ZIRAL and Franciscan Herald Press, Chicago, Ill.
Library of Congress Cataloging in Publication Data:

SIVRIĆ, Ivo: *Bishop J. G. Strossmayer; ney light on Vatican I.*
1. Strossmayer, Josip Juraj, Bp., 1815-1905.
2. Vatican Council, 1869-1870.
BX4705.S845S56   262'.5'20924 [B]   73-22014
ISBN 0-8199-0491-0

Cum permissu superiorum

PREFACE

Originally the purpose of this work was simpy to present the role of Bishop Joseph G. Strossmayer at the First Vatican Council of 1869-1870. However, even the most superficial reading of his speeches convinced me that such a presentation of him would be incomplete: neither doing justice to Strossmayer nor to the reader. The Bishop's picture would be blurred. It was this conviction which induced me to broaden my research into the man and his activities.

Why had Strossmayer and a significant minority of bishops at Vatican I fought against the dogmatization of papal infallibility? My already intense curiosity on this point was further enhanced when almost by an accident I came across some recently published documents concerning Vatican I. At the same time, I learned of the existence of more unpublished documents. The realization, that in all this documentation the person of Bishop J. G. Strossmayer occupies one of the most prominent places, encouraged me still more to concentrate on him.

Papal infallibility was debated intensely at Vatican I and one can hardly believe that the opposing bishops — with such great minds as Strossmayer's in their midst — were unable to offer anything more than sheer resistance. Hopefully this presentation of J. G. Strossmayer, his theology, ecclesiology, and ecumenism can serve as an insight into the thoughts of his colleagues since he was one of the leaders of this group.

This investigation also attempts to indicate the atmosphere and spirit in which this Ecumenical Council was conducted. Also, this work might point out that the Fathers of the Minority at Vatican I were in many respects not far from the spirit of Vatican II. What I wish to imply is that whatever is newly grown in the Church must have been planted in the past. Therefore, my attempt has been to expose these wholesome seeds to students of ecclesiology.

I honestly admit that there are weaknesses in this work. I can only say that when an author must synthesize the wide scope of

4

Strossmayer's activities and sift out so huge a documentation much depends on his taste and on his approach to the problem. The last Chapter « Role in Europe » and part of Chapter II may be considered by some to be out of range of the proposed work, but in my judgment Strossmayer's role in European politics cannot be precluded from his other activities and ideas.

Finally, I would like to express my particular gratitude to Rev. Marion Habig, OFM of Chicago and Prof. Ann Paton, Ph. D. of Geneva College, Beaver Falls, Pa. for having prepared the manuscript for the publisher. My thanks are also due to Prof. Jerome Jareb, Ph. D. of St. Francis College, Loretto, Pa. who placed his library at my disposal and also to Mrs. Ginger Bupp of Farrell, Pa, and Rev. Charles Zovko, OFM of Rankin, Pa. who typed the entire manuscript. I also wish to express my gratitude to Mrs. Patricia M. Coghlan, Prof. Thomas Minder of Pittsburgh University and Rev. Romano S. Almagno, OFM for their interest and encouragement. I am especially indebted to my editors, Rev. Mark Hegener, OFM of Franciscan Herald Press and Rev. Vincent D. Lasić, OFM of ZIRAL.

Ivo Sivrić, OFM

ABBREVIATIONS

AJA : Arhiv Jugoslavenske Akademije, Zagreb, Croatia (Yugoslavia).

BS : *Bogoslovska Smotra,* Zagreb.

CBSG : The Correspondence between Bishop Strossmayer and Lord W. Gladstone, Appendix XVII to *The Southern Slav Question and the Habsburg Monarchy,* by R. W. SETON-WATSON (New York, 1969 - first published in 1911).

CP : CEPELIĆ M.-PAVIĆ M., *Josip Juraj Strossmayer biskup bosansko-djakovački i sriemski, god. 1850-1900,* Zagreb, 1900-1904.

GBBS : *Glasnik biskupija bosanske i srijemske* I-XXXII (1873-1905.

JAZU : Jugoslavenska Akademija Znanosti i Umjetnosti, Zagreb.

JJS-DK : *Josip Juraj Strossmayer - Dokumenti i Korespondencija,* vol. I, edited by Dr. FERDO ŠIŠIĆ, Zagreb, 1933.

KRS : *Korespondencija Rački-Strossmayer,* edited by Dr. FERDO ŠIŠIĆ, voll. IV: 1st in 1928, 2nd in 1929, 3rd in 1930, and 4th in 1931, Zagreb.

MANSI : J. D. MANSI, *Sacrorum Conciliorum nova et amplissima collectio.*

RSCV : Rapporti sul Concilio Vaticano (Lettere particolari di Emerico Tkalac al Ministro degli Esteri E. Visconti Venosta - Roma, 20 gennaio - 25 luglio 1870. Archivio Storico del ministero degli Esteri, Archivio di Gabineto (1861-1870), Concilio Ecumenico, Busta 209 fasc. 4), Roma, 1966, in *Imbro I. Tkalac e L'Italia,* by ANGELO TAMBORRA.

TS : TADE SMIČIKLAS, *Nacrt života i djela biskupa J. J. Strossmayera i izabrani njegovi spisi: govori, rasprave i okružnice,* Zagreb, 1906.

I

A NEW APPRAISAL

At the very outset of this work we feel compelled to state that we experienced a great deal of apprehension when we undertook the task of writing about Joseph George Strossmayer (1815-1905), Bishop of Djakovo, Croatia (Yugoslavia). The reasons were many and various. Undoubtedly, his diversified activities and involments in so many undertakings of an ecclesiastical, political, national, and international character were a factor. Also the huge amount of documentation on his life and enterprises contributed enormously to this state of mind.

It is practically impossible to depict Strossmayer or his contributions in relation to any particular cause without presenting his basic ideas on man, human conscience and freedom, and his ideas on theology in general and ecclesiology in particular. All these concepts overlap and are so intertwined that they are found in every sphere of his activities.

We reached this conclusion after laboriously having read, analyzed, and studied his correspondence, writings, addresses, and speeches. The lack of knowledge of these essential matters most likely accounts for the fact that he was quite often misjudged and misinterpreted by historians. He was and still is equally misunderstood in his native land, and not seldom contradictory statements were and are being made about him and his ideas. It appears that he is still a controversial figure, viewed either as a dreamer without much sense for realities or as a visionary with ideas which his contemporaries were unable to comprehend or did not believe were feasible.

Our primary aim, therefore, is to present Strossmayer's ideas in perspective so as to derive a truer picture of the man. These will include his ideas on the mission of the Church, the reformation of the Church's central government, the reorganization of Europe, the liberation of southeast Europe from the Turks, and so on.

All these undertakings and involvements of his cannot be correctly understood without having a lucid notion of his fundamental ideas which brought him into confrontation with the Austrian Emperor Francis Joseph, Pope Pius IX, and the Roman Curia. His theological and ecclesiological concepts will illustrate best his deep involvement in ecumenism and his endeavors to bring about the reunion of the Eastern and Western Churches.

Though a great deal has been written about Strossmayer, some of it true and interesting, no one has so far succeeded in encompassing his whole personality and no one has attempted to make a synthesis of his ideas and activities. It is true that several books and numbers of articles have been written on his life and activities, but unfortunately these works are nothing else but collections of his letters, addresses, and various documents.[1]

---

[1] The book of Cepelić-Pavić is the most comprehensive work on the life and activities of Joseph G. Strossmayer. It convers well over 900 pages of small print. Undoubtedly, it contains many good observations, but it seems to us that its main aim was to reproduce as many as possible of Strossmayer's speeches, pastoral letters, memoranda and writings. They had no pretensions of bringing him out of his native land nor did they care to present his ideas. It is difficult for any reader – if not impossible – to obtain any picture of the Bishop from this book.

Two or three years later anoter book was written by Tade Smičiklas, *Nacrt života i djela biskupa J. J. Strossmayera i izabrani njegovi spisi: govori, rasprave i okružnice* (Sketch of the Life and Work of Bishop J. G. Strossmayer and Selected Documents: Speeches, Studies, and Encyclicals) (Zagreb, Dionička Tiskara, 1906). Tade Smičiklas (a historian ex professo) admits that he was unable to do justice either to the life or the activities of the Bishop since he had only a short time to write the book, *ibid*, pp. VII-VIII. Smičiklas' taste in choosing Strossmayer's best addresses and pastoral letters was excellent.

The third book was written by Dr. Andrew Spiletak, *Strossmayer i pape* (Strossmayer and the Popes) (Djakovo, Biskupijska Tiskara, 1934). This book is a compilation of his own articles published in *Glasnik Biskupije Djakovačke* (Herald of the Diocese of Djakovo) during the years of 1925 and 1929. Spiletak, in this book, presents Strossmayer documents to prove the Bishop's loyalty to the Holy See. It is repetitious and shares the same faults of Cepelić-Pavić's work. Furthermore, Spiletak omits the documents which might « incriminate » Strossmayer in the eyes of the public.

The articles on Strossmayer written by A. Spiletak and published in *Bogoslovska Smotra* (Ephemerides Theologicae), Zagreb, are: « Was Bishop Strossmayer a Liberal Catholic and the Promoter of the Movement for Establishing a National Church?, » XIX (1931), 313-338. « Strossmayer o slobodnim zidarima » (Strossmayer and the Freemasons), XX (1932), 295-324. « Strossmayerova okružnica uoči Vatikanskog Sabora » (Strossmayer's En-

Dr. Andrew Spiletak, a great admirer of Bishop Strossmayer, author of *Strossmayer i Pape* (Strossmayer and the Popes) – published in 1934 –, and a writer of many articles pertaining to the Bishop affirmed in 1937 it was a national disgrace that as yet no scientific book on the life and works of Strossmyer had been written.[2] In 1959 Dr. Vladimir Košćak, an historian and the greatest expert on Strossmayer's legacy, stated that « the reason why no biography of Joseph G. Strossmayer which was complete and based on scientific research, not to mention a critical appraisal of the role he had played, is found not only in the wealth and the variety of his ideas and activities but more so in the fact that the documents

---

cyclical on the Eve of the Vatican Council), XXII (1934), 1-19. The latter is merely the text of Strossmayer's encyclical which was never published previously in any form except that the clergy received a copy of it. (No commentary of any kind is given). « Biskup Strossmayer i pravoslavlje » (Bishop J. G. Strossmayer and the Eastern Church), XXIII (1935), 121-144 and 277-304. « Tres casus a J. Strossmayer propositi et soluti » (Three Cases of Conscience Proposed by J. Strossmayer), XXII (1934), 283-294 and 377-383, and XXIII (1935), 81-92. « Neke i danas savremene misli Strossmayerove » (Some of Strossmayer's Ideas Are Still Actual), XXV (1937), 161-172 and 291-300. (All these articles of Dr. Spiletak are more or less a collecton of documents).

Other articles are: TADE SMIČIKLAS, « Misli i djela biskupa Strossmayera » (The ideas and the Achievements of Bishop Strossmayer), in *Rad Jugoslavenske Akademije znanosti i umjetnosti*, Zagreb, LXXXIX (1888), 210-224. Dr. RATSKO DRLJIĆ, O.F.M., « Iz korespondencije biskupa Strossmayera sa bogoslovnim zborom bosanskih franjevaca u Pečuhu » (Bishop's Straossmayer's correspondence with the Bosnian Franciscan Students of Theology in Pecuh), in *Franjevački Vjesnik*, Sarajevo, 1937, nos. VI-VIII. Dr. BERISLAV GAVRANOVIĆ, O.F.M., « Dr. Josip Juraj Strossmayer », in *Dobri Pastir* (Edited and published by the Bosnian Franciscans) *ibid.*, XVII-XVIII (1968), Sarajevo 160-202.

We would like to add to this list of studies, the articles which were written on Strossmayer outside his native land: BEN HURST, « The Founder of Modern Croatia,» in *The Catholic World*, New York, vol. 81 (1905), 773-789. This author gives some insight into the life and achievements of the Bishop, although there are several historical and geographical inaccuracies. LOUIS LEGER, « L'Eveque Strossmayer,» in *La Nouvelle Revue*, Paris 1908, 215-224. (L. Leger was a personal friend of the Bishop and was financially supported by him in publishing some books and articles on the South Slavs. His writings are accurate.) ANTE KADIĆ, « Vladimir Soloviev and Bishop Strossmayer,» in *The American Slavic and East European Review*, vol. 20 (1961), 163-188. ANDRIAN FORTESCUE, « A Slav Bishop: Joseph George Strossmayer », in *The Dublin Review*, 164 (1918), 234-257. (This article is greatly lacking in historical accuracy and is somewhat hostile to the Bishop, but it has its merits in appraising the Bishop's achievements. A. Fortescue follows the writings of Emilie de Laveley and Louis Leger).

[2] *BS*, XXV, 161.

are not easly accessible...»³ These two observations show that our apprehension and uneasiness regarding this undertaking are not unfounded.

We do not, however, share completely the opinion of Košćak since most of the documents have already been published by Dr. Ferdo Šišić in five huge volumes and many documents are contained also in the works of Spiletak and in the voluminous work by Cepelić and Pavić. However, we must grant to Košćak that at least some documents are not available as yet. Furthermore, the two « Pro memoria » of Strossmayer to the Italian goverment on how to solve the Roman Question were unknown until recently.⁴

In spite of these sporadic lacunae, we believe it is possible to reconstruct Strossmayer's ideas and plans from the massive documentation published by Šišić and others. Of course, we did not neglect the Archives of the Yugoslav Academy of Zagreb. If we add Strossmayer's « Lenten Pastoral Letters, » published in the Diocesan Review GBBS, scholars will have enough material at their disposal to form clearer opinion and ideas; for, his pastoral letters, in many instances, deal actually with all the human and religious problems of the Strossmayer epoch. Every year since 1873 when this review was founded, Strossmayer published his pastoral letters, some of them very lengthy.⁵ Some letters are published also by Šišić.

It is well to mention at this point that the Bishop is repetitious in many instances. This is evident not solely in his pastoral letters, but also in his correspondence with Lord Gladstone, in his « Pro

---

³ Dr. VLADIMIR Košćak, « Strossmayerova ostavština u arhivu JAZU » (Strossmayer's Legacy in the Archives of the Yugoslav Academy of Science and Art), in *Historijski Zbornik* (Historical Review), published by the Croatian Historical Society, Zagreb, XI-XII (1958-1959), 351.

⁴ Cf. ANGELO TAMBORRA, *Imbro I. Tkalac e l'Italia* (Roma, Istituto per la Storia del Risorgimento Italiano, 1966), 148-150.

⁵ For the present we would like to mention only a few encyclicals of his: Pastoral letter of 1877 « On the Unity of the Church » in GBBS, V (no. 3), 17-33. (We quote this pastoral from TADE SMIČIKLAS, *op. cit.,* pp. 377-404). « On Sts. Cyril and Methodius » in GBBS, IX (1881), 25-53. (We quote this letter from T. SMIČIKLAS, *op cit.,* pp. 405-443). Two other encyclicals of Strossmayer are: « The Reply (of Bishop Strossmayer) to the Three Greek Orthodox Bishops », dated Febr. 4, 1882, quoted by F. Šišić, KRS, IV, 461-513; and his Lenten letter of January 18, 1891, which is actually Strossmayer's « apologia pro vita sua », quoter also by F. Šišić, KRS, IV, 221-253, except the first part which Šišić did not reprint, and it is quoted by GBBS.

memoria » to the Russian government, and in other documents. Some of his ideas expounded at the First Vatican Council are found in other writings as well.

Šišić did not limit himself merely to the Archives of the Yugoslav Academy of Science and Art. He did research work also in others: the Archives of the University of Budapest; the Archives of the Cultural and Religious Ministry in Vienna; the Archives of the University of Vienna; the Archives of the Augustineum (now known by the name of the College of St. Thomas) in Vienna; the Archives of the Bosnian-Herzegovinian Museum in Sarajevo; the Archives of the Brlić Family in Slavonski Brod, Croatia; the Diocesan Archives of Djakovo, Croatia; the Archives of the Archdiocese of Zagreb; the State Archives of Zagreb; the Archives of the University of Zagreb, Croatia; and the Archives of the parish and high school (gymnasium) of Osijek, Croatia.[6]

It was Šišić's principal goal to publish all the available documents written either by Strossmayer or to him by other distinguished personalities. Undoubtedly, the most valuable and the most comprehensive documents are the correspondence between Strossmayer and his intimate friend Dr. Francis Rački.[7] In this voluminous cor-

---

[6] Cf. the Preface, written by Dr. Ferdo Šišić, in JJS-DK, I, pp. V-VI.

[7] Canon Dr. Francis Rački was born in Fužine, Croatia (Yugoslavia), on Nov. 25, 1828. High school and college studies he pursued in Rijeka and Varaždin and theology in Senj and at the University of Vienna, Austria, where he obtained a doctorate in sacred theology in 1855. He was ordained to the priesthood on August 15, 1852. Thereafter he taught for a while in Senj and in 1857 he was sent to St. Jerome in Rome where he remained until 1861. In 1863 he was appointed the school supervisor for Croatia, and he served in this capacity until he was elected president of the Yugoslav Academy of Science and Art. He died on Febr. 13, 1894.

He wrote a great number of books and studies and others were edited by him. All his works treat historical subjects. F. Rački is considered the father of modern Croatian historiography. Cf. CHARLES and BARBARA JELA-VICH, The Balkans in Transition (Berkeley and Los Angeles, University of California Press, 1963), p. 427; cf. also VLADIMIR ZAGORSKI, François Rački et la Renaissance Scientifique and Politique de la Croatie (1828-1894), Paris, 1909.

In 1884 he went to Russia and spent some time in Moscow and St. Petersburg (Leningrad) where he met Vladimir Soloviev. While in St. Petersburg he discussed with Soloviev and other leading Russian intellectuals the possibility of the reunion between the Eastern and Western Churches. Through this encounter of Rački with Soloviev the Bishop of Djakovo was brought into direct contract with this Russian theologian and philosopher. Cf. KRS, III, 141-143. Rački was nominated an honorary faculty member of the University of Moscow,

respondence of four volumes they withheld no secrets from each other, whether they dealt with the Church or the political and cultural matters of the time. This documentation strikingly reveals the character and the sentiments of the Bishop and his innermost reactions to various personalities and incidents.[8]

The correspondence between Canon Dr. Nicholas Voršak and Strossmayer, and Voršak and Dr. Rački, which is also found in the Archives of the Yugoslav Academy of Zagreb,[9] is of great interest and significance particularly for Voršak's native land Croatia and southeast Europe, though in some respects it also deals with problems of general historical interest. It is regrettable that these documents have been totally neglected and have never been published; for, they offer a deep insight into some incidents of the First Vatican Council, into the life and case of Fr. Augustine Theiner, and also into the negotiations between the Vatican and the Russian government and between the Holy See and Montenegro. In quite

---

which, of course, he regarded to be of « a special significance to him since a Greek Orthodox University was honoring a Catholic priest ». Cf. KRS, IV, 438 (Rački's letter to Strossmayer, dated Dec. 27, 1885).

Strossmayer and Rački were very close to each other; they shared the same ecclesiastical, political, cultural, and other views. As far as the execution of their ideas and plans is concerned this is expressed best by Strossmayer himself in his letter on the occasion of the death of F. Rački: « Whatever I have done for the glory of God, for faith, country, and nation, the same thing was done in his noble soul and heart. More than a half of everything that I have accomplished was initiated by him, and it is his merit and glory. It can be said rightly that he was one of the purest, most honest, most learned, and most meritorious priests that the Church of Croatia and the Croatian State ever had... The late (Rački), since his early years, was my special brother and friend who was to me, in the trials and difficulties of my life, the greatest support and consolation. I can sincerely say that with him I have lost a good half of my soul and heart, and it is more so in these days when I am too old and weak... ». Cf. GBBS, XXII (1894), no. 4), 49-50, and KRS, IV, 415). A list of the works of the F. Rački is found in the article written by Velimir Deželić, « Franjo Rački », in Znameniti i zaslužni Hrvati (Zagreb, 1925), p. 223.

[8] F. Šišić in his Preface to the four volumes of KRS writes: « Whatever I considered in the correspondence of Strossmayer to be of any significance I did not omit. For this reason I did not overlook the letters of Strossmayer in which he manifests his reactions to persons and events or in whatever manner he expresses his intimate feelings with bitter words even though they are of a subjective character. Had I done otherwise, I would violate the sincerety of the psychological structure of this man and consequently the importance of his historical appearance ». (KRS, I, pp. VIII-IX).

[9] Dr. Nicholas Voršak was born in Ilok, Croatia, 1833. He was a mem-

a few instances Voršak acted on behalf of Strossmayer, and this brought him into friendly contacts with some leading European personalities.

The Bishop also wrote a few articles in « Vienac » (The Wreath).[10] He published his « Opis puta u Njemačkoj » (Travelog in Germany) in twelve issues of GBBS.[11] His other studies will be mentioned later on.

His doctoral dissertation, presented at the University of Vienna, Austria, was « De schismate Graecorum cum praecipuo ad Primatum Romani Pontificis respectu » (The Oriental Schism Especially in Regard to the Primacy of the Roman Pontiff). He also wrote another dissertation — intended principally for discussions in major seminaries and monasteries — under the title « Dissertatio historico-dogmatica de doctrina Ecclesiae Christianae trium primorum saeculorum » (A Historical-Dogmatical Dissertation about the Doctrine on the Structure of the Christian Church during the First Three centuries). Undoubtedly it is a great loss that neither of these works have been preserved.[12]

If these two dissertations were available, the former would help us greatly to know his early ideas on the problem of the Eastern Church, and from the latter we would learn his thinking concerning the concept of the Church of God in the first three centuries. In all probability these two missing documents would furnish us or rather they would show us how the seed of ecumenism and his unquenchable desire for the reunion of the Churches had grown in his mind and how they gradually had developed and had assumed such tremendous proportions that they almost reached

---

ber of the Chapter of St. Jerome in Rome for many years and died on February 4, 1880 in Rome.

[10] Cf. CP, op. cit., p. 229« The Bishop also wrote in *Pozor* and in *Katolički List* of Zagreb. Cf. TS, op. cit., p. VIII. Tade Smičiklas has two studies written by the Bishop: « Opis katedrale u Djakovu » (The Description of the Cathedral of Djakovo), pp. 203-246, and « Slike u katedrali u Djakovu » (The Paintings in the Cathedral of Djakovo), pp. 246-303. Both studies were originally published in GBBS. We quote from Tade Smičiklas.

[11] GBBS, vol. III, Nos. 2-14 (1875). This serialized article was reprinted by Tade Smičiklas in op. cit., pp. 322-359. A list of Strossmayer's Lenten letters is found in CP, pp. 231-233. Ho wrote an encyclical each year except 1873, 1904, and 1905. Cf. A. SPILETAK, *Strossmayer ı Pape*, pp. 323-324.

[12] Cf. JJS-DK, p. 19.

the stage of obsession. It would be entirely wrong to suppose that he believed the renunion of the Eastern and Western Churches would take place during his life. In this regard he always considered himself to be a « tool » in the hands of Providence to pave the way for reunification.[13]

Pursuant to Strossmayer's interest in this area, we would like to mention one of his plans. Had the plan been realized, most likely many of the difficulties in presenting Strossmayer's general ideas would have been eliminated, especially in regard to his ecclesiology; and, one would not have to go over hundreds and hundreds of pages to compile a synthesis of his ideas. For some time after Vatican I Strossmayer kept toying with the idea of writing a book on the structure of the Church (her internationalization in particular) and her mission in the modern world. It appears that this concept had taken deep roots, and it was apparent in a debate with three Orthodox bishops in 1882. In reply to them, he wrote a letter which was in reality a medium sized book;[14] and in this document, among other things, he elaborated the subject of the structure of the Chuch.

Almost a year later he comunicated his thoughts to Rački,[15] but the latter did not react at all. He remained silent without offering any suggestion or encouragement to the Bishop. We have been puzzled by this attitude of Rački, even more so in view of the fact that he was a « Guardian Angel » and advisor to the Bishop, and one who was wont to encourage him in his undertakings. The only reasonable solution that we can offer is Rački's prudent fear for the future and the illustrious name of the Bishop who had wanted to write a book in Latin for the benefit of the educated Catholic public in Europe. Rački being well acquainted with Strossmayer's thoughts also knew that the Church was not yet ready and ripe to accept all of his ideas, and that undoubtedly his book would create a tremendous commotion because of his popularity in Europe and because of his bold as well as anti-Italian proposals. We do not maintain it was a too far

---

[13] KRS, IV, 470. He always advocated that every priest must work for the reunion of the Churches.
[14] KRS, IV, 461-513.
[15] KRS, III, 55. (The letter was dated February 7, 1883).

fetched assumption in the mind of Rački that such a book could have been the end of the Bishop since there would have been a good possibility that the Roman Curia would force him into retirement.

It would not be fair to the person of the Bishop if we overlooked what he himself said about his writings after Prof. Kosta Vojnović initiated a campaign of sorts among the Bishop's friends to publish his writings and addresses. When this news reached him, he wrote the following to Rački on February 26, 1888:

« I do not know if it is opportune at the present time, while I am still alive, to be preoccupied with the trifles which I have written until now. This is the idea of Dr. Kosta Vojnović. I am not sure if it is well planned. As far as the Vatican Council is concerned, I doubt if it would be wise to write anything about it now. Since I am an impatient and sickly man, whatever I have written was written hastily. My annotations on the Vatican Council are tried up together. I will hand them over to you, and once I am gone, then you can do with them whatever you please. I will also give you all my correspondence and all the significant documents which are pertinent to our times and to the present happenings. I have been a pratical man rather than a writer. This reminds me – now at the end of my life – of the words of our Ban Jelačić who, during his illness, very often used to point to his heart. 'Hardly anyone,' he said, 'will ever know how much love this heart had for my people'. Poor Ban! The sad end of his life will remain an eternal monument to his love for his nation.[16] Thanks to God! Servus inutilis sum; quod facere debui, feci (I am an unuseful servant; whatever I had to do, I did). »[17]

Since we shall also deal in this book with the orations of the Bishop, delivered at Vatican I, it should be of some significance at least to know how be used to prepare his speeches. This will also illustrate how he approached serious problems. « If notes of my speeches – delivered at the Vatican Council – are in your hands », he

---

[16] KRS, III, 357. Strossmayer exclaims « Poor Ban » because at that time everybody maintained that Ban Jelačić had been poisoned by the Emperor's court, poison being gradually served to him by his cook.

[17] KRS, III, p. 356.

writes to Rački on July 5, 1889, « then I must say, and I will eventually make it clearer, that in these notes only my principal ideas
are indicated. According to my old custom I would study a subject
thoroughly, and then I would improvise a speech. Every commenta-
tor must keep this in mind.» [18] To the Fathers at te Council he said
the very same thing. [19]

Most probably the best description of Strossmayer's speech de-
livery has been given by the French statesman and historian and the
Bishop's acquaitance Emile Ollivier: « (Strossmayer) is above all
else an incomparable orator. He ignores a written speech. After
having condensed his ideas in a few notes, he abandons himself to
the good luck of improvisation. He is sometimes audacious, at times
resilient, occasionally ample, sometimes stirring, not seldom spiritual, but fascinating all the time ».[20]

By now it becomes obvious that Strossmayer's role in the First
Vatican Council will be thoroughly discussed. It is unnecessary and
superfluous to discuss the First Vatican Council in detail; for many
standard books have been written about it.[21] Strossmayer's role in

------

[18]   KRS, IV, p. 82.
[19]   « The extremely important problem (papal infallibility) which is under
the discussion, I have studied conscienciously and with great diligence for
a long time; here I am before God and this holy Council to bring out candidly
and humbly the results of my research as my weakness permits; I beg you to
consider me worthy of your patience and benevolence. Since I am accustomed
to speak extemporaneously – and I cannot do it otherwise – it sometimes
happens unintentionally to me that I pronounce a word which is not so correct
and which is less worthy of your attention and listening. But believe me I am
always willing to take back such a word, and it is pleasing to me if you
correct me ». Cf. MANSI 52, 391-392.
[20]   EMILE OLLIVIER, L'Eglise et l'Etat au Concil du Vatican (Paris, 1877),
II, 12. In another place he says that « Strossmayer is universally admired »
(ibid., p. 40 and 41).
[21]   C. BUTLER, The Vatican Council 1869-1870, based on Bishop Ullathorne's Letters (Westminster, Maryland, The Newman Press, 1962). JAMES
HENNESEY, S. J., The First Council of Vatican: The American Experience
(New York, Herder and Herder, 1963). EMILE OLLIVIER, op. cit., (2 vols.).
R. AUBERT, Le Pontificat de Pie IX (Paris, Bloud et Gay, 1952) which is volume 21 of the Histoire de L'Eglise, edited by A. Fliche and V. Martin. THEO-
DORE GRANDERATH, S. J., Geschichte des vatikanischen Conzils, 3 vols. which
appeared in 1903-1906. JOHN ACTON, « The Vatican Council », in The North
British Review, XIV (1870), 183-229, and also in The History of Freedom
and Other Essays, by JOHN E. E. D. ACTON (London, Macmillan and Co., Limited, St. Martin's St., 1907), pp. 492-550. (We shall quote this article from

Vatican I has been mentioned by Cepelić-Pavić,[22] Andrew Spiletak,[23] and Janko Oberški;[24] but their works are incomplete and totally one-sided due to the lack of availability of documentation when they were written. This becomes even more evident in view of the reports of their countrymen Nicholas Voršak and Imbro I. Tkalac who happened to be close collaborators of the Bishop during Vatican I, and who spoke his mind. Neither Cepelić-Pavić nor Spiletak nor Oberški have made any attempt to sort out or synthesize Strossmayer's ideas. In one place Oberški even accuses him of being heterodox and a Gallican.[25]

Whether or not the presentation of Strossmayer's ideas and plans

---

the latter work). HURERT JEDIN, *Ecumenical Councils of the Catholic Church* translation by Ernest Graf, O. S. B. (New York, Herder and Herder, 1960), pp. 187-239. PHILIP HUGHES, *The Church in Crisis: A History of the General Councils 325-1870* (Garden City, N. Y., Hanover House, a division of Doubleday and Co., Inc., 1961), 333-365. E. E. HALES, *The Catholic Church in the Modern World* (A Survey from the French Revolution to the Present) (Garden City, N. Y., Image Books, a division of Doubleday and Co., Inc., 1961) pp. 133-147. NEWMAN C. EBERHARDT, *A Summary of Catholic History*, II (Modern History) (St. Louis and London, B. Herder Book Co., 1962), pp. 534-542. JAMES Cardinal GIBBONS, *A Retrospect of Fifty Years*, I (Baltimore, John Murphy Co., 1916). E. AMMAN, « Vatican », in *Dictionnaire de Theologie Catholique*, XV, cols 2536-2585, etc.

[22] CP, *op. cit.*, pp. 283-297. The chapter « Strossmayer at the Vatican Council » was written around 1900. Cepelić and Pavić had at hand only some of Strossmayer's notes.

[23] Dr. SPILETAK, *Biskup J .J. Strossmayer u Vatikanskon Saboru-Govori, predstavke, prosvjedi* (Bishop J. G. Strossmayer in the Vatican Council – His Orations, Proposals, and the Notes of Protest) (Hrvatska Bogoslovska Akademija, vol. XII, Zagreb, 1929). This work is a translation of Strossmayer's orations delivered in the Vatican Council, and it has some footnotes. Its greatest merit is the fact that it assembles the notes of protest submitted by the opposing bishops either to the presidents of the Council or to the Pontiff.

[24] Dr. J. OBERŠKI, *Strossmayerovi govori na Vatikanskom Koncilu* (Zagreb, 1929). This is another translation of Strossmayer's speeches in the Vatican Council. It has some annotations which are not of much value. Another work of Dr. J. OBERŠKI, *Hrvati prema nepogrješivosti papinoj prigodom Vatikanskog Sabora 1869-1870* (Croatians and Papal Infallibility in the Vatican Council of 1868-1870) (Križevci, 1921). Oberški bases his research on T. Granderath's work and shares his views in regard to Bishop Strossmayer which are in many instances biased. Dr. ANTE KADIĆ, *Bishop Strossmayer and the First Vatican Council*, a reprint by Cambridge University Press from *The Slavonic and East European Review* (pp. 382-409). This study is the interpretation of Strossmayer's speeches, delivered in the Council, accompanied with some incidents.

[25] J. OBERŠKI, *Strossmayerovi govori...*, *op. cit.*, p. 120, note 19.

will offer us a new insight and approach to the First Vatican Council we leave to the reader to decide. At any rate this was in the back of our mind when we entered upon our task. Our attempt is warranted by the books and articles written on Vatican I which made it look as though the bishops gathered at this ecumenical council solely to fight over the dogma of papal infallibility and as if the bishops of the minority or, as we sometimes refer to them, the opposition had nothing constructive to offer but their objections. Undoubtedly, the bishops of the opposition were regarded and appraised only in the perspective of infallibility, and their proposals were almost completely consigned to oblivion.

It is hardly possible to do justice to the opposing bishops whithout evaluating their ideas and suggestions and considering what they would have contributed to the general welfare of the Church; or, phrasing it another way, would their suggestions – provided, of course, that they had been accepted by the Council – have enriched the Church and spared her and Europe of many evils.

In our judgement a work comprising the main ideas of the opposing bishops at Vatican I and comparing them with the present situation would be of great interest. Many excellent ideas were sown by them, but they were lost because of the feuding over infallibility and also because a great number of bishops of the majority were still entrenched in the medieval mentality and unsusceptible to modern ideas.

The presentation of Strossmayer's ideas deserves special consideration since he held the most discordant position among those bishops who opposed infallibility. Even the opinion of so distinguished a Pontiff as Pius XI can hardly discredit entirely the wholesomeness of their ideas and proposals, especially if they are viewed in the light of our era. One can hardly accept at face value the assertion that the Church has taken the best possible approach at all times to every problem and the best possible course in every age.

We, of course, refer to the letter of November 5, 1924, addressed to Msgr. Louis Petit, editor of the Acts of Vatican I, in which Pius XI lauded Vatican I and Pope Pius IX for taking care not only of the needs of that epoch but also of the future necessities of the Church. Pius XI most certainly had in mind the dogmatization of the primacy and infallibility of the Roman Pontiff when he referred to the opposing bishops (he called them « censores ») as being of a « short vision » (acies imbecilla).[26]

Almost as a rule, Catholic historians and theologians, in their writings concerning Vatican I and particulary in reference to the bishops of the opposition have tried to discover the ecclesiological concepts which made them oppose the dogma of papal infallibility at this Council. It is evident that the expression « inopportunism » – which is occasionally ascribed to them – is somewhat relegated into the background, and the opinion that they were influenced by Gallicanism, Febronianism, and Episcopalianism, and acted as followers of various German theological schools is given a prominent place.[27]

While these scholars put the emphasis on these movements within the Catholic Church of France, Germany, and the Austrian Empire, Lord Acton – a layman and one of the principal actors among the opposing bishops at Vatican I – places rather a strong stress on liberalism which was so prevalent among them.[28] If anyone was competent enough to appraise the position of these prelates and their motivation, it was certainly this British scholar who was so intimately connected with the leading forces of the opposition. In our estimation we should be more attentive to what he said of Vatican I because no one can doubt his versatility and competence in historical and theological matters. Unfortunately, Acton's study, *The Vatican Council*, is almost totally neglected by Catholic historians and as well theologians. In all probability the reason for this reality was the fact that Acton was a layman and was involved in

---

[26] MRNSI, vol. 51. The photostatic copy of the Pontiff's letter is found at the very beginning of this volume which is not paged.

[27] R. AUBERT, *op. cit.*, pp. 327-329 and passim; PHILIP HUGHES, *op. cit.*, pp. 337-338; DOM C. BUTLER, *op. cit.*, pp. 27-28, 85-108 and passim; E. E., Y. HALES, *op. cit.*, p. 136; N. C. EBERHARDT, *op. cit.*, II, 534-542; (This author even places emphasis on the « Expediency of (the) definition – of papal infallibility – at this particular time » *ibid.*, 534). Cfr. HANS KÜNG, *The Council, Reform and Reunion* (Garden City, N. Y., Doubleday and Co., Inc., 1962), pp. 147-183; HANS KÜNG, *Structures of the Church* (New York, Edinburgh, Toronto, Thomas Nelson and Sons, 1964), pp. 352-377; HANS KÜNG, *The Church* (New York, Sheed and Ward, 1967), pp. 11-12 and passim. For more literature see D. Butler, R. Aubert, and Hans Küng.

[28] « The only bishops whose position made them capable of resisting were Germans and the French; and all that Rome would have to contend with

the controversy at Vatican I; and consequently his competence and objectivity have been questioned.

Many historians seem to have a problem with Strossmayer and do not know where to place him in regard to both ecclesiology and motivation at Vatican I. It would appear that a lack of knowledge concerning his background and theological ideas induced many a writer to attribute all sorts of things to him. It may have been that his ideas and designs and their projection into the future of the Catholic Church confounded some of his contemporaries.[29]

For an unknown reason one writer states that he was « l'agitateur »,[30] that he was constantly in a state of excitement at the Council,[31] that he ran away from the bishops of Hungary to the French opposing bishops on account of political reasons and his dislike for the Hungarians.[32] Another affirms that the Bishops of Djakovo was not only « one of the best speakers in the Council but also one of the most temperamental... »[33] One attributes to him the use of « blunt language, » and says he was an « ardent Croatian nationalist. »[35] Another refers to him as a « storm centre of the Council. »[35]

From the report of his intimate friend, Lord Acton, to I. Döllinger, it appears that Strossmayer was not afraid of a « head-on confrontation » with the entire Council.[36] Other characterizations of

---

was the modern liberalism and decrepit Gallicanism of France; and the science of Germany. The Gallican school was nearly extinct; it had no footing in other countries, and it was odious essentially to the liberals. The most serious minds of the liberal party were conscious that Rome was as dangerous to ecclesiastical liberty as Paris » (History of Freedom..., op. cit., p. 534).

[29] Compte Begouen, « Souvenirs sur Mgr. Strossmayer », in Spomen-Spis prigodom otkrivenja spomenika hrvatskom rodoljubu i narodnom prosvjetitelju (J. G. Strossmayer), edited by Dr. S. Rittig and R. Maixner (Zagreb, 1926), p. 72.

[30] R. Aubert, op. cit., p. 327.

[31] Ibid., p. 340.

[32] Ibid., p. 327, note 1. Here we must remark that Strossmayer never mixed religious issues with those of politics. This was his « credo ». The leading Hungarian bishops, Mgrs. John Simor and Louis Haynald, were at least good acquaintances, if not good friends, with whom he did not only use to share dinners but did some favors to them.

[33] Hubert Jedin, op. cit., p. 205.

[34] N. C. Eberhardt, op. cit., p. 540.

[35] D. C. Butler, op. cit., p. 111.

[36] « I now believe, and so does Strossmayer, that they should let it come

Strossmayer have corroborated this appraisal. Mgr. Ullathorne, Bishop of Birmingham (Great Britain) described him in these words: « Strossmayer sits just under me (in assembly hall in St. Peter's Basilica). He is a warm-hearted affectionate Croat, as eloquent as he is warm, but apt to get over vehement. We have taken quite an affection for each other ».[37] James Cardinal Gibbons considered him « the most eloquent prelate of the Council », but does not attribute to him the power of convincing the hearers.[38] The Secretary of State Cardinal Antonelli was a little more specific. After having heard Strossmayer's third oration, he said confidentially to Odo Russell that Strossmayer « is the world's greatest orator, even though I do no share all his views ». [39]

In spite of their critical remarks, some eye-witnesses and historians, however did give him credit for defending the Protestant Christians and for his audacious attacks on the schema which made unfounded accusations against Protestants; and the result was that the Schema in this particular instance was revised and considerably toned down.[40] Regarding Strossmayer's proposals and ideas at Vatican I, it was generally acknowledged that he fought valiantly for the decentralization and internationalization of the central government of the Catholic Church.[41]

We should mention another reason why we regard it necessary to discuss Strossmayer. First of all in relation to the opposition at the Council. Pope Pius IX did not consider Cardinal Rauscher, nor Cardinal Schwarzenberg, nor Bishop Felix Dupanloup, nor Archbishop Darboy of Paris, but Strossmayer as the « ring-leader » (capo-setta), and referred to him as the « enemy of God and his own

---

to a head once more, and then, in the Council itself, denounce the Council » (quoted by JAMES HENNESEY, op. cit., p. 178).

[37] Cited by D. C. BUTLER, op. cit., p. 112.

[38] JAMES Cardinal GIBBONS, op. cit., I, pp. 26-27.

[39] AJA, XII A 810/24 (Voršak's report from Rome to F. Rački, February 9, 1870).

[40] Cf. D. C. BUTLER, op. cit., p. 240; H. JEDIN, op. cit., pp. 206-207; and J. HENNESEY, op. cit., pp. 146-147. Strossmayer next day was supported by Mgr. Richard V. Whelan, Bishop of Wheeling, W. Virginia, on the issue of the Protestants.

[41] R. AUBERT, op. cit., p. 410.

personal anemy».[42] It is interesting that Lord Odo Russell,[43] the British accredited envoy in Rome, and Imbro Tkalac,[44] the unaccredited envoy of the Italian government of Florence, in their dispatches to their respective governments shared the opinion of Pius IX. According to these brilliant reporters of Vatican I, Strossmayer was a leader of the opposition for at least the first two months of the Council.

Most likely no one perceived the significance of Strossmayer's designs and dynamic ideas concerning the Church of God as did Mgr. Felix Dupanloup of Orleans, when he told the Bishop of Djakovo, after he had delivered his first speech in the assembly of December 30, 1869, that « the Council has discovered its man ».[45]

---

[42] These words were addressed to Filipo M. Cardinal Guidi when Pius IX reprimanded him for proposing some modifications in the dogma of papal infallibility: « Vous êtes tous corrompus, s'écrie le Pape, ces protestants allemands et américains vous ont inspiré des idées hérétique, et vous particulièrement, vous conférez ce misérable 'capo-setta' croate qui est l'ennemi de Dieu et le mien » (Tkalac's dispatch to Venosta, June 21, 1870, RSCV, pp. 313-314). This conversation was communicated to Tkalac either by Strossmayer or by one of Cardinal friends.

[43] Lord Russell in his dispatch of January 26, 1870, informs the British government: « The speech of Bishop Strossmayer of Bosnia is universally said to have proved him to be the best Latinist, the ablest debater, and the greatest orator of the Council. He spoke in favour of special privileges of the episcopacy and against the spirit of centralization of the Vatican, Bishop Strossmayer may now be considered the leader of the opposition ». Cf. Noel Blakinston, The Roman Question - Extracts from the Despatches of Odo Russell from Rome 1858-1870 (London, Chapman and Hall, 37 Essex St. WC2, 1962), p. 386.

[44] Imbro I. Tkalac, in his report of January 25, 1870, informs Venosta on the proceedings of the Council: « The event of the day is still the speech of Strossmayer, delivered, in the yesterday's session. Last night in the close circles nothing was talked about but this speech of his; today it is publicy discussed with admiration and enthusiasm, and it is considered to be fantastic in theological matters. The most distinguished French, German, and American bishops came to congratulate him; he was embraced, flattered, called the St. Ambrose and St. John Chrysostom of the Council. And it looks as if the history of the Vatican Council will be essentially the history of Mgr. Strossmayer » (RSCV, pp. 233-234). Tkalac, in another dispatch of January 20, 1870, wrote that Strossmayer « has placed himself at the head of the opposition » (ibid., p. 227).

[45] AJA, XII A 810/22 (Voršak's report from Rome to F. Rački, Dec. 31, 1869). Voršak himself heard Bishop Dupanloup say this to Strossmayer in the assembly hall in St. Peter's Basilica. The bishop of Orleans highly complemented Strossmayer by telling him: « Vous êtes le premier orateur du Council » (ibid.).

This oration by Strossmayer was a topic of daily conversation in the city of Rome among the bishops and statesmen convened there from all over Europe and lasted for quite a few days afterwards. It almost seemed that the Council would move in the direction of his bold proposals according to Tkalac's and Voršak's reports. A great number of the prelates and the representatives of various governments came to Strossmayer's quarters to congratulate him.[46]

In relating some other observations on Strossmayer, an attempt is also made to extricate him from the politics and the ecclesiastical and cultural activities of his native land (Croatia) and of the Austrio-Hungarian Empire in which he was deeply involved for quite some time. However, the mention of some occurences and activities of interest to the general public for the sake of presenting Strossmayer in a clearer light is understandably necessary.

Of special interest is the opinion of the Roman Curia concerning Strossmayer and his activities. It should be kept in mind that only a very small number of the leading personalities of the Roman Court were acquainted with his undertakings; or if there were more, they did not perceive their significance.

The entire matter is best illustrated in the interview between the Secretary of State Cardinal Rampolla and Fr. Politeo. This interview took place in Rome on October 1, 1888, and was published in the newspaper « Narod » (The People) in Split, Dalmatia. Rampolla said to Fr. Politeo: « Strossmayer as a bishop, man, and patriot is so great that he should be of concern to entire Europe, and he really is that as we are able to see ». The Secretary of State admitted that there were some individuals in te immediate vicinity of the Pope (Leo XIII) who do not care for Strossmayer. After having stated his, Rampolla continued: « A man of Strossmayer's intellect, heart, and achievements cannot produce the same effect in every man; it simply is not in the nature of man. When Strossmayer greeted the Pope the last time on behalf of the Croatian pilgrims, there were some around the Pontiff who were simply elated by the river of his sublime oratory, and with a smile or a gesture they ma-

---

[46] Cf. AJA, XII A 810/22. Voršak's report and Tkalac's dispatch have a greaty similarity.

nifested their joy to the Bishop; but there were some here and there who did not do this. The memory of the Vatican Council, at which Strossmayer had become famous all over the world, had much to do with it.

« If you understand by the Vatican only the Pope (Leo XIII), » continued Rampolla, « then I would like to assure you, Fr. Politeo, that His Holiness is not only attached to Strossmayer but he loves him, and has unlimited confidence in him, and the Pontiff treasures and appreciates his activities and aims... » At the end of this long interview Rampolla added: « I am sorry that Strossmayer is not young any more, and that we do not have five or six Strossmayers ».[47]

---

[47]   KRS, IV, 36-39. It was a well known fact that the Bishop of Djakovo was a very close friend of Pope Leo XIII. Cf. D. C. BUTLER, *op. cit.,* p. 112.

II

LIFE AND CHARACTER

A famous British historian and expert on the southeast European problems wrote the following about J. G. Strossmayer: « The well-known Italian statesman Marco Minghetti once assured the Belgian publicist Emile de Laveley that he had the opportunity of observing at close quarters almost all the eminent men of his time. 'There are only two', he added, 'who gave the impression of belonging to another species than ourselves. These two were Bismarck and Strossmayer'. The man of whom this high attribute was spoken arrested the attention of Western Europe on the memorable occasion of the Vatican Council ».[1]

Strossmayer's great-grandfather Paul came originally from Linz, Austria, and served in the capacity of a sergeant in the city of Osijek (Croatia) where he fell in love with Helen Benaković, married her, and settled for good in that city. At the very beginning, their Croatian neighbors called them and their family « Paulovi » or « Paulović ». As a matter of fact, some Paul's children, as the baptismal register shows, were named « Paulović ». Strossmayer occasionally expressed his regret that he had not been named either « Paulović » or « Pavlović ».[2]

He was born on February 4, 1815, in Osijek, and was baptized on the very same day. Very probably, he was one of twin bro-

---

[1] R. W. SETON-WATSON, *The Southern Slav Question and the Habsburg Monarchy* (New York, Howard Ferting, 1969. – First published by Constable and Co. Ltd. in 1911), p. 118. It is interesting to note that Otto von Bismarck tried to arrange a metting with Strossmayer through the Consul Schlozer, but it was never held. Cf. TS, p. 120.

[2] The documents of Strossmayer's family tree are graphically presented by Dr. F. Šišić. Cr. JJS-DK, I, 451-456. On these pages excerpts from various parish registers are found.

thers.[3] He attended the high school (gymnasium) conducted by the Franciscan Fathers in the same city (1826-1831), and college (philosophy) in the major seminary of Djakovo (1831-1833). From 1833 to 1837 he pursued theological studies at the University of Budapest (then called Pest), Hungary. His ordination to the priesthood took place on February 16, 1838, after a postponement, partly due to his illness and partly to the lack of the canonical age.

His first priestly assignment was in the parish in Petrovaradin, where he served in the capacity of an assistant pastor from 1838-1840. Just at the time when a disagreement arose between the pastor and young Strossmayer, the latter received a letter from Emperor Ferdinand informing him that he had been accepted in the Augustineum in Vienna, Austria, to continue higher theological studies. He remained in Vienna from December, 1840, to August, 1842, when he obtained a doctorate in sacred theology. From then until September, 1847, we find him teaching in the major seminary of Djakovo.

On July 16, 1847, Dr I. Feigerle, court pastor and principal director of the Augustineum, asked Mgr. Kuković, Bishop of Djakovo, to relieve J. G. Strossmayer of his duties in his diocese so he could become a court chaplain and one of the three directors in the Augustineum. Bishop Kuković gave his approval on July 22, 1847, and Emperor Ferdinand's confirmation followed on August 27 in the same year. Strossmayer served in this capacity until he was appointed Bishop of Djakovo on November 18, 1849, after Bishop Kuković had resigned. He was consecrated a bishop on September 8, 1850, and solemny installed in Djakovo on September 29, 1850.[4] After he had served as bishop of Djakovo for almost fiftyfive years he died on April 10, 1905.

---

[3] F. Šišić claims that he was unable to locate the baptismal record of the Bishop's twin brother who died several months after his birth. Cf. JJS-DK, I, 3, note 1. Cepelić and Pavić (*op. cit.,* p. 27) and Tade Smičiklas (*op. cit.,* 3) claim that he had a twin brother. Strossmayer himself affirms in his letter to Utješenović that his twin brother died and « perhaps the good Lord has showered his brother's blessings upon me ». Cf. V. Košćak, « Strossmayerova ostavština u arhivu JAZU », *Historijski Zbornik,* XI-XII (1958-1959), 375, note 16. Most probably Strossamayer himself had told his friends Cepelić, Pavić, and Smičiklas about his twin brother.

[4] The transcripts of all the available documents are found in JJS-DK, I, 1-40.

While he was a theology student he distinguished himself in all branches of theology, especially in dogmatic theology. Before reaching the age of twenty years he had already earned a Ph. D. at the University of Budapest.[5] Besides being a brilliant student, as is apparent from all the records, he developed what was an inborn talent and became an unparalled debater and dialectician.

Once when he happened to be taking examinations, the president of the examining board, astonished by his ability in dialectics, exclaimed: « Strossmayer will be either the chief heretic of the nineteenth century or the main pillar of the Catholic Church ».[6] This trait of his never left him. It came to the fore in his debates in the Expanded Council of the Emperor in Vienna (of which he was a member); it manifested itself in the Diet of Zagreb; and it became strikingly evident in the debates in the First Vatican Council. During a Council session Mgr. Ginoulhiac, Bishop of Grenoble, told Strossmayer: « You simply terrify me with your pitiless logic ».[7] On another occasion when he disagreed with Mgr. Ketteler and his proposal, he challenged Ketteler to enter into debate with him on the involved issue. After an hour of discussion in front of other bishops, Ketteler shook Strossmayer's hand and said: « I will vote against (my own proposal) ».[8]

Undoubtedly, he was cognizant of his prowess in the art of discussion; and for this reason, during Vatican I, he kept insisting, whenever an opportunity offered itself, on having genuine debates on various matters. This also motivated him to suggest in one of the general assemblies that the Pontiff should attend the general assemblies so that he might see for himself the force and the value of the argumentation. This ability did not puff him up, nor did it induce him to humiliate anybody. His extraordinary respect for other people's convictions and opinions simply precluded him from becoming engaged in any of these human shortcomings. « Man, who is in search of truth », he wrote to the students and the faculty of

---

5 CP, p. 30.
6 *Ibid.*
7 ACTON, *Te History of Freedom,* p. 536.
8 RSCV, p. 328.

the University of Zagreb, « is also expected to steer his look to his opponents and their convictions. A proud man despises 'Ex professo' mankind and human traditions; he shuns the authority of God and every other authority, and of course he refutes the convictions and opinions of other people ».[9]

Before we attempt to offer a survey of Strossmayer's activities and involvements and before we place them in some sort of chronological order, we deem it necessary to point out some his personal characheristics and his basic ideas which have a direct bearing on his general outlook and on his personal formation. This, of course, will help us greatly to grasp better the significance of his historical role. His other fundamental ideas will be treated elsewhere.

Unfortunately, it must be said that his abilities and his dynamic and appealing personality arrested the attention of the foreigners more forcefully than that of his own compatriots. Eugene Perrot, a perpetual secretary of the Academy of Inscriptions in Paris, after having paid a visit to the Bishop in Djakovo in 1869, has this to say about him in his study, *Tour du Mond:*

« The Bishop is a man who is born to play the most important role if the circumstances are going to be in his favor. He is in possession of a lively, inquisitive, and lofty mind, but at the same time his soul is warm and compassionate; and nature has given him all this so that he can influence all those who come in contact with him: to win them to his side and to enrich them, to become an orator and a leader. In parlance he is eloquent without becoming emphatic and declamatory; everything is marvelously arranged for the presentation of his ideas: his gaze is glowing; his gestures are noble and vivacious; his voice is clear, resonant, and emphatic; his language is rich, firm, and full of delightful and colorful images. Once he is either in a church or in an assembly, he cannot but leave a tremendous effect ».[10]

---

[9]   TS, p. 308. (This address, under the title « Three Words to our University, » was originally published in GBBS in 1874, nos. 23-24, and in 1875, nos. 1-2, and was reproduced in its entirety by T. Smičiklas. We shall quote it from T. Smičiklas, TS.)

[10]   Quoted by Louis Leger, *loc. cit.,* p. 217.

In the eyes of the Italian historian Angelo Tamborra, « Stros-smayer is a man of exceptional religious, cultural, and intellectual stature »,[11] and another Italian writer characterizes him as « a Slav socialist who became a priest..., a genius who is more vivacious than mature..., more a revolutionary than a politician, more Croat than a bishop, more Slav than a Christian ».[12]

Perhaps, the best descriptive picture of the Bishop was given by his two friends: Tade Smičiklas, the Croatian historian, and Emile de Laveleye, a Belgian publicist. These two descriptions were written independently, but they are amazingly similar. We shall quote de Laveleye:

« Strossmayer appeard to me like a saint of the Middle Ages, such as fra Angelico painted on the walls of the cells of San Marco in Florence. His face was refined, thin, ascetic; his light hair, bru-shed back, surrounded his head like a halo; his grey eyes were clear, luminous, inspired. A sharp yet gentle flame beamed from them, the reflection of a great intellect and a noble heart. His speech is easy, glowing, full of imagery; but although he speaks French, Ger-man, Italian, and Latin, besides the Slav languages, with equal ease, none of these languages can furnish him with terms sufficiently expressive for the complete rendering of his thought, and so he uses them by turns. He takes from each the word, the epithet, he needs, or he even uses the synonyms that come from them all. It is when he finally arrives at Latin that his sentences flow with unequal breath and power. He says precisely what he thinks, without reti-cence, without diplomatic reserve, with the abandon of a child and the insight of genius. Entirely devoted to his country, desiring no-thing for himself, he fears no one here below; as he seeks only what he belives to be good, just and true, he has nothing to conceal ».[13]

However, it seems to us that the picture of the Bishop would be somewhat incomplete without adding the appraisal of his admi-rer, the British historian R. W. Seton-Watson, which at the same time furnishes a new insight into his political role. According to him,

---

[11] ANGELO TAMBORRA, *Imbro I. Tkalac e L'Italia*, p. 127.
[12] Quoted by A. TAMBORRA, *op cit.*, p. 128.
[13] R. W. SETON-WATSON, *op. cit.*, p. 128.

Strossmayer « as a politician... lacked balance and restraint, and was swayed by sentiment to an excessive degree. But as an intellectual and moral force, as the patron and inspirer of thought and culture, his influence upon Croatia and the Southern Slav world cannot be exaggerated. As Jelačić typifies the military prowess and loyalty of the Croat, so Strossmayer stands foi those qualities of faith and romantic idealism for which the best sons of the race have been distinguished ».[14]

This sober appraisal, given by a British historian, certainly should not be overlooked. It is regrettable that the writer did not have more documents, none except Strossmayer's correspondence with Lord W. Gladstone; for we maintain that he would have been able to shed more light on the complexity of the Bishop's personality.

Anyhow, it is evident from his letters to Rački that Strossmayei was impatient; they sometimes sound as if he was too passionate and unrestrained. His idealism went to extremes, and he sometimes exceeded the limits of his available time and energies. This holds particularly for his ecumenism and for his endeavors to bring about the reunification of the Churches and to obtain the cultural unity of the South Slav nations. From time to time he was cognizant of this tendency, for istance when he thanked F. Rački for toning down some of his letters.[15]

On the other hand, in some instances, it is evident that he made serious efforts to be realistic especially in his appraisals of the Russian Eastern Church and her position vis à vis the Russian government and also Russian politics. How much his constant stomach trouble and his occasional but intensive moods of depression, of which he wrote so often,[15] contributed to his state of mind we do not know for certain, but on the other hand we cannot disassociate the fact that he was « passionate » and « impatient » from such psychological factors. These traits remained with him until he died. His inner disposition – due partly to the heavy demands upon

---

14   *Ibid.*
15   KRS, I, 294.
16   *Ibid.,* pp. 47-48, and passim. Quite often he refers to these personal occurrences as « my miseries ».

his energies and time and partly most likely to his infrequent moods of depression – made him think of abandoning the arena of political, cultural, and church activities and of retiring to the island of Lokrum near Dubrovnik. Rački, of course, each time dissuaded him from taking such drastic steps.[17]

In other matters he grew and changed considerably as time went on; and this is particulary true in regard to his ambitions and aspirations. It is almost obvious that he was not content with working in a parish, nor with teaching in the major seminary of Djakovo, nor with teaching at the University of Vienna; he wanted to obtain a more important position which – to his mind – would be more suitable to his abilities.

When in October, 1840, he received a rescript from Emperor Ferdinand that he had been accepted in the Augustineum in Vienna, he told his bishop, Msgr. J. Kuković: « I want you to konw, Your Excellency, that I am going to be your successor ».[18] While he was teaching in Djakovo, he entered a contest to obtain a chair of dogmatic theology at the University of Budapest.[19] Most likely he would have gotten it, if it had not been for the fact that he was not Hungarian. At the same time he wrote to his personal friend, Dr. I. Feigerle, and asked him to obtain a position for him in the Augustineum in case he should fail to come into possession of a chair in the University of Budapest.[20] As we have already seen, Dr. Freigerle complied with Strossmayer's wish. Dr. J. Hausle, a court chaplain and one of the directors of the Augustineum, was also of help to him; and not a small part was played also by A. T. Brlić.

When Msgr. J. Kuković, bishop of Djakovo, on April 10, 1849, resigned due to his poor health, Strossmayer became extremely in-

---

[17] *Ibid.*, pp. 229-231.
[18] CP, p. 32. On the 8th of October, 1840, he noted in his diary that « Divine Providence has special plans for me », and that « I have to pray constantly and thank God for his graces ». The piece of paper, on which these words were written, is found in the Archives of the Yugoslav Academy of Zagreb (*ibid.*).
[19] See the letter of Mato Topalović (dated May 21, 1846) to Lj. Gaj, JJS-DK, I, 23-30; Strossmayer's letter (dated March 12, 1847) to Andrija T. Brlić, *ibid.*, pp. 30-31.
[20] *Ibid.*, p. 32, note 3.

terested in becoming bishop of Djakovo. There was no rival candidate for this post except perhaps Canon Stephen Mojses. It is apparent from the Bishop's correspondence with A. T. Brlić that he made use of all his connections and of persons of influence at the Austrian court to obtain the see of Djakovo. On one occasion he wrote to Brlić that « it would be a great loss to Slavonia, if I would not become the bishop of Djakovo ».[21] Persons of fame and influence, for instance, Ban J. Jelačić, Metel Ožegović, and secretary of Culture and Religion in the Austrian government Leo Thun, were behind him regardless of his age. He was thirty four years old at that time.[22]

When George Cardinal Haulik,[23] Archbishop of Zagreb, died on May 11, 1869, there was a strong movement among the clergy and the faithful of Zagreb favoring the transfer of Strossmayer from Djakovo to Zagreb.[24] After he had learned about the situation in Zagreb, the Bishop actually begged F. Rački to use his influence on the clergy to restrain them from requesting his appointment to the archbishopric of Zagreb.

For a host of reasons he wanted to remain in Djakovo. He was almost on the border of Bosnia and Serbia, and here he was better able to exercise his influence upon the Catholic population. He had started many things in Djakovo and wanted to see them finished. He was also afraid that, once he would be romoved from Djakovo, the Hungarians might impose their man on this diocese. He therefore expressed his gratitude that « divine Providence has arranged

---

[21]   *Ibid.*, pp. 33-34.
[22]   All the pertinent rescripts are found in JJS-DK, I, 40-46.
[23]   George Cardinal Haulik (born April 20, 1788 and died May 11, 1869) was a Slovak. In spite of his relatively great achievements in the diocese of Zagreb, he never was popular either among the clergy or the faithful. In 1848 there was even a strong movement among Croatian politicians to force him into retirement. Not seldom Haulik was referred to as « retrogressive », since he did not want to participate either in the political or cultural movements. Strossmayer himself calls him « Retrogressive George ». Cf. JJS-DK, I, 46 and 47, note 17. Haulik's biography was never written. Cf. Dr. Anto Livajušić's article in *Danica* (weekly newspaper), Chicago, nos. 48-49, December 3 and 10, 1968. Cardinal Haulik had a great collection of paintings which he bequeathed to his relatives in Slovakia, and finally quite a number of them were purchased by Strossmayer. Cf. KRS, I, 77, 81, and passim.
[24]   KRS, I, 86-87.

things in such a way that I cannot become the archbishop of Zagreb ».[25]

He preferred to remain in the practically unknown small town of Djakovo, where he was able to work undisturbed and unostentatiously for the realization of his goals. It appears that neither promotions nor titles were of great concern to him. When Italian newspapers of March, 1878, unceasingly kept trumpeting that Pope Leo XIII would make Dupanloup and him cardinals, and he was notified about it by F. Rački, he simply answered the letter: « What a joke! With the great expenses I already have it would be a sin to spend money on such futile titles ».[26]

In view of his fame and friendly associations with practically all European leading personalities, one would expect that he would kept himself aloof from the common people; but, as we shall see during the course of his work, it was just the other way around. He was a genuine Christian humanitarian, full of compassion for the poor, the downtrodden and the oppressed; and these were his first consideration in all his undertakings. On quite a few occasions he declared that he was the happiest man when he was « in the company of his good people ». He used to look forward to the days when he had to go around to administer the sacrament of confirmation or to dedicate a church in some small village.[27]

Poor university students were particularly close to his heart. He asked F. Rački to search out such students so that he could pay their transportation and school expenses, especially the post-graduate students who happened to be taking final exams to obtain academic degrees.[28]

From his correspondence it appears that he spent fantastic sums of money on the students, regardless of their church affiliation.

Undoubtedly, he was a man of occasional impulsivness, but this trait never blinded him to such a degree that he would hate

---

[25] *Ibid.*, pp. 87-89. Strossmayer's letter to Rački (dated July 30, 1869). He refers here to the governments of Vienna and Budapest which were so hostile to him.
[26] KRS, II, 156.
[27] *Ibid.*, IV, 180, and passim.
[28] *Ibid.*, I, 27, and passim.

anybody or fail to show the Cristian charity which was a favorite subject of his writings and speeches. In spite of his numerous confrontations with various people, one can state that he preserved his global outlook and Christian composure in the most trying moments of his life.

Now and then he had reason enough to lose his patience and temper, not only with his opponents, but equally with his friends when they happened to go against his plans and ideas. In August, 1876, when he learned that his intimate friend Fr. Gregory Martić, O.F.M. of Sarajevo had signed the note of protest against Serbia, he became so angered that he called Martić all sorts of names, and he concluded by saying that Martić « had deserved to be hanged ».[29] However, their friendship was only temporarily disrupted; for, some time later the possibility of making Martić a member of the Yugoslav Accademy was a matter which the Bishop discussed with its president F. Rački.

Two prominent individuals in the public life of Croatia with whom the Bishop of Djakovo was unable to get along were: Dr. Ante Starčević (1823-1896), the leader of the Croatian Party of the Right, and Joseph Cardinal Mihalović (1814-1891), archbishop of Zagreb. We believe it was not Starčević's political program that disturbed the Bishop so much as his intransigence toward the Serbs. In reality, Starčević's ideology happened to be pan-Croatism as the answer to the pan-Serbianism which was so rampant in the second half of the nineteenth century. Since it was Strossmayer's ardent desire all along to bring the Serbs and the Croats closer and closer into a friendly – if not cordial – relationship with each other[30] and since both movements (pan-Croatism and pan-Serbianism), in his mind, were pernicious to the welfare of their respective nations, there is no wonder that he reacted so vehemently to this symptomatic

---

[29] Ibid., II, 40-41.
[30] « The best and most prominent men in Croatia, such as Bishop Strossmayer and the historian Rački, cultivated cordial relations with the princes of Serbia and Montenegro and did everything in their power for the further promotion of a brotherly union of both branches of the Southern Slavs, the Roman Catholics and the Greek Orthodox », writes Serbian historian VLADISLAV R. SAVIĆ, South-Eastern Europe: The Main Problem of the Present World Struggle (New York, Chicago, Toronto, London: Fleming H. Revel Co., 1918), p. 89.

national plight. In addition, Starčević exercised great influence upon the university youth of Zagreb, and actually more than half of them opted for his political program.[31] This fact greatly worried both Strossmayer and Rački. And the former called Starčević a « genuine stupid man, » regarded him « to be out of his mind » and a « crazy writer ».[32]

At moment it looked as though he was not so really against Starčević provided, of course, he (Starčević) « would be more moderate, more refined and more just », as he put it in one of his letter to Rački.[33] During the year 1883 he would not have been so critical of Starčević had the latter not responded so vigorously to the Serbian claims.[34] On June 20, 1893, Strossmayer and Starčević exchanged visits with each other;[35] and prior to these meetings, at the time that Starčević became seriously ill, the Bishop of Djakovo wrote to Rački « I do not know if one should wish him (Starčević) to be dead because he poisoned our youth ».[36]

In spite of his fluctuations and impulsiveness toward Starčević and his politics, one thing remains certain: namely, that his severe criticism was motivated principally by the fact that the cleavage between the Serbs and the Croats had become so acute that it appeared that all his plans of bringing the Southern Slavs to cooperate with one another had commenced to crumble.

At this place it is well to note that only the principality of Montenegro and its leaders had understood the situation and had acted accordingly. In this state of affairs he expected Croatian po-

---

[31] Cf. KRS, II, 219 and 226.

[32] *Ibid.*, II, 205; *ibid.*, III, 165 and 191.

[33] *Ibid.*, III, 18. « Starčević's impossible attitude on the Serb question », writes R. W. Seton-Watson, « was largely responsible for the succes of the Khuen regime and the complete subordination of Croatia to the Magyars; and it cannot be denied that by his policy of unrestrained fanaticism he showed himself lacking in the most essential qualities of statesmanship and played into the hands of his enemies. Yet it is impossible to withhold our admiration from his passionate consistency and rigid patriotic creed and still more impossible to doubt his sincerity and honour. So long as the name of Cato commands the respect of the modern world, so long must Croatia honour the memory of Anthony Starčević » (*op. cit.*, p. 109).

[34] KRS, III, 82 and 106.

[35] *Ibid.*, IV, 378-379.

[36] *Ibid.*, 361.

liticians and the univeristy youth to be more understanding and
more conciliatory than those of Serbia, and hence he was so saddened by the unpleassant incidents between the Croats and the Serbs
that his correspondence with F. Rački is full of lamentations. What
is more, he knew that both the Serbs and the Croats played into
the hands of their enemies, the Hungarians and the Austrians, according to the old motto « divide et impera ».

Joseph Cardinal Mihalović,[37] Archbishop of Zagreb, was a
thorn in Strossmayer's side. The views of Mihalović and his occu-
pancy of the see of Zagreb were unbearable to the Bishop, for both
were in direct conflict with his basic principles. First of all, he did
not want to mix politics and the Church, and secondly, he held
that the priestly vocation should not be used for political purposes.
Cardinal Mihalović violated both principles: he was an exponent
of the Hungarian government -- some sort of an agent – and he
employed his priesthood and position to work for the government
wich was inimical to the people whose spiritual shepherd he happened to be.[38]

Another target of his criticism was the Roman Curia. His basic
idea was always that the Church's central government had to be
internationlaized if the Church wished to fulfil her mission in the
world. He was also extremelv critical of the Italian prelates « who
run the Roman Curia, who have exhausted themselves, and who
have made the Church inadequate and relatively unfruitful ». What
is more, the Roman prelates, in his judgment, were nothing more
than mediocre persons who had brought the Church from the top
of a mountain into the valley where vision is totally obstructed.
This deplorable situation in Rome was strikingly evident to foreigners but not to the Roman prelates. Time and time again he said
that only a man (meaning a pope) of genius be capable to interna-
tionalize the Church. « When this will be realized », he writes to

---

[37] He was a son of a Hungarianized Croatian family. For a few years he
served as chaplain in the Hungarian army and then he became a pastor in the
suburbs of Temeswar.

[38] KRS, I, 234-235 and 143. Strossmayer was not officially invited to
Mihalović's funeral nor did he make any efforts to come. F. Rački tried to persuade him to attend the funeral but to no avail (cf. KRS, IV, 220 and passim).

F. Rački, « despite the hardness of heart, blindness, and selfcompla-
cency of the Roman prelates, only God knows. It seems to me,
what men do not want to do willingly, they will do unwillingly
when all sorts of evil and difficulties assail them ».[39]

We mention these incidents of Strossmayer's attitude toward
various personalities and institutions so that the reader can easily
see what kind of man he was. In spite of the many adversities and
disappointements that he had to face, it looks as though his idealism and hope for better days never abandoned him. His soul might
have screamed occasionally out of deep sorrow, but this sorrowful
outcry was accompanied by unconquerable hope, faith, and trust.

This is forcefully mirrored in the following incident. Undoubtedly, the most difficult years that his nation went through were the
years of the tyrannical rule in Croatia of Count Charles Khuen-
Herdervary (1883-1893), when even the railroad signs were written
in Hungarian, a language that the Croatian people did not understand. At his period he poured out his heart to his friend Lord
W. Gladstone, after having expressed his heartfelt congratulations
on the Liberal victory at the polls in Great Britain: « The Hungarians are a proud, egotistical, and in the highest degree tyrannical
race, and my poor nation is persecuted, oppresed, and ill-treated;
but I hope that the cause of the Slavs in general, restored by providential events to its natural destiny, to the adventage of universal
culture and liberty, will also deliver my own nation, which is worthy of all the favor of God and man ».[40]

1. - A Survey of Strossmayer's Chief Activities

At the very outset we would like to remind the reader that we
have no intention of displaying either a strict chronological order
of the events in which he actively participated or of dwelling on
certain activities of his for any lenght of time, for some of them
will be discussed later.

---

[39] KRS, III, 68-69; see also *ibid.*, IV, 1-2 and passim.
[40] CBSG, p. 444. This was the last letter that the Bishop wrote to Lord
Gladstone.

During the years which he spent at the universities of Budapest and Vienna, he was always engaged in various extracurricular
activities. It was customary in those times for university students
to be involved either in social or political movements, and Strossmayer was no exception. He used to associate in Budapest with
the Lutheran minister Jan Kollar and with the Croatian politicians
and students who happened to live in that city. The very same
thing appened during his student's years in Vienna, Austria.

When he was court chaplain and director of the Augustineum
in Vienna, his political and cultural activities assumed greater dimensions. At that time he had already became a center of attention
among the Croatian politicians in Vienna and Zagreb and also to
a great extent among the leading men of the Czechs, Poles, Slo-
vaks, and so on. Due to his enormous popularity among the Slav
groups he was called a « Slav Knight ». On account of his sermons
he was equally famous among non-Slav intellectuals and politicians
in Vienna.

In 1848 there was a widespread rumor in Vienna and Zagreb
that he might become bishop of Zagreb. This was the special desire of the Croatian politicians who were greatly dissatisfied with
Msgr Haulik, Bishop of Zagreb. Something else of much greater
significance had happaned in the assembly of April 25 of that
year in the Diet of Zagreb. In this assembly it was decided that
the celebacy of the Catholic clergy should be abolished in the territory of Croatia and that the vernacular (Old Slavonic language)
should be introduced in the Catholic liturgy of Croatia. The latter
was still in use in sereval dioceses of Dalmatia, and this perennial
Croatian privilege was to be extended to all other Croatian dioceses.
A special delegation was formed to present these proposals to the
Emperor of Austria for final approval. Croatian leaders not only
regarded young Strossmayer as liberal and amenable to modern
ideas, but they also thought of him as the clergyman best equipped
to put their decisions in practice.[41]

---

[41]   Cf. Andrija T. Brlić's letter to Lj. Gaj of May 5, 1848 in JJS-DK, I,
37-39. Note 2 on page 38 is extremely important. Cf. also the article of Dr.
Djuro Šurmin « Strossmayer u 1848 godini » (Strossmayer in the Year of 1848),
in *Strossmayer -- Koledar za God, 1909*, III (Zagreb, 1909), 30-32.

There is no doubt that Strossmayer was notified about these matters. Although we have no available documents telling us what stand he took on the issue of celibacy, there are great number about his advocacy of the vernacular, at least in the administration of the sacraments and in the breviary. Besides recognizing its practical value, he regarded the vernacular « as a means which God may use in the future to reunite the Yugoslav nations in faith... ».[42] In May, 1859, Strossmayer, in cooperation with F. Rački, wrote a « pro memoria » to Pope Pius IX in regard to the use of the vernacular; and the Pontiff issued an order to the Secretariat of State, that this topic « must be discussed without delay and as far as it is possible it ought to be put into practice ».[43] The purpose of this radical enterprise, undertaken by the Diet of Zagreb, is obvious: to strengthen Croatian national identity vis-à-vis the Austrians and Hungarians.

During the stormy events of the year 1848 Strossmayer did not remain neutral and inactive. The Hungarian revolt erupted on the territory of the Austrian Empire; and Ban J. Jelačić, who was chosen to crush it, did this with an army of 40,000 Serbs and Croats. Strossmayer was unofficially requested by the Archduke Francis Karl and his wife Sophia (parents of the then Archduke Francis Joseph, the later Emperor) to serve as an intermediary between the Emperor's court and Ban Jelačić. On August 30, 1848, he conveyed to Jelačić the wish of the Emperor's court, that he should attack Hungary instantly and that he should move toward Budapest as fast as possible.[44] Jelačić crossed the Drave River on September 11, 1848, and attacked Hungary, rallying the Croats and Serbs around him with his warlike motto, « What God brings and the hero's fate ». Strossmayer also supplied Jelačić with information concerning the rout it would be best to take; and a young Serb who served as his messenger, was killed while performing his duty.[45]

---

[42] KRS, I, 56. See also pp. 57-58 and passim.
[43] JJS-DK, I, 422-423.
[44] Ibid., p. 40.
[45] Cf. TS, p. 5. Strossmayer, later on, became dissatisfied with Ban Jelačić

When he became bishop of Djakovo or, to use his official title, « Bishop of Bosnia and Syrmium », and served as such for almost a decade, he did not intervene in politics, because during this period Bach's Absolutism was in full force in the Austrian Monarchy and there was no liberty of any sort. From 1850 to 1860 he devoted all his energies to the improvement of his diocese and the diocesan estates which were very large but poorly organized.[45] The following year, on September 23, 1851, he was appointed apostolic administrator of the Catholics who lived in the province of Serbia. This initiated his correspondence with the Prince Alexander Karadjordjević and his government, and he tried by all means to establish cordial relations with the Serbs.[47] Seven times he visited Serbia while he served in this capacity.

He was Bishop of Bosnia only in name. Bosnia was in the hands of the Ottoman Turks. As soon as he took possession of the bishopric of Djakovo he instantly came into contact with Fr. Andrew Kunjundžić, O.F.M., the Father Provincial of the Bosnian Franciscan Fathers. Franciscans were the only clergy in Bosnia. Strossmayer and Fr. Kujundžić reached an agreement that the Franciscan students of Bosnia should be brought to Djakovo to pursue their studies. This took a lot of effort on the part of the Bishop. He had to erect a house of studies for them; but first he had to obtain the approval of the Austrian king and of Rome, and this was not an easy task. By the end of 1852 the Franciscan students arrived in

---

since the latter did not use his power and prestige to secure the proper place for the Slavs in the Monarchy. He performed the ceremony of Jelačić marriage.

[46] Perhaps the best and the most succinct survey of Strossmayer's activities has been given by his secretary of many years, Fr. Milko Cepelić, in GBBS, XXVIII, no. 3 (1889), pp. 20-28, under the title « Josip Juraj Strossmayer ». It looks as though Dr. V. Košćak, *loc. cit.*, in *Historijski Zbornik*, XI-XII (1958-1959), 252-253 has followed Cepelić. (Košćak's survey is much shorter). It also seems that the British historian R. W. Seton-Watson was acquainted with Cepelić's article. Cf. *The Southern Slav Question*, pp. 118-128, Chapter VI, « Bishop Strossmayer and the Renaissance of Croatian Culture ». In Seton-Watson's work there are some inaccuracies which do not mar its value. For various reasons all of these authors do not mention many important works of the Bishop.

[47] Cf. JJS-DK, I, 184-189. On these pages and elsewhere, there are quite a few letters of Strossmayer and the princes of Serbia.

Djakovo.[48] The education of young Bosnian friars progressed very nicely, and the arrangement between the Bishop and the Franciscans remained undisturbed until 1875 when the University of Zagreb became a reality.

Prior to this, Strossmayer had championed the idea that all major seminaries in the historical territory of Croatia should be closed and all Croatian students of theology, Bosnia included, should be sent to the theological shool of Zagreb which was a part of the university. When the Hungarian government learned the plans of Strossmayer, they began to urge the Vatican to issue an order that the Franciscan students of Bosnia should instantly be removed from Djakovo and sent to Hungary. A fierce struggle between Strossmayer and the Hungarians ensued, and Strossmayer lost the case to the Hungarians. The Vatican and Cardinal Miha-lović, Archbishop of Zagreb, sided completely with the Hungarians, disregarding the interest of the Church in Bosnia. In June, 1876, the Bosnian Franciscan students had to leave the seminary of Dja-kovo and go to Hungary.[49] The Bishop, however, continued to communicate with the students of Bosnia.[50]

By 1860, immediatelly after the despotic rule and forceful Germanization of the Austrian Monarchy had ceased, the Bishop entered into domestic politics. In political circles, he was known because of his earlier articles, published in the Czech and Croatian newspapers during his sojourn in Vienna in 1848 and 1849, in which he had advocated the federation of nations in the Austrian Monarchy. His political program called for complete decentraliza-tion of the Austrian government, and the granting of freedom to each nation. These were the themes of his speeches and debates in Vienna, Budapest, and Zagreb. He was a staunch enemy of pro-vincialism, which Austria and Hungary favored according to the old proverb « divide et impera », and he wanted to see each nation united in its historical and ethnical territory. This stand brought him into conflict with the Emperor Francis Joseph in 1867, and

---

[48] *Ibid.*, 216-217, 240-241 and passim.
[49] KRS, I, 337-341 and passim.
[50] Cf. Dr. RASTKO DRLJIĆ, OFM, *loc. cit.*, in *Franjevački Vjesnik*.

as a result he had to go into exile in France for a few months. In accordance with his plan, he also urged the government to free the Southern Slavs from Turkish domination.

While he attempted to achieve these goals in political chambers, he knew deep in his heart they could not be fully and satisfactorily realized if the nations did not have their higher educational and scientific institutions. Therefore, his advocacy of national freedom ran parallel with his promotion of enlightment among the Southern Slavs. Naturally, the enlightment of a people – as he stressed so often – has to be in harmony with the principles of the gospel; in this way national independence and unity can be achieved. Through gradual growth each nation must find and develop its own course in elevating its people, not only in spiritual and intellectual but also in the material domain. All of this again must be guided by Christian ideas and based on Christian principles.

He had had these convictions already in 1848, when he discussed with his friend Thun, the Secretary of Culture and Religion in the Austrian government, the possibility of founding a university of Zagreb and a Law School in Osijek (Croatia).[51] In his letter of December 10, 1860, to Ban Sokčević the Bishop pledged the sum of 50.000 florins for the founding of the Yugoslav Academy of Science and Art which was intended to serve the Slovenians, Croatians, Serbs, and Bulgarians.[52] Into this institution he later on poured money as though it were water. Finally, after many difficulties and obstacles had been overcome, the Yugoslav Academy was formally opened on July 28, 1867, in the presence not only of the Slavs, but also of many representatives of the European academies.

The achievements of the Yugoslav Academy among the Southern Slavs can be seen best in the report which its president, Dr. F. Rački, gave to the members of the Academy on the occasion of its twenty-fifth anniversary. During this period of time – according to Rački report – there were 117 active members of the Academy (46 Croats, 15 Serbs, 7 Slovenians, 3 Bulgarians, 20 Czechs,

---

51   JJS-DK, I, 60.
52   TS, p. 81.

15 Russians, 4 Poles, 4 Germans, 2 Frenchmen and 1 Italian) and 241 volumes of scientific work in various fields of the sciences were published.[53]

In like manner he kept pouring money into another institution, the University of Zagreb, which was officially opened on October 19, 1874. Great sums of money were contributed by him to the Art Gallery of Zagreb which he dedicated on November 8, 1884. In 1866 he began to build the Cathedral of Djakovo, and it was consecrated by Bishop Posilović of Senj on October 1, 1882.[54] He also established many other educational institutions, as for instance the academies for the girls in Osijek and Djakovo.

The First Vatican Council of 1869-1870 and his role in it brought about a great change in his life and activities. This must be attributed to the fame he acquired at the Council by advocating modern ideas which endeared him to many European statesmen. Prior to the Council, in 1867, he ceased to participate actively in local politics and in those of the Austrian Monarchy. This by no means indicates that he abandoned the political arena; rather he preferred to work behind the scenes until he died. By the middle of 1870's he began to take part in the political affairs of other European countries, sometimes on his own initiative and at times because he was asked. All of his political activities either concerned the reorganization of Europe or pertained to the liberation of the Southern Slavs from the Turks.

2. - Strossmayer in the European Political Arena (1870-1880)

It should be noted that Strossmayer had a great sympathy and love for France. In 1867, while in France, he came in contact with the French leading politicians, for istance L. Thiers, E. Ollivier, and Charles Montalembert. These contacts were more than just a mere acquaintance.

---

[53] KRS, IV, 334-349. The Report was given on December 10, 1892.

[54] For more information on these topics, cf. CP, pp. 326-390 (the Cathedral of Djakovo), pp. 671-692 (the Picture Gallery in Zagreb), pp. 622-655 (the Yugoslav Academy of Science and Art). See also M. Cepelić, *loc. cit.*, in GBBS, pp. 24-27; R. W. Seton-Watson, *op. cit.*, pp. 120-124; and TS, pp. 78-101.

As soon as the First Vatican Council ended and the Franco-Prussian War (1870-1871) was in progress, he rushed to Vienna, Austria, to see the Russian ambasador E. Novikov. He begged Novikov to induce the Russian Tsar Alexander II to intervene and prevent the Prussians from destroying France. Strossmayer's plea was conveyed to the Tsar, but the intervention he asked for did not take place. However, according to the Croatian historian Tade Smičiklas, Tsar Alexander II in 1875 followed the advice of the Bishop when Prussia once again threatened France.[55]

It may appear thas Strossmayer's request of the Russian Ambassador in Vienna was out of place and too presumptuous, and that he regarded himself and his renown too highly. It should be known, however, that in February, 1870, the Russian Government, through its representatives, had contacted the Bishop in Rome and wanted him to be its intermediary with the Vatican in establishing friendly relations. Strossmayer responded promptly by putting in writing what steps should be undertaken on the part of the Russian government in order to achieve the desired goals.[56] There are no documents telling us what these steps were. Subsequently, the Bishop was in contact with the Russian Prince Leo Ouroussoff in Rome through Canon N. Voršak in regard to the reconciliation of Russia with the Vatican and so tried to pave the road for the eventual concordat between Russia and the Rome.[57] Undoubtedly, these incidents induced him to seek out Novikov in Vienna and to ask him for immediate intervention by the Russian government in bealf of France.

Immediately after the closing of the First Vatican Council he began with the utmost secrecy to act as an « unofficial » adviser to the Italian government. His cordial friendship with the Italian leading politicians, Marco Minghetti, Visconti Venosta, Giuseppe Massari, the Duke of Sermoneta, and many others, led him to deal with the extremely touchy topic of the Roman Question. In March,

---

[55] TS, p. 118.
[56] Voršak's report from Rome to Dr. F. Rački of February 9, 1870. AJA, XIIA, 810/24.
[57] AJA, XIA/132, and passim in the correspondence between Voršak and Strossmayer. Cf. also KRS, II, 227.

1871, he addressed a « pro memoria » in Latin to the Italian government[58] in which he suggested what attitude and what steps were to be taken vis-à-vis the Pontiff. A year later he wrote for them another « pro memoria » in Italian which is much broader and more precise.[59] It appears from these documents that he urged them to exercise the utmost patience and understanding.

In his letter of May 5, 1871, to G. Massari who had sent him a copy of two speeches he delivered in the Italian chamber of Deputies, Strossmayer praised him and his political comates for employing wisdom and patience in solving the acute Roman Question.[60] It is evident that the Italian statesmen asked him for advice on this burning issue. On one occasion when Strossmayer accompanied by Dr. Rački happened to be in Rome many Italian politicians rallied around him in the house of Odescalchi and begged him to settle in Rome for the winter in order to reconcile them with the Pope. The whole incident was told to Tade Smičiklas by F. Rački, and most probably it took place in 1884. Once Strossmayer became so impatient with the standstill process in solving the Roman Question that he decided to act on his own, by-passing the Roman Curia and going directely to the Pontiff on behalf of the Italian government, but he was persuaded by Canon Rački not to do it.[61] Most probably he would have provoked and even enraged the Roman prelates.

Toward the end of 1873 he entered into correspondence with the Russian Princess Lisse Trubeckoi who happened to be very close to the Russian statesman Prince Alexander Gorchakov (1798-1883).[62] She traveled all over Europe on a political mission. We have no documents which might indicate when Strossmayer and Trubeckoi became acquainted. There is every reason to presume that it took place while he was in Paris in 1867. He corresponded with her until the begining of 1893. Most of the letters were ex-

---

[58] Carthe Minghetti (Biblioteca dell'Archiginnasio, Bologna, Italy), Cartone 84, fasc. III.

[59] Ibid.

[60] Archivio del Risorgimento, Roma, Busta 817, no. 49.

[61] TS, p. 119.

[62] Strossmayer became a friend of Alexander Gorchakov's son who was also in the Russian diplomatic service in Rome. Cf. KRS, III, 59.

changed between them during the years of 1877 and 1878 when the crisis of the Eastern Question was at its peak.

By the end of 1873 L. Thiers cherished high hopes that he would once again become the prime minister of France. Princess Trubeckoi wanted Strossmayer to come to Paris since at that time a great conflict arose between the liberal republican party, of which L. Thiers was the leader, and the clerical royalist party. It was known to both Trubeckoi and Thiers that Strossmayer's sympathies were on the side of the liberal republican party, but he did not want to compromise himself or rather to come into conflict with the French hierarchy and the clergy[63] among whom he enjoyed a great fame.

Most probably Thiers wanted to use the Bishop's name in his political compaign. For this reason, Strossmayer did not want to write directely to Thiers, but sent a long letter to Princess Trubeckoi in which he expounded his ideas on the European situation in general and on that of France and of southeast Europe in particular. This approach was adopted by the Bishop with the hope that she would communicate the contents of his letter to Thiers and Prince Gorchakov.[64]

In all likelihood this letter of the Bishop contained the same ideas and proposals which are found in his « pro memoria » to the Russian government and in his correspondence with Lord W. Gladstone which will he treated elsewhere. The princess kept communicating the Bishop's proposals (how to solve the southeast European question) to Gorchakov, and she also kept posting Strossmayer on the opinion of Gorchakov and of Count Nicholas Ignatyev.[65]

It appears that Strossmayer's activities were known to some circles in Russia, for as early as 1875 he was given an honorary Ph. D. by the University of Moscow,[66] and in 1888 he was made

---

[63]   KRS, I, 249-250.
[64]   Ibid., p. 250, and see also p. 279.
[65]   Ibid., II, 65, 159, 179 and passim. There are about 58 letters of Trubeckoi to Strossmayer which are kept in the Archives of the Yugoslav Academy of Science and Art in Zagreb. They are of interest to the historian who wishes to become acquainted with the Turco-Russian War.
[66]   Ibid., II, 349-351.

an honorary member of the Slav Benevolent Society in St. Petersburg.[67] Certainly this generosity on the part of the Greek Orthodox toward a Roman Catholic prelate was extremely unusual.

The year 1876 marks another turn in the political and religious activities of the Bishop of Djakovo. In this year he came into direct contact with the Russian dynasty and government and also began to correspond with Lord W. Gladstone. The Russian dynasty and its government wanted to come into closer contact with the Bishop, and the execution of this plan was entrusted to Princess Trubeckoi and Dr. Augustine Heesen (who was a convert to Catholicism and a secret adviser to the Russian government). Sometime in August, 1876, Princess Trubeckoi wrote a lengthy letter to Strossmayer, but unfortunately the letter got lost and he never received it. However, we know its contents from Dr. Ladislav Rieger (a leading Czech politician and Strossmayer's intimate friend) to whom she communicated the principal ideas of the letter; and Dr. Rieger, believing that the letter in question had been confiscated by the Austrian government, immediately conveyed them to Dr. Rački in Zagreb. According to Rieger's report, it was her wish and the wish of her cousins (perhaps « the cousins » were the members of the Russian dynasty) that the Bishop should immediately go to London and through his friends and acquaintance establish contact with the British government and present to the leading British politicians the situation of the South Slavs, and thus win the British sympathies for the Russians in case the latter decided to interfere militantly in the Balkans. Dr. F. Rački was of the opinion that the Bishop should not undertake such a risky mission at that time, because the Austrian-Hungarian official policy was one of friendship with the Turks; and since Baron F. Beust who was then the Austrian ambassador in London would report every move of the Bishop to the government of Vienna, the Bishop might eventually be considered a traitor.[68] Strossmayer followed Rački's advice.

Just about that time Dr. A. Heesen was sent by the Russian government to study the curriculum of the universities in Germa-

---

[67] *Ibid.*, III, 346.
[68] *Ibid.*, II, 44-45.

ny and Austria, and he was also instructed to come into direct
contact with the Bishop. Through their mutual friend Dr. Peter
Matković, Dr. Heesen and Strossmayer met in Vienna by the middle
of August, 1876. At this meeting they discussed what steps Russia
was expected to take in order to establish friendly relations with
the Vatican.[69]

From Vienna Dr. Heesen proceeded to Rome where he had
an audience with Cardinal Franchi (Prefect of the Sacred congregation of the Propagation of the Faith, and also an intimate friend
of Strossmayer who recomended Heesen to him). Dr. Heesen also
had a private audience with Pope Pius IX. Afterwards, Cardinal
Franchi asked Dr. Heesen to convey to the Bishop his ardent desire that he should at once write a « pro memoria » to the Russian
government. While Strossmayer kept working on the « pro memoria », Dr. Heesen went to London. In spite of Heesen's advice
that the « pro memoria » be written in German, the Bishop chose
to write it in Latin and to supply Dr. Heesen with a summary
in German.[70]

The original of the « pro memoria » was sent to Canon Rački,
and two copies of it were made under his direct supervision. One
was to be sent to the Russian government, and the other was preserved by Rački for posterity and history. Since Strossmayer did
not trust the Russian Ambassador Novikov in Vienna and so did
not want to transmit this document through him, F. Rački sent it
to his friend in St. Petersburg, I. Sreznevsky, who was a famous
Russian academician and a secret adviser to the Russian government; and, of course, he was asked to hand it over to Dr. Heesen.
On November 15, 1876, Heesen placed the document « in the
hands of the one for whom it was intended ».[71] Out of fear of the
Austrian and Hungarian authorities the whole thing was executed
in an atmosphere of utmost secrecy. The « pro memoria » in
question was dated September 8, 1876, the feast of the Nativity

---

[69] *Ibid.*, p. 46.
[70] *Ibid.*, pp. 48-49. Heesen continued to correspond with the Bishop
and in October, 1879, he even paid him a visit in Djakovo. Cf. KRS, II, 329
and 379-382.
[71] *Ibid.*, pp. 68-73.

of the Bl. Virgin Mary; but it is apparent from Strossmayer's other correspondence that the document was given its final form by the end of September.

This « pro memoria » deals with the European political situation, the reorganization of Europe, and the role Russia was expected to play in Europe. Two other most significant points were the prospective concordat between Russia and the Holy See, and the liberation of the South Slavs from the Turks, or, as the latter is better known, « The Sourthen Slav Question ». The contents of the document are mentioned here solely perfunctorily; they will be treated more extensively elsewhere.

Since the Southern Slav problem had become so acute in the 1870's that it became of great concern to every European government, naturally the Bishop was intensively preoccupied with it; and he tried by every means to arouse the conscience of the Christian world to come to the rescue of the Southern Slavs who had been maltreated by the Turks for centuries. The question of liberating the South Slavs was on the mind of the Bishop for many years, and, not being able to find any support either from the Hungarians or from the Austrians who were in reality Turcophils and anti-Slavs, he had to look elsewhere for help.

It is noteworthy that the Bishop actually initiated the correspondence with Lord W. Gladstone and the Russians at the same time and asked both of them for their intervention in Southeast Europe. While he was working on his « pro memoria » to the Russian government, two leading British clergymen, Canon Liddon and Rev. Malcolm MacColl, on their way back home from Serbia, stopped in Djakovo to see the Bishop in order to get more reliable information on the Turkish atrocities perpetrated on the Christians in Bosnia, Herzegovina, and elsewhere. They were introduced to the Bishop by a letter of recommendation of Dr. I. Döllinger; and when they (Liddon and MacColl) begged him to write to Mr. Gladstone, he immediately complied with their wish.[72]

---

[72] *Ibid.*, p. 45 (Strossmayer's letter to Rački – dated September 6, 1876). It appears from this letter that the Bishop wrote his first letter to Lord Gladstone by the sixth of September even though it was dated October 1, 1876 (*ibid.*). Cf. also R. W. SETON-WATSON, *Disraeli, Gladstone, and the Eastern Question* (London: Frank Cass and Co. Ltd, 1962), pp. 85-87.

The correspondence between Gladstone and Strossmayer went on until July, 1892. Though both expressed their eagerness to meet each other the meeting never took place because of unforseen obstacles. They had a great affection and admiration for each other, and the Bishop regarded Gladstone as the best British statesman and also one of the greatest statesmen of that time.[73]

It was regrettable that the Bishop's letters to Gladstone were not instantly published in the British press, which was what Gladstone wanted; but the Bishop did not agree to this desire of the British statesman because he feared the reprisals by the Austrian and Hungarian authorities. The publication of the letters would have helped Gladstone in his political campaign, and it would also have greatly promoted the cause of the Southern Slavs among the British public.

For many years afterwards, the British government (Gladstone's party) maintained contact with the Bishop and F. Rački. This was done by various political personalities close to Gladstone, for instance, Mr. Bryce (secretary in Gladstone's cabinet),[74] Donald Crawford,[75] and the British General Consul Nicolson.[76] Gladstone's intimate friend Emile de Laveley also acted as an intermediary between the British Statesman and the Bishop, asking the latter's advice for solving the Egyptian problem.[77]

The British public and press were very sympathetic toward the Bishop; and this became evident especially in September, 1888, when the Bishop came into conflict with Francis Joseph over the telegram sent to the president of the Kiev University.[78] We do not,

---

[73]   KRS, II, 74 and passim. Neither Strossmayer nor Gladstone gave up the hope of meeting each other. As late as September 21, 1886, Lord Gladstone wrote to his wife: « Bishop Strossmayer may make a journey all the way to Hawarden, and it seems that Acton may even accompany him, which would make it much more manageable. His coming would be a great compliment, and cannot be discouraged or refused ». Quoted by JOHN MORLEY, The Life of W. E. Gladstone (New York: The Macmillan Co., 1903), III, 352-353.

[74]   KRS, IV, 89-90. Bryce was only with Rački in Zagreb and was prevented by his wife's illness from going to Djakovo to pay a visit to the Bishop (ibid.).

[75]   Ibid., p. 39.

[76]   Ibid., p. 96.

[77]   Ibid., III, 130.

[78]   The British historian Edward A. Freeman wrote an article in The

of course, here present a complete account of all the Bishop's connections with the British government for the purpose of speeding up the liberation of the Southern Slavs. There are some remote indications that the Bishop wanted to make the United States of America interested in the South Slav Question. He was in contact with the American Ambassador in Rome, Mr. Morsh.[79]

Prior to the opening of the Congress of Berlin (1878), Strossmayer begged his friend Gladstone to use his influence and make it possible for him to appear before the Congress in order to present the cause of the people of Bosnia and Herzegovina over which he had at least nominal spiritual jurisdiction.[80] The British historian R. Seton-Watson offers the following commentary on the Bishop's plea: « It is impossible not to regret that nothing ever came of this (Strossmayer's) tentative suggestion that he should appear before the Congress (of Berlin) to plead the cause of his Bosnian kinsmen. The sight of the great Christian orator before that distinguished gathering of diplomatic freebooters would have afforded equal food for reflection to the cynic and the moralist ».[81]

It is very difficult to offer an account of Strossmayer's activities from 1880 on, except the fact that his direct involvements diminished considerably. Of course, he continued to function politically, but all this was done behind the scenes and in much lesser measure. During 1880's he became acquainted with Vladimir Soloviev, and with whom he exchanged views on reconciling the Eastern and Western Churches. Undoubtedly, during these years he also continued to work on the task of establishing the pact between the Holy See and Russia.

This period was highlighted by the confrontation between the Bishop and the Emperor Francis Joseph. The whole incident was precipitated by the Bishop's telegram, sent to the president of St. Vladimir's University on the occasion of the ninth centennial

---

Manchester Guardian about the incident in which he highly praised the Bishop for his courage and ecumenism. Cf. KRS, IV, 40.

[79] KRS, I, 206 (Strossmayer's letter to Francis Rački from Rome, dated January 25, 1873). Morsh invited the Bishop for dinner (*ibid.*). Cf. also KRS, I, 47.

[80] CBSG, p. 445.

[81] R. W. SETON-WATSON, *The Southern Slav Question*, p. 127.

of Russia's acceptance of Christianity. Since this telegram created such a great commotion in Europe, we would like to cite it here in its entirety: « To the President of St. Vladimir's University, Kiev, Russia. It is my honor to join your celebration today with the most heartfelt joy. The heritage of St. Vladimir is the holy faith; it is an Easter and life; it was the light and glory, and still is such to the great Russian nation. May God bless Russia and enable her to fulfill with living faith, with exemplary life, with help from above, and with Christian heroism – not to mention her other roles – her glorious international role happily, salutarily, and victoriously, a role assigned to her by Divine Providence. These are the most sincere whishes of my heart. Please, be an interpreter of my sentiments, to the other brothers whom I am amicably greeting and paternally blessing, Signed: Strossmayer, Bishop ».[82]

This telegram was sent in July, 1888, and it was acknowledged with thanks by Kiev University's President Demchenko on his own behalf and that of Kiev's Bishop Platon.[83] The publicity which this telegram received in the European press (especially the Italian and the French), greatly disturbed Pope Leo XIII and Cardinal Rampolla; and this publicity was heightened by the coincidence of Strossmayer's telegram with that of the archbishop of Canterbury.[84]

It did not take Strossmayer too long to straighten out the whole problem with Rampolla and Pope Leo XIII;[85] but Emperor Francis Joseph, on account of political motives and implications, remained very resentful and waited for the opportunity to attack the Bishop. This took place in Bjelovar (Croatia) on September 12, 1888, when the Emperor came to Bjelovar to observe the military maneuvers. All the Croatian bishops (Strossmayer included) were invited to pay a visit to the Emperor, and the bishop of Djakovo complied with this order with a heavy heart, most probably because he had some presentiments of what was in store for him in the

---

[82] KRS, IV, 5.
[83] V. Košćak, loc. cit., in Historijski Zbornik, XI-XII, 366.
[84] KRS, IV, 6-7.
[85] Ibid., pp. 9-13 and especially pp. 34-35. Naturally, this telegram made the Bishop more popular among the Greek Orthodox of Russia, Bulgaria,

forthcoming encounter with the sovereign. At first the Emperor tried to ignore the Bishop, but later on he insulted him by implying that he had been mentally sick when he sent the telegram to Kiev. Naturally, the Bishop politely but fearlessly made a rejoinder to the Emperor; and if it had not been for the intervention of Cardinal Mihalović, much more serious complications might have developed.[86]

Before we bring this chapter to an end we would like to mention another battle that the Bishop fought in the early 1890's. The whole struggle was over who would become the archbishop of Zagreb after Cardinal Mihalović died on Febraury 19, 1891. The struggle ensued between Strossmayer and the Hungarians who wanted to give the see of Zagreb to their man as had been the case with Cardinal Mihalović. This contest lasted three years, and it was conducted in secret, except of course for occasional news items in various newspapers which appreared from time to time, and usually were unfounded. It was not only a question of whether or not a Hungarian or a pro-Hungarian would come into possession of one of the largest dioceses in the world and thus subjugate Croatia to some extent in the ecclesiastical sphere to the Hungarians, but there was a justified fear that the Hungarians would take the province of Medjumurje, which was one hundred percent ethnically Croatian, and annex it to the nearest Hungarian diocese.

From the moment that Cardinal Mihalović became seriously ill, Strossmayer increased his correspondence about the archdiocese of Zagreb with the apostolic nuncio in Vienna Msgr. Luigi Galimberti, and with Pope Leo XIII and Cardinal Rampolla, the Secretary of State.[87] Everybody knew that he was an intimate friend of Leo XIII and Rampolla and was using all his influence to stop the plans of the Hungarians and thus prevent them from humilia-

---

Bohemia, Serbia etc. See Rački's letter to Strossmayer of August 24, 1888 (*ibid.,* p. 9).
[86] KRS, IV, 21-22.
[87] « In regard to the successor of the Cardinal (Mihalović) in Zagreb I have done everything possible in Rome and Vienna that my conscience dictated to me. Now my conscience is at peace », he wrote to Rački on February 8, 1891. KRS, IV, 219.

ting the Croats and from dividing Croatia.[88] It appears from some documents that Galimberti, the apostolic nuncio, had sided with the Hungarians, and this, of course, irritated Strossmayer.[89] The latters' candidate for the see of Zagreb was Msgr. Joseph Stadler, archbishop of Sarajevo.[90] The Holy See proposed to the Emperor Francis Joseph the following three candidates: Msgr. Joseph Stadler, Msgr. George Posilović, and Msgr. Matthias Stepinac, spiritual director of the theological students in Zagreb;[91] and in 1894 Bishop Posilović[92] was appointed archbishop of Zagreb.

---

[88] *Ibid.*, pp. 259-260.
[89] *Ibid.*, p. 303 and passim.
[90] *Ibid.*, p. 312.
[91] *Ibid.*, p. 318.
[92] Msgr. G. Posilović was a professor at the University of Zagreb and the editor of *Katolički List*. He became the bishop of Senj (Croatia) in 1876 and served in that capacity until he was transferred to Zagreb where he remained until he died in 1914.

III

THOUGHTS AND PROPOSALS

To gain a close insight into the personality and character of Bishop Strossmayer it is necessary to take a look at his moral stature and also to see by what principles his life, activities, and enterprises were motivated and guided.

1. - Human Conscience and Convictions

There is no doubt in our mind that one cannot achieve this withtout becoming acquainted with his conception of human conscience and of human persuasions. His speeches and writings are permeated with his extremely vigorous feelings on the value of an individual's conscience and convictions. As a consequence, he also deals on numerous occasions with a person's good name and honor. It seems to us that our interpretation of his thoughts on these topics would mar rather than illustrate his ideas; and so we have decided to let the Bishop speak for himself. It ought to be said at his place, however, that some of his reflections on this subjects were expressed at moments of personal crises, trials, confrontations, and others when he was totally undisturbed and calm.

When on September 3, 1888, the Bishop came in conflict with the Emperor Francis Joseph and with the Vatican authorities, and when, as it seems, the Vatican and the Austrian-Hungarian government came to an agreement to remove him from his position because he had sent a telegram to the president of the Kiev's University on the occasion of Russia's ninth centennial of Christendom, he wrote the following to F. Rački:

« It seems to me that in Vienna and Budapest they have decided to remove me from this position by all means and to force me into retirement. The reason will be: salus reipublicae suprema lex (the welfare of the state is the supreme law). Under this motto hundreds and hundreds of injustices have been perpetrated. The Vatican, it seems to me, will follow the same pattern, that is, it will say: well, you are innocent but maius Ecclesiae bonum exigit, ut loco tuo cedas (the welfare of the Church requires your resignation). One more formula under which many injustices are hidden. However, I am totally calm and undisturbed... My conscience is clear, and a clear conscience is the voice of the majesty of God, to which any other majesty must be subject ».[1]

This does not mean that he thought of himself as being sinless and without faults and shortcomings. In his Lenten Pastoral of 1891 he esplains what he meant or rather he is more specific:

« I am a man and like any other man I am liable to make mistakes, and indeed I did make some. However, nobody can prove that I would exchange my conscience and my convictions for anything in the world. The Holy Spirit speaks to me through my conscience and convictions. Therefore, I would rather be dead a hundred times than to become unfaithful to my conscience and convictions, that is, to the Holy Spirit... The greates value in this world is an honorable and honest name which is worthier than life itself, and which God has placed under His special care and under the protection of our conscience; and nobody can take it away from us without personal guilt ».[2] This reasoning of his bears a great resemblance to St. Paul, Rom. 9, 1-2: « I speak the truth in Christ, I do not lie, my conscience bearing me witness in the Holy Spirit... ».

In his most difficult moments and especially when he was seized by melancholia, which afflicted him in his later years, he used to find great comfort in this principle of his spiritual life. In his letter of February 7, 1883, he confides his inner trouble to F. Rački:

« Your every letter brings a great consolation to my aching heart. My brother, very often such an intensive melancholia seizes me that I do not know what to do with myself. If it were not for

---

[1] KRS, IV, 20. When he touched upon the topic of jurisprudence, he said: « ... (judge's decisions) must not rely upon anything else but on his conscience and on God who speaks to him through his conscience and naturally on the existing law). Cf. Strossmayer's address delivered on July 28, 1867 (TS, p. 157). This oration was originally published in a series of books known by the name *Rad Jugoslavenske Akademije*, v. I, pp. 27-43.

[2] His Pastoral letter of January 18, 1891 (cf. KRS, IV, 253).

God and faith, I would despair. Everything is simply pulling me into solitude. My brother, if I did not feel in my soul the voice of God which keeps telling me: persevere and continue... I would retire from all activities. I will bear with myself as long as I can ».[3]

After the Bishop was calumniated by the Orthodox bishops of Karlovci, Kotor, Zadar, in their respective postoral letters, he wrote a lengthy reply to them which is an exposition of the structure of the Church of God, and he addressed these words to them:

« God knows and sees that I am telling you the truth when I state that I love our (Slav) race with equal love regardless of how each nation is called; and what is more, I would like to free them from all the evils which are vexing them with the sacrifice of my life. Whatever I have done so far, I have done for our entire (Slav) race... and whatever I will do in the future I will do for both (Catholics and Greek Orthodox). The only thing that I am not able to give even to my own people is my conscience and my convictions which I wish to bring unmarred before the throne of God... »[4]

While he was in Rome during the First Vatican Council, and in March, 1870, the debates and confrontation between the majority and minority had reached their peak, he said to Rački: « I must remain true to my convictions in order to save my conscience and honesty before God and mankind. Afterwards, may God and the luck of a hero allot to me whatever it might be. I will do what I must do... ».[5]

Strossmayer cherished the value of a person's conscience and convictions so much that no power was capable of making him go against his own conscience or change his convictions. If anyone attempted to do this, his entire being would scream in protest, and he would remain faithful to his firm persuasions regardless of consequences and threats. On one occasion he preferred to go into exile temporarily instead of giving up the convictions which he thought to be correct.

This was manifested best in his confrontation with the Emperor Francis Joseph which had taken place by the end of April, 1867.

---

[3] KRS, III, 55.
[4] *Ibid.*, IV, 512.
[5] Letter of March 8, 1870 (cf. KRS, I, 101).

In that year the Emperor was to be crowned in Budapest and Francis Joseph wanted the Croatian deputies to come to that city for the occasion. Meanwhile, the Croatian Diet of Zagreb, of which Strossmayer was a member, kept insisting that Francis Joseph must be crowned in the city of Zagreb too, to show their national identity and political independence from the Hungarians.

The Emperor imagined that the Croats would comply with his wishes if Bishop Strossmayer stayed away from the meeting of the Diet which was scheduled to be held on May 1, 1867, to decide whether or not they would send a delegation to Budapest.[6] Prior to this the Emperor called Strossmayer to Vienna and told him: « It is my will and my command that you defend the Hungarian program (in the Diet). If you don't wish to do it, then you are forbidden to attend the meeting of the Diet in Zagreb. I am telling you most decidedly: in case you resist me, I am ready to use reprisals against you ».[7]

« You can just imagine, » he commented on this in his letter to Rački, « how my honest soul reacted to it and what my mouth spoke out.. I do not change my convictions for anybody in the world, and how can I fight against this brutal force. Therefore, there is no other alternative for me but to go to France for awhile... »[8] Subsequently a strong rumor persisted in Vienna that the Emperor and his court would annihilate him one way or another; but « they will never destroy either my conscience or my convictions ». he wrote to Rački.[9] The outcome was that he went to France, where he spent a few months as an expatriated person.

It was the custom of the Bishop, whenever he happened to be confronted with a serious problem concerning which he had to make a decision, to study it from all angles, and then to draw his conclusions. Whatever the results of his thorough study might be, he would adhere to them. He employed the same policy in forming his conscience. And once his conscience was formed, he became as immovable as a cliff. Perhaps, on account of these traits of his,

---

6   *Ibid.*, I, p. 46.
7   *Ibid.*, p.45.
8   *Ibid.*
9   *Ibid.*

he might appear on the surface to be stubborn or proud. Whether or not he was really obstinate and unyielding in some instances is difficult to say because of the sincerity of his mental attitude.

Most probably nobody was aware of the Bishop's complexity as much as his intimate friend Rački. The following examples of Bishop's attitude will illustrate best what we mean. During the year 1871, Rački pleaded with him on two occasions. Both cases deal with the Bishop's position in regard to the decrees of the First Vatican Council, which he refused to sign. (After the Council, the Vatican required those bishops who had not affixed their signatures to its decrees to do so). Rački was worried what steps the Bishop might take in case he received such a letter of command from Rome.

On My 19, 1871, Rački wrote to him: « I beg you for one favor. In case you receive a letter from Rome demanding that you accept the decrees of the Vatican Council, please, be so kind as to notify me immediately about it, in that case I will come at once to you in Djakovo. Please, have two things in mind: do not offer weapons either to your personal or to our national enemies, and try by all means to preserve your reputation which you earned in the world. It is my conviction that this question (papal infallibility) will not be solved definitely by the Roman Curia but by Divine Providence ».[10]

Two months later Rački sent another warning to the Bishop concerning a trip he planned to make to Kissinger, Germany. « I sincerely confess, » he writes, « that I am fearful that the German opponents of infallibility might crowd around you, and this may offer an opportunity for various ovations and demonstrations which might provoke the Roman Curia. In case you go there for the sake of your health, your prudence will know how to avoid such things which might bring on any crisis ».[11]

To both letters of Rački the Bishop replied, but there is not a word of comment on Rački's recommendations and admonitions. It appears that the Bishop had definitely formed his conscience on the topic of papal infallibility already at the Council and he could not go against his conscience. What is more, anyone who examines

---

[10] *Ibid.*, p. 136.
[11] *Ibid.*, pp. 137-138.

the letters he wrote immediately after the Council will see that there is not a word about the Council. The Bishop did not moan or gripe over the past; he did what he thought was right in the Council. After the Council he simply plunged into ecclesiastical, cultural, and political activities as though the Vatican Council had never been held and he had no part in it. In short, he had done his duty, and the matter was closed.

To his mind, even in the Church, one must remain true to his conscience and convictions. He advocated a certain freedom of disagreement under certain qualifications whithin the Church. This will be illustrated best by something already mentioned, namely, the incident of the Bishop's telegram to Kiev. When the news of the telegram (which had already created a grett commotion in the Austria-Hungarian Empire) reached the Pontiff, and after the Bishop was officially notified by his friend Secretary of State Cardinal Rampolla, that the Pontiff had been greatly disturbed by the incident and he was asked for an explanation, the Bishop – before sending a reply to Rampolla – wrote this to Rački:

« This indicates that the Pope follows the foreign policy of the Austrian-Hngarian government too much. Whatever may happen, you know how I shall answer Rampolla.... I shall answer as God, my conscience, my faith, and my position demand. The answer will be calm and considerate but nonetheless a resolute one. It is evident that our enemies have more influence in the Vatican... than we can imagine. Let them have it... This is the weakness of the present Vatican. As you know, I do not care for myself. I am only concerned with my reputation and conscience – the rest is just a joke. Those for whom I feel sorry, as you know, are my friends and the faithful who are going to be immensely saddened if I, on account of this, have to go into retirement; and this is liable to happen if the Vatican will require me to do something which might be contrary to my conscience and position. Regardless of what may happen, one has to tell the truth sincerely and openly, and everything else must be confided to God ».[12]

In his copious correspondence with Rački and elsewhere he

---

[12] Letter of August 20, 1888 (cf. KRS, IV, 7).

strongly advocates that a bishop in the Catholic Church — whenever an occasion warrants — must take the stand of St. Paul (« I opposed him to his face, since he was manifestly in the wrong » — Gal. 2, 11) versus St. Peter, if a bishop thinks that the pope is in the wrong. In his long reply to Rampolla's letter, Strossmayer says: « I genuinely respect and admire the Supreme Pontiff Leo from the botton of my heart, and although I consider myself to be worthy of St. Paul by convincing Peter from time to time that he is in the wrong, I will never either in life or death separate myself from him (Pope Leo) ».[13]

Certainly it is deserving admiration that the Bishop appropriated the role of St. Paul versus St. Peter not only for himself but also for all other bishops; and he extended the same privilege to his clergy in their dealings and communications with himself. As a matter of fact, he encouraged his clergy to stand by their convictions vis-à-vis him. In his classical encyclical of 1877 on « Unity in the Church », in which, among other things, he set forth so exquisitely the role of a bishop within the Church, and that of the clergy and also their relationship with one another, he wrote:

« They (the priests) are expected to be sincere and openminded toward their bishop; they should declare decidedly although modestly their convictions in serious and significant matters; this must be done in such a manner that the virtue of charity is never violated. As you know, on one very important occasion the Great Apostle of the Nations determinedly expressed his opinion straight in the

------

[13] Letter to Cardinal Rampolla of August 20, 1888 (*ibid.*, pp. 12-13). Cf. also Strossmayer's letter to Rački of January 11, 1888: « I can hardly hope that I will ever again see Rome and the Pope; if, however, a chance be offered to me to see the Pope, I will moderately — but firmly — tell him my mind not only on current politics but also on its ultimate source and reason. I will do it the way St. Paul did to St. Peter... Bismarck is evidently after conquering all of Europe, which means a terrible war; once this takes place, the good soul of Pope Leo will become frightened since his soul will begin to feel remorse on account of his contribution to this evil » (cf. *ibid.*, III, p. 347). In Vatican I he also discussed the matter of conscience and human convictions of the bishops vs. the pope. He says that « Regardless of what has been said so far from this podium, in my opinion and persuasion, it belongs to the essence of the power of bishop's not only to judge, to confirm, to explicate, and to approve in the ecumenical councils but the bishops in their conscience and convictions can also sometimes refute ». Mansi, 52, 397.

face of the Prince of the Apostles St. Peter. By this St. Paul's holy subordination – which comes from Jesus Christ himself – was not marred, and much less was the holy and constant love between these two apostles violated, a love by which they remained united as one body and one soul until death ».[14]

Before closing this topic, we would like to make a few more pertinent remarks. Strossmayer always thought of himself and considered himself a liberal. In fact, he asserted this position of his with a certain amount of pride, and he did so especially at the Vatican Council. [15] From the writings it becomes apparent that he regarded being a liberal as identical with being a progressive, that is, one who is cognizant of new movements and ideologies in the secular world, who is open and accessible to the achievements of modern science, and who is not afraid to introduce wholesome attainments into the life stream of the Church.

« Today the Church of God, » he wrote to his clergy on the eve of the Vatican Council, « is primarily concerned with the establishing of closer and more lively communication with her center and within herself, and in her holy unity the Church is searching for new forces and means to resist onsloughts and above else to insure and preserve with new means her independence and freedom in matters which pertain to her divine mission ».[16]

He showed his astuteness when he made the following observation: « The world bestows praise, a praise that is well merited, on those men who employ greater and greater diligence in studying nature, and are attempting every day to penetrate deeper and deeper into her mysteries in order to draw out of them an abundance

---

[14] TS, p. 382. This Pastoral « Unity in the Church » was originally published in GBBS in 1877, no. 3, pp. 17-33. It is reprinted by TS.

[15] Strossmayer writes to Rački from Rome on November 23, 1869: « We the liberal bishops do not know one another, and it is feard that we will not come to an agreement and that we will not have sufficient courage, without which nothing can be accomplished and especially here in Rome » (KRS, I, 100).

[16] BS, XXII (1934), 10. (The original of this Pastoral was in the archives of the Diocese of Djakovo under no. 817. See BS, loc. cit., 1. At the present time it is found in the archives of the Yugoslav Academy of Science and Art in Zagreb. The entire text of the document is reprinted in the above cited volume of BS).

of new resources for the benefit of the human race and for the glory of the human spirit. This is praiseworthy, and from the bottom of her heart the Church should rejoice over it ».[17] He did not disdain material progress: « To earn and accumulate benefits is not contradicting the will of the One who endowed nature with so many resources as long as man uses them for his own good and shares them with other people ».[18]

His awareness of these modern achievements and of the strivings of nations to be free and independent, concerning which we shall have more to say later on, made him speak once again of human conscience which is the chief regulator of human behavior and of mankind's relationships. In quite a few instances he discussed the question whether anyone is entitled to influence human conscience. He is unequivocal on this subject when he writes: « Nobody is allowed to influence immortal soul, conscience, faith, and eternal law except the true and living God and the institution which he founded for this purpose ».[19] However in regard to the control which the Church has over human conscience, he specified how the official Church is expected to exercise this influence, how far the Church can go in this direction, and what means she is empowered to use in this matter.

In his opinion, neither the Church nor any other institution is allowed to employ « external and compulsory ways and means ». No organized society can exercise any influence upon human conscience but the Church which is the product of God's hands, but in this assignment she is allowed to emply only « spiritual means ».[20] From the context it becomes apparent that the Church

---

[17] BS, *loc. cit.*, p. 7.
[18] *Ibid.*, p. 6.
[19] Strossmayer's Pastoral of 2891 (cf. KRS, IV, 228). In the same document he treats the subject of children's education and of parents' conscience in mixed marriages, and concludes with these words: « The education of the children in mixed marriages must be confided to the conscience and to the free will of parents who in this matter stand under the influence of Jesus Christ and of holy Church. A Cristian State must guarantee full freedom of conscience, and must remove any forceful and unjust means which would tend to regulate holy faith, conscience, and the salvation of men, since forceful means are not in accordance with the spirit and with the heart of Jesus Christ » (KRS, IV, 241).
[20] BS, *loc. cit.*, 16. He is very precise on this point in his Pastoral of

carries out her mission by correctly presenting the truths of God
to the faithful and reasoning with them. Naturally, « spiritual
means » also imply the work of God's grace in the human soul
and mind. Furthermore, according to him, « if human conscience
and persuasions are not free » then one can hardly talk about freedom in the Church and much less so in other human institutions.[21]
On account of his resolute stand on these questions, as Imbro
I. Tkalac reports, both religious and secular tyranny were odious
to him regardless of what shape or disguise they might assume.[22]

2. - Ideas of Freedom

Undoubtely, Stossmayer's views on freedom are corollaries of
his notion of the individual's conscience and convictions, on which
he focussed his attention and by which his activities were guided
all his life. Personal freedom and all other freedoms were the fa-

---

1881 « Sts. Cyril and Methodius » in which he says: « Today the Church
must courageously defend her own freedom and human conscience. I repeat:
(today) it is genuine hypocricy to even imagine that the Church would attempt to influence states and nations by any other means except by those
which Christ had used, that is, by recommending holy faith and (Christian)
virtues along those principles which are alone able to tame human passions
and lust in order to enoble human society and to save it from the abyss
toward which it is heading. Today the Church, by protecting her own liberty
– as it used to do previously – carries within herself freedom and enlightenment to all nations, by teaching them, that freedom can be saved and enjoyed
if the freedom of the Church and of conscience are guaranteed and if evangelical principles and the right of Christian virtues are thoroughly grounded
in public and private life » TS, p. 439. (This document was originally published in GBBS, no. 4, pp. 25-53).

21 BS, loc. cit., 16. The Bishop said time and again that « it is a sin
against the Holy Spirit to go against someone's faith and convictions » (cf.
GBBS, V, no. 9, p. 90). This is taken from his Pastoral of 1877 under the
title « The Office of St. Peter's Successors in the Church of God ».

22 « By placing himself (Strossmayer) at the head of the opposition », I.
Tkalac notifies V. Venosta in his report of January 20, 1870, « against the
pretensions of the other party, he (Strossmayer) does not listen to anything
else but to his human conscience and to that of the bishop, and he simply
wishes to carry out the duties of his office... he strives to save the Church
and human society from the evils by which they are menaced, and he will
never omit a chance to defend human rigts against any sort of tyranny, be
it spiritual or secular. No person deplores, as he does, the existing confusion

vorite topics of his long time reflections, even during his student years at the University of Budapest, and more so a few years later at the University of Vienna, where he came into direct contact with various leaders who took an active part in the national awakening of the Slav nations.

While he was in Budapest as a student of theology, he was in constant communion with the Croatian lay students, Steve Mlinarić, Pacific Dražić and Fran Kurelac, who later on played significant roles in the Croatian cultural and political life (this was done especially by the latter). During his student years in Budapest he also used to pay a visit from time to time to the well known poet and Lutheran minister Jan Kollar, who was a pan-Slavist to such a degree that he almost thought of pan-Slavism as a religion within which there was a lot of room for free worship for the Lutherans, the Calvinists, the Greek Orthodox, and the Catholics as well, and who was looked upon as an apostle of religious tolerance.[23] It is hard to ascertain whether or to what extent this Lutheran minister exercised any influence upon Strossmayer, who subsequently became the most eloquent champion of religious tolerance in southeast Europe and the chief proponent of the reunion of the Eastern and Western Churches.

A few years later we find Strossmayer as a student at the University of Vienna. During these years and much more so in the succeeding years when he came back to Vienna in the capacity of a court chaplain and prefect of the Augustineum (the college where the ecclesiastical students lived) he was steadily seen in the company of Croatian politicians and those of other nations. His circle of closest friends was composed of Metel Ožegović, John Kukuljević Andrew Brlić, Ban Jelačić, and many others.[24] All his friends were progressives and strong protagonists of modern ideas and movements which were so rampant all over Europe in those years.

How much his sporadic involvement in politics up to the time

---

within religion and the Church in regard to their interests which are alien to both (the Church and religion)» RSCV, pp. 227-228.

[23] Louis Leger, « L'Evêque Strossmayer », in *Nouvelle Revue*, 1908, 215-216. Cf. also CP, p. 30.

[24] CP, pp. 34-37.

when he became bishop of Djakovo contributed to the formation
of his notion of national freedom and authonomy, it is hard to say.
However, we do not entertain any doubts that prior to his conse-
cration as bishop – when he was only 35 years old – his ideas on
freedom were well developed and systematically formulated in his
mind. During his two sojourns of several years in Vienna he co-
piously contributed to various newspapers which are not available
to us, but we know from other sources that in his articles he discussed the freedom of an individual and that of a nation.[25]

Most probably the most eloquent statement on the freedom
of an individual is found in his speech (which lasted at least an
hour and an half) which he delivered to his faithful on September 29, 1850, on the occasion of his episcopal installation:

« As far as freedom is concerned, it is true that man is created
to enjoy it; it is equally true that the dignity of man cannot be
reconciled with slavery; it is true that tyranny of one man over
another is a crime; it is true that man was called into existence by
God with the gift of a free will; it is true that the Redemption
and its grace – earned by Christ – is so moderate that it never
violates the freedom of the human will; it is true that without
freedom of choice we cannot talk about virtue and merits; it is
true that Christianity protects freedom as long as it considers
man as son of God, a brother of Christ, and the temple of the
Holy Spirit..., it is true that every government must take into consideration the mission of Christianity and also this dignity of man
if it wishes to be of any benefit to human society and to be blessed by God ».[25]

His writings also show that he used to tackle the problem of
reconciling the individual's freedom with the redemptive grace
of Christ. Human freedom is so sublime that it is never violated,
and « God, in spite of his power and his redemptive grace, leaves
every man free to save himself through his free will and his de-

---

[25] *Ibid.,* p. 36.
[26] JJS-DK, I, 156. This speech, delivered in Croatian to his faithful,
and his speech, delivered to the clergy in Latin on the same occasion, were
printed in separate brochures under the title « Oratio qua clerum suum, dum
regimen dioecesium suarum ritu solemni caperet in Domino salutavit anno
1850, die 29 Septembris. Viennae typis Congregationis Mechitarum ».

cision to use the grace of God ».[27] This he repeated in quite a number of places.

Human freedom and conscience must be preserved in all their facets. When he discussed the relationship between a State and the Church and the role and duties of a citizen in a State, he unequivocally maintained that a citizen – being created into an image of God and sanctified by the sacrament of baptism – is allowed to resort to prudent, ethical, and moral means to oppose the civil authority if he feels that the latter is neglecting its duty in promoting the welfare of an individual and that of a certain group of people. (There is no doubt that the Bishop referred in this instance to the political set-up in the Austrian-Hungarian Empire where the national minority groups where maltreated). However, he disapproved of revolution and of using any violent means.[28]

When the Bishop embarked upon the subject of how prisoners and the accused should be treated by the authorities, he vehemently defended their rights to be heard in a human and Christian way. Any confession on their side, extorted by tortures, or by means of force or trickery, is nil and void since their freedom was violated. Furthermore, a State is obligated to employ suitable means in reforming and making them fit to live honestly in human society.[29]

Before we proceed any further we would like to make a brief digression. It has been mentioned several times in passing that Strossmayer issued a special pastoral letter on the forthcoming Council. This letter was dated June 29, 1869. (The original copy is kept in the archives of the Yugoslav Academy of Science and Art in Zagreb, and in 1934 it was published in its entirety in Bogoslovska Smotra (Ephemerides Theologicae), a review of the Croatian Theological Academy, XXII, 1-19). In this pastoral, he presented a complete outline of all the topics which, to his mind, should be on the agenda of the scheduled Council. For some of these subjects he offered solid reasons why they should be discussed. More or less

---

[27] His Pastoral of 1891 (KRS, IV, 235-236); cf. also his Pastoral of 1869, BS, *ibid.*, 14.
[28] Pastoral of 1891 (KRS, IV, 235).
[29] Pastoral on « Sts. Cyril and Methodius » (TS, p. 416); cf. Pastoral of 1891 (KRS, IV, 234), and also « Three Words to our University » (TS, p. 310).

all of them were propounded by him in the Vatican Council to a much greater extent. Prior to the Council his hopes and expectations from the forthcoming Council were high, and certainly he did not anticipate any confrontation and heated arguments in the Council. Some of his basic proposals were: freedom of the individual, freedom of nations, freedom of the Church in the world, freedom of the pope, and religious tolerance. It appears from this pastoral that there was no doubt in his mind that these topics would be thoroughly discussed in the Council.

Let us return to personal freedom and the freedom of nations. Before the Vatican Council, Strossmayer was a strong advocate not only of personal freedom but equally so of freedom of any nation regardless of its size. As a matter of fact, this problem of freedom was extensively debated in 1860 in the so-called Expanded Council of the Emperor in Vienna, of which council he was a member. « It is necessary, » he said in one of the sessions, « that Austria must be made uniform because she is destined to perform a sublime mission in Europe; and for this reason she must be strong and enjoy good repute; if she wishes to meet these requirements, she is, above all else, expected to be harmonious. Since I am convinced of this, I must declare that in her integrity Austria must be so organized that each nation and every people, no matter who they are, must find security for their national existence and for their institutions. Regardless of how gladly I support the just strivings of the Hungarians..., I cannot fathom how public affairs (in any State) can be correctly and justly conducted if only one nation has all the rights while the others are deprived of them. Furthermore, it is recognized rule that nobody is allowed to violate the personal liberty of a citizen and that the individual's freedom must be safeguarded by the State, and consequently by the same token every nation is entitled to the same right; and this freedom of a nation must be so protected and supported that the nation may freely grow and progress».[30]

---

[30] TS, p. 41. This text and the entire debate between Count Borelli – who advocated that Dalmatia must remain a separate political body from the other Croatian provinces – and Strossmayer – who on historical and national basis was strongly in favor of reunion of the Croatian provinces (Dalmatia

Quite a few years later, when the Eastern Question became actual, he offered the same idea to the Lord Gladstone saying that the nations in southeast Europe – once they were liberated from the Turks – must be given an opportunity to form their own government according to their needs and desires.[31]

In the same year, in the Expanded Council of the Emperor, he eleborated the notion of a nation. This idea he unfolded when he defended the right of the Croatian provinces (Dalmatia, Istria, Hrvatsko Primorje, and eventually Bosnia and Herzegovina) to be reunited with Croatia Proper. His point of departure on the topic of nationel consciousness was especially the politico-historical particularity of a nation, namely, a people sharing the same history and the same qualities and, of course, wishing to live together as one national entity.[32]

This outlook of his had to be mentioned if we are to comprehend correctly his stand on the reunion of the Italian states and his opposition to the papal temporal power. He strongly favored the fusion of the Italians states – Papal States included – into one. Therefore it is apparent that he was against papal temporal power for a twofold reasons: first of all, the Church – by mingling and managing secular affairs – was liable to neglect her divine mission, entrusted to her by God; secondly, the Papal States and the pope's temporal power stood in the way of the just strivings of the Italian people for national reunification.

At this point we must mention several facts which pertain to the topic of the Roman Question, which was in reality question of preserving papal temporal power. In his « pro memoria » of January 20, 1872, to the Italian government, Strossmayer expresses his satisfaction that the Italian armed forces have occupied the

---

included) into one political and independent entity – is found in TS. Cf. Strossmayer's speech in the Diet of Zagreb, delivered on July 5, 1861 on « The Relations between the Kingdom of Croatia, Slavonia and Dalmatia and the Kingdom of Hungary » (TS, pp. 135-156). This speech was printed as a brochure in Zagreb, 1861.

[31] Strossmayer's letter to Gladstone of October 24, 1876 (CBSG, p. 422).

[32] TS, pp. 42-77. « Nations, like individual », the Bishop writes to the Literary Club of Gorica, Slovenia, in 1863, « have their own psychological characteristics » (TS, p. 86).

city of Rome. What is more, the Italian government by accomplishing this had actually rendered a great service not only to the Italian nation but also to the entire Catholic world by liberating the Holy See from earthly occupations.[33] From his other « pro memoria » of March, 1871, also addressed to the Italian government, it appears that he wanted the Italian government to give to the pope a certain portion of the city of Rome where the pope and his various offices could function freely and independently. We base this on the fact that Strossmayer disapproved the occupation of the Quirinal by the Italian troops, he wanted it to remain in the hands of the pope, and expressed a strong desire that the Italian government give back the Quirinal to the pontiff.[34] In both of these documents he strongly advocated that the Italian government grant total freedom to the Holy See. In his other writings, he not only disapproved but strongly condemned the Italian government's confiscation of the property of the Catholic Church, for instance, convents and monasteries, and its enactment of special laws which could be applied against the Catholic clergy.[35] Even though we do not possess any written documents which might indicate that Strossmayer informed Italian officials of his views on these matters, knowing his character and his love for the Church we feel justified in assuming that he did communicate his criticism to them.

Although he earnestly desired to see every nation autonomous, free, and independent, and clearly perceived in the unity of a nation its growth, strength, and progress, the Bishop did not fail to recognize the fact that the movement had to be qualified inasmuch as it could become detrimental to the welfare of other nations. « We all know, » he states, « that in recent times a national awakening has become a governing principle – and this is right and just, since national unity, after the holy faith, is the most precious

---

[33] Carthe Minghetti (Bibliteca dell'archiginnasio, Bologna, Italy), cartone 84, fasc. III. In all probability Strossmayer had sent this « pro memoria » to his intimate friend Marco Minghetti, and then the latter handed it over to his political colleagues.

[34] *Ibid.*

[35] GBBS, v. V (1877), no. 9, p. 89 and passim, and also in so many other documents.

gift of God; but, in my judgment and according to my convictions, » he adds, « the principle of national unity must be ennobled, elevated, sanctified... by the spirit of the holy Gospel, and it must be inspired by that justice which says 'Do not do to others what you do not wish to be done to you'. Otherwise the principle of national unity may and will become the source of pride, intolerance, selfishness, and of all kinds of injustices ».[36]

Better to understand the position of the Bishop on various aspects of freedom, we quote several excerpts from his pastoral lettere of June 29, 1869:

a. *Freedom in General*

« Today the world is earnestly striving for nothing so much as for its own freedom. Every nation and individual would like to be master in his own house; everybody whishes to be the architect of his own future. The Church does not find fault with this tendency because she knows that our relationship with God and with his divine will is based on freedom... Man and the entire human society, which were worthy to be redeemed by the blood of the Son of God, deserve to live in and to enjoy freedom ».[37]

b. *Freedom of Nations*

« In my opinion the Vatican Council will be preoccupied also with the following issue. It is known that today all the nations of the world are longing for their freedom and unity. As far as this is concerned, every nation that forms a unity by its nature and its history and origin is entitled to become united, and in this unity it is justified to seek its strength, its life, and its progress. The Church is not opposed to this tendency ».[38]

---

[36] Strossmayer's speech delivered at Zagreb on the occasion on the opening of the Art Gallery, November 9, 1884. This address was originally printed in *Rad Jugoslavenske Akademije*, v. 73, pp. 162-185. We cite according to TS, p. 195.

[37] BS, XXII (1934), p. 14.

[38] *Ibid.*, p.10.

c. *Freedom of the Church*

« Essentially necessary for the Church in performing her mission are her freedom and independence; and it can be affirmed with every right that this is the first fruit of the Redemption. When Christ redeemed the world through his blood and death, he redeemed the entire earth and all nations that dwell on it. When he handed them over to his Father, he acquired the eternal right for himself and for the eternal truth to preach it freely (through his Church) and freely to live and reign (on this earth)... For this reason the Church at present is striving to insure freedom for her mission in the world with new methods because the old international agreements have become inefficient. This is not only for the benefit of the Church but also of great concern to all nations since the Church's freedom and independence will serve as pledge of their own liberty and independence ».[39]

d. *Freedom of the Pope*

« It is self-evident that in the first place freedom and independence must be guaranteed to the Pope who is the foundation of unity not only in the Church but in every aspect of a free life; it is obvious that the Church cannot be considered free as long as her supreme authority... is not free and independent... Hence it is evident how important it is, not only for the Church but also for the entire world, that the Church enjoy freedom and progress and that the successor of St. Peter does not become a subject of any nation; by its very nature and human weakness every secular power always tends to use the immense moral force which is found in the supreme authority of the Church for its own selfish interests; if this happens, it will become detrimental not only to the Church but to the entire human society as well. In regard to this view, not only ecclesiastics but also the most learned and broadminded statesmen agree that civil and ecclesiastical powers must be united

---

[39] *Ibid.*, pp. 14-15. Cf. also his Pastoral of 1891 in which he says that « holy Church in her mission guards her freedom and independence like an eye in the head, for Christ-God and our Redeemer ordered her to do so » (KRS, IV, p.. 233).

in the city of Rome but in the rest of the world they must remain separated... ».[40]

When the freedom of the Church came up at the Vatican Council in the Schema « De disciplina ecclesiastica », in which the drafters proposed that the Church should find protection and safety for her freedom through the patronage of the rulers and of the civil authorities, especially in the matter of the election of the bishops, Strossmayer, who saw a great peril in this for the Church, opposed it very vehemently. Considering himself to be a liberal and a strong proponent of every kind of freedom and liberty, he could not have found security for the freedom of the Church in anything else but in freedom itself. He formulated his proposal in the following manner:

« There is no doubt that the authors of the mentioned Schema had pious and holy intentions in proposing that it is necessary to call upon the rulers of this world and on the civil authorities to be protectors of the freedom of the Church. At this point, in order to put the minds of the dafters at ease, let me say that their proposal is dangerous and fruitless as well. It is dangerous since this patronage and protection of the rulers have brought the Church into slavery and humiliation. It is fruitless: as things stand today, the rulers -- in spite of their noble intentions – cannot be protectors of the freedom of the Church since in many countries they are forbidden by their constitutional laws (to do this) – sometimes even by an oath they have taken... Neither the civil authority nor the severity of penal laws can offer us any provisions in this respect; on the contrary, they (the rulers) would embitter and provoke their constituents and nations not only against themselves but also against the Church and against her clergy in particular... In my opinion, if the Church is really in need of outside protection to safeguard her freedom, she should not look for it nor will she find it in any other means but in promoting civil rights and the freedom of nations. In this way the Church will take this holy weapon (of freedom) out of the hands of those who are warring

---

[40] BS, XXII (1934), p 16. It appears from his Pastoral letter of 1877 that two French statesmen: F. Guizot and E. Thiers were the first who had coined this slogan on freedom and independence (see GBBS, V, no. 9, p. 88).

against her and who are trying to destroy moral values. And the Church, by employing this means of freedom with vigorous strength and perseverance, will make it serve her own protection, and at the same time it will become the protection of nations and of a good and holy cause ».[41]

To present a complete picture of the Bishop's notion of personal and national freedom, it is necessary to mention another view of his which has a close relation with the subjects under discussion. He was known to be a strong opponent of any kind of administrative centralism in a state. Of course, this centralized governmental power primarily pertained to the situation in the Austria-Hungarian Empire in which the Austrians or the Hungarians held all the power in their hands while the other national groups were the victims of that absolute power or at best they were not permitted to express themselves to any extent in their own favor and in behalf of their national interests.

At any rate, in the speech which Strossmayer delivered in the Diet in Zagreb on July 5, 1861 (which lasted almost two hours) – after having exposed the evils of centralized power – urged the Croatian deputies that « it is our sacred duty to oppose centralism... Centralism is in accordance neither with the spirit of justice nor with that of the Gospel... it makes little difference whether a slave is kept in golden or in iron chains ».[42] He was a staunch enemy – and such he remained for the rest of his life – of any sort of absolute power and excessive centralism. What we wish to inculcate is that in his already formed mind there was a strong desire to see democracy in every human organization and to some extent in the Catholic Church, too. From perusing his voluminous documentation one can hardly escape seeing this trait of his nor can resist the temptation to state that he carried his political or social convictions into the structure of the Church. It seems that the ultimate cause for his political and ecclesiastical views is to be sought in the Bishop's studies of the structure of the Church in the first three centuries. Furthermore, the Prelate was almost obsessed by the desire to discover

---

[41] Mansi, 50, 480.
[42] TS, pp. 153-154, and also CP, p. 513.

a balance of power in every instance, be it in State or within the Church. This prompted him to search for an equilibrium of might on the international level in order to preserve peace and tranquility among the states and nations. At least he envisioned this neutralization of forces on the European continent as we shall see elsewhere.

It seems to us that one of the basic reason why he was in continuous struggle to discover a balance of power and why he was against absolutism is found in his awareness of human weakness, human selfishness and pride; consequently he was apprehensive to see much power deposited in one man's hands. Whenever an opportunity arose he elaborated on this topic of « human inborn weakness ». When his friend Lord Gladstone complained to him that the holiest people worked against him, the following answer the Bishop gave him: « As to your comment, my most honoured friend, that often the most pious people work against you, while other less pious support you, let me rimark this: that, as the Apostle Paul complains, in every man there are, in our present state, two opposing laws, the 'anima naturaliter christiana,' as Tertulian calls it, and the 'anima pagana'. Unfortunately, even in the best and noblest souls the 'anima pagana' often triumphs ».[43]

Having all this in mind one should not be surprise to hear him say in the Vatican Council that « ... our nations will accept more

---

[43] Bishop's letter to Gladstone of April 11, 1878 (CBSG, p. 437). Cf. also his address « Three Words to our University » (TS, pp. 311-313) and Mansi 50, 481. The Bishop depicts the two opposing forces at work in man in the following fashion: « It is the duty of every man, of every State, and of human society to practice truth and justice in the world. This is a daily bread upon which every human being and every sort of organization must feed itself if it wishes to exist and to be fruitful. Since harmony and love (in the human society) are the noblest goals and the noblest fruit of truth, and since every individual, every society, and all mankind struggle to come into possession of truth, by the same token they are to strive for harmony and unity, too. This is found in human nature and in the holy Gospel which contains all the mysteries of human nature and of human society. In my opinion », the Bishop continues, « this unity of mankind, founded upon truth and justice and also upon mutual respect, sooner or later will become a reality. In the meantime, the wild instinct of weakened man's human nature turns this holy and genuine sentiment into a tendency for tyranny and supremacy which lack truth, justice, mutual understanding, and love. Man is prone to transfer this blind impulse into life of family, of State, and of human society; hence there are so many evils in the family and in the State as well » (TS, p. 332).

willingly, more readily, and more heartedly if the decrees, which we recommend to them, are given in the name of the entire Council; and if we tell them that our decisions are not based on the authority of one person even though he posseses the supreme authority but in the name of all of us in the Council ».[44] This stand of his he substantiated with the practice of the Apostolic Council of Jerusalem and with the mentality of the age in which Vatican I was held. « The title of the decree (of the Jerusalem Council), he argued, « is this 'It has been decided by the Holy Spirit and by ourselves' (Acts 15, 28). First of all, thanks, honor and glory are given to the Holy Spirit... then it says 'ourselves.' I perceive in this word 'ourselves' that unity and cooperation (beween the pope and the bishops) which I have recommended a moment ago. In this expression 'ourselves' there is no doubt that Peter retained the first and principal place – not excluding the rest (of the apostles) who are not on the equal level with him – but who (the apostles) with their common right, mutual consensus and cooperation contributed to the formulating of that decree... ».[45] He further argued that: « ... in our own days there is a movement among cultural nations and peoples to define and to determine their own common interests and rights with mutual consensus, »[46] and he cannot see why this should not be practiced in the Council. In his subsequent speech he picked up this thread of thought for awhile once again by stating that many cultural nations have learned from the Church councils how matters of grave nature and importance are to be discussed and decisions mutually reached. The Church is the mother and the teacher of all nations, and she should set an example.[47]

---

[44] MANSI 50, pp. 140-141.
[45] Ibid., p. 141.
[46] Ibid.
[47] Ibid., pp. 482-483. Strossmayer in his fifth and last oration (of June 2, 1870) in the Council argued for some time against papal infallibility, and among so many other arguments he alleged that in modern times people – especially the young and educated -- are against any absolute authority. On this point St. Augustine served him as the point of departure. According to St. Augustine the educated were misled and trapped by the Manicheans because of the extreme authority of the Catholic Church. First of all, he states « we have to realize that it is hard on human frivolity and vanity to bear the yoke of authority... and that we have to be cautious and farsighted while we are defining the qualities of authority, and we can offer unwillingly and unintentionally an oppor-

It almost seems that he was arguing that all the decrees should be issued in the name of the Council, not only in the name of the Pontiff, as though he did not want to see that « supreme power » turned into « absolute ».

Furthermore, he ventured in the same speech to introduce one more proposal even more daring than the previous ones. Being imbued with liberal and democratic tendencies and wishing to see the Church as closely united as possible either in the current Council or otherwise, and its being detestable to him that the Pontiff might appear to the world – even in this Council – to be overlording, he suggested on the basis of practice of some former ecumenical councils that it would be extremely desirable to see the Pontiff preside in general sessions instead of only in public congregations in which already redacted decrees are solemnly promulgated. In this way the Pontiff would become better acquainted with the issues under the discussion, and would be able to see the force of arguments on all sides, and consequently all these factors would help him to form a better judgment on the current matters.[48] However, he did not get far with this argumentaion; he was interrupted by Cardinal de Luca, one of the Cardinal Presidents, with the remark « First of all, what our Holy Father has confirmed in his Bull cannot be dragged into discussion ».[49]

Strossmayer in his speech of December 30, 1869, at the Vati-

---

tunity that the supreme authority (papacy)... becomes diminished » (MANSI 52, 402). Secondly, he affirms that papal infallibility, « which is about to be defined, will make the Catholic Church odious to the nations and to the youth, by accusing her of being full of superstition and of blind faith since the ultimate foundation to authority and to faith is entrusted to the judgment of one man (pope) of whom it is said that he is a sinner and exposed to all human weaknesses » (MANSI 52, 403). Naturally, during this speech of his, now and then, many of the council fathers kept murmuring. Pope Pius IX in his congratulatory letter « Dolendum profecto » of March 12, 1870 to Dom Gueranger, Abbot of Solesmes, for having written a book *The Pontifical Monarchy* had touched upon these topics. The letter itself is full of bitterness toward those Catholic laymen who did not submit themselves without questioning to the Holy See, and dared to advocate some sort of democracy in the Church. The Pontiff had also in mind the bishops of the minority (Cf. *Papal Theaching, the Church,* selected and arranged by the Benedictine Monks of Solesmes, and translated by Mother E. O'Gorman, R.S.C. J. [Boston, St. Paul Editions, 1962], pp. 201-202).
[48] MANSI 50, 142.
[49] *Ibid.,* 143.

can Council did not limit himself solely to criticism of the Schema
(Constitutio dogmatica de doctrina catholica) but this drafted document was a means for him to introduce some suggestions of his
which deserve our attention for two reasons: first, because they
fall within the scope of this topic under the discussion; secondly,
because they reveal his attitude and his program which he wanted
to have implemented into the agenda of the current Council.

Time and again he kept urging that the Council should not overlook the strivings of nations for individual and national freedom. The
implication was that these were some of the current issues which the
Fathers should take into consideration and discuss them. As a result, he turned his criticism on the drafters of the Schema, by stating, that « they (the drafters) being enclosured within the shool
walls are better acquainted with the needs and debates of the school
than with the necessities of the Church and of the people ».[50] In his
judgment the best equipped people to know and to deal with the
needs of the Church were the bishops who worked in the large cities and who were in constant ad immediate contact with the
ills and with the problems of the modern society – and especially
those bishops who have come out with sound recommendations.
He argued that those bishops should be given more opportunity
to eleborate on these problems and to give their opinions.[51]

The Bishop candidly admited that the proposition of the originators of the Schema were correct in themselves, but he believed that
they were irrelevant to the society of the present age; and it looks as
though the initiators of the Schema « have resurrected from the
tombs the propositions and theses which had been debated in the
shools a long time ago but which are now a passe », he said.[52]
Thereafter, he urged the Fathers and various commissions to desist from writing books full of laws and recommendations; instead
he suggested that « on the contrary, if we write just a several pages and if these pages meet the needs and expectations of the Church
and of the faithful, then this Council will earn for itself an eternal
name, and will deserve to be complimented by all nations ».[53]

---

50   *Ibid.*, 144.
51   *Ibid.*
52   *Ibid.*, 145.
53   *Ibid.*

What is more, he opposed any definition of a new dogma, and argued that « to cure the wounds of the human society we do not need new dogmatic definitions; the old ones will suffice, since they are divine and consequently inexhaustible, to remedy the miseries of all nations of all ages provided, of course, they are properly explained and correctly applied ».[54] Finally he has attacked the abusive language, which had been applied to the separated Christians, with these words « I am dissatisfied with the form (of the Schema) because I find in it abusive expressions – and I repeat abusive expressions – as for instance: anti-Christs, shame, disgrace, abomination, detestation, impiety, monstrous errors, cancer, etc. I beg your pardon, Venerable Fathers, but I wish to tell you that these expressions (applied to the other Christians) are not in accordance with our age and let alone with the spirit of the Church. Those are terribly mistaken who opine that the present generation can be converted and brought back into the bosom of the holy Church by way of these opprobrious utterances and anathemata ».[55] After having mentioned the incident how Christ rebuked the Apostles when they asked him to punish those who did not believe, he added his opinion « In my judgment, while the Church is exercising her authority and power in condemning errors in accordance with her mission and duty, she remains and will remain the mother of all races and of all nations, which (the Church) all of us – especially those in error – has in her heart. While she adjudges errors by way of her power, she constantly tries through her love and sympathy to win those in error to herself and to bring them into unity ».[56]

In his judgment the unity and the universality of the Church must be manifested in all aspects, be it in the ecumenical councils or in her supreme government. He considered ecumenical councils as the best manifestations of the unity as well as the abundant inner life of the Church. In advocating holding an ecumenical council every ten years, he asserted that had this been done and practiced most probably the Reformation would have never occured.[57] What

---

54   *Ibid.*, 146.
55   *Ibid.*
56   *Ibid.*, 147.
57   *Ibid.*, 483.

is more, he looked upon an ecumenical council as a means to prevent a « total absolutism » within the Church. For this very reason in his last speech of June 2, 1870, in which he had brought out a host of arguments against the papal infallibility, he argued this way:

« If however, Venerable Fathers, the personal and absolute infallibility of the Roman Pontiff is ratified, then, in my judgment, it becomes evident that ecumenical councils will become superfluous and unnecessary (the bishops are protesting — but he continues). The following question can be justifiably posed: why the bishops from the farthest corners of the Catholic world, leaving their flock and relinquishing the most sacred duties of their office, must meet frequently, if there is always in the center of the Church the personal and absolute authority which is present all the time and which suffices to solve all the controversies concerning faith and morals and to reestablish peace in the Church in case it is disturbed?[58]

It would be wrong to deduce thas Strossmayer wanted to do away with the monarchical structural set-up within the Church. On the other hand he came out with some strong proposals at the Vatican Council which had been in practice in the early Church or which are in accordance with those practices *per deductionem*. These recommendations of his were to serve as to prevent this monarchical power from turning into an absolutism which might work totally independent of the rest of the Church, especially from the episcopate. The unity of the Church — which is centered and realized in papacy and only in papacy — and his notion of the universalism (or as we call it at present internationalisation) of the Church are her two essential factors. His notion of the universalism of the Church was so powerful that in his opinion the head of the Church had to grow out or to be born out of his international organic entity in order to present and to function on behalf of the entire Christian community. He was so clear and precise on these

---

[58] MANSI 52, 397. For this very reason, namely, that ecumenical councils are going to be brought to an end, if papal infallibility will be defined, he declared himself in the assembly of the bishops « nor do I wish to contribute to the fourth chapter of the Schema by casting my vote in favor of it (papal infallibility) and thus becoming an accomplice in making this ecumenical Council be the last one » (*ibid.*).

points that there is no need of commentary; simply the extracts from his speeches will suffice. It must also be kept in mind that, besides wishing to debate the current problems, he wanted to see the Church to be reformed *in capite et in membris,* « constantly in the process of reforming and improving regardless who we are and how holy and perfect we might be, as long as we live in this mortal body of ours and as long as we dwell in earthly life, everyone of us every moment and until our last breath needs reformation; and if I am not mistaken, this humble and sincere acceptance of this reality is our salvation and the pivot of our hope... After all, he continues to say, « this Council is convoked to reform whatever in the Church is in need of reformation ».[59]

3. - Strossmayer's Proposals on Changes in the Structure of the Church

a. *Cardinals*

Since the reformation, according to him, must begin from the highest to the lowest in the Church, the college of cardinals was his first topic. His point of departure on this problem was the Council of Trent which had been preoccupied with the reformation of this college. « It is known, » he says, « that the Council of Trent was engrossed in this problem; if I am not mistaken in the fourteenth session of the said Council the decision was made... that the college of cardinals must be composed, in as far as it can be realized, from all peoples and nations. Following the footsteps of that Council... let me express the same wish. It is my desire that this college of cardinals becomes genuine and real image of the Church... thus each people and every nation according to its number... will be able to see in this sacred body its members and its representatives ».[60]

He brought forth two principal reasons for choosing cardinals from among all nations:

« From this college (of cardinals), first of all, proceeds the

---

[59] MANSI 50, 478.
[60] *Ibid.*

highest and indeed divine power (papacy) which is necessary to
the Church. This is her (Church's) eternal and immovable foundation, and it is also foundation to the entire mankind since it is a
keystone to the harmony which must prevail in the human society...
I would like, following the Council of Trent, that this power (papacy) in its very origin bears the sign of universalism; let the pope
who is the common father, teacher, judge of all cardinals, come
out of the bosom of the entire mother Church, and thus it will become evident that he was elected and approved by all from the
very beginning ». [61]

« The second reason... is that college of cardinals... is preoccup-
pied with the most difficult problems of the entire Catholic world.
(Of coure, Strossmayer speaks here of cardinals residing in Rome).
And the very same nature of the problem requires that the college, which is destined to solve and to bring decisions on these most
troublesome issues of the world, be also the representation of its
constitutive parts, that is, that each Catholic nation may find in
this college its advocates and protectors of its interests... trying
to adjust their (cardinals') decisions to the genuine and real needs
not only of one church but of all churches... ».[62]

b. *Roman Congregations*

He strongly implied in elaborating on the Roman Congregations that quite a few of their concerns must be relinquished to
the bishops. This is what he said about the Congregations:

« What I have said, pursuing the spirit of the Council of Trent,
about the illustrious college of cardinals, I deem necessary to ap-
ply the very same thing to the excellent Congregations which are
engaged in solving the most serious questions of the Church. They,
in my judgment, should have a character of universalism, too;
thus it will not happen that the most capable and most learned men
of only one church (of Italy) participate in them but also the pious,
learned and distinguished men of all other nations. What is more,
the reformation of these Congregations will be brought to perfection

---

[61] *Ibid.*, 478-479.
[62] *Ibid.*, 479.

il they are freed from the matters of less importance which can be solved elsewhere. There is a general and universally accepted maxim (which says) the one, who is preoccupied with the insignicant, less necessary and superfluous matters, ordinarily neglects the essential ».[63]

c. *Provincial and Diocesan Synods*

The holding of the provincial and diocesan synods is the manifestation of the life of the Church, and they are of great advantage to the universal welfare of the Church. He insisted that provincial and diocesan synods refrain from publishing their recommendations and regulations in volumes if they wished to be effective and up to date.[64] Afterwards he elaborated on the relationship between provincial and diocesan synods with the Roman Congregations for the approval of their decisions. He made the following comment:

« As far as the provincial synods are concerned, I repeat, if they are held frequently they will be of great aid to the Church of God. It is my desire that in the future the Roman Congregations desist from mutilating and changing the acts and decrees of the provincial synods: first of all, they must abandon their practice of adding new decrees which are very often unacceptable due to the needs of that particular church. I know positively that some zealous advocates of holding provincial synods just on account of these mutilations and additions had totally abstained from having these synods. As far as I know the provincial synods used to have their inner and domestic rights... I propose... that the inner and domestic rights of these synods be preserved in the future, of course, not violating the authority of the Holy See and its power in watching that nothing is decided what would be contrary to the authority of the Church, her doctrine, of the rights of the Holy See or of the ecclesiastical universal discipline; otherwise, let nothing be added or changed or interpolated ».[65]

---

[63] *Ibid.*
[64] *Ibid.*, 482.
[65] *Ibid.*, 487. In the Schema on the bishops and on the synods many reasons are alleged why the acts of the provincial synods are to be sent to Rome,

d. *Election of Bishops*

This topic was very closely connected in the Bishop's mind with the provincial synods and the freedom of the Church. Since he was a firm believer all his life that the Church and the State must be separated, then his proposal how the bishops are to be elected is not a surprise. He gave a strong indication that the rulers and the governments must be deprived of any interference in choosing and appointing bishops. Furthermore, he reasoned that if the governments are given any right in appointing bishops, then there is a great danger that some priests will do all sorts of things to please a government in order to get appointed to the bishopric.[66] Thereafter he came out with the following:

« The Vatican Council must prevent and liquidate this evil (outside interference in electing bishops) as far as it is possible. If this evil enters into the Church, it will pervade her and erode her like a cancer. Therefore, I believe that Church will have to return sooner or later to the old practice by increasing the power of the provincial synods and thus enabling them to influence the election of bishops, and in this manner they will remove the danger from the Church. It is true, however, that this proposal is a serious and touchy matter, on the other hand I maintain that the Vatican Council was convoked not to be preoccupied with trivial matters and problems which are easly solved but it is its duty to tackle the most difficult problems and to offer the appropriate aid to the solution of the extraordinary evils and dangers ».[67]

---

and one of the reasons is that Rome may examine « that nothing is decided that would be too strict or what might be contrary to or not in accordance with the human mind ». This quotation is taken out of Strossmayer's speech, and he says that it is found on page 29 of the Schema. He offers the following comment on the quoted statement: « I may say that I have read this statement ten times, and I could have hardly believed my eyes. Is it possible that the metropolitan bishop with his suffragans can decide or pass as a law something which would not be in accordance with the sane mind? I have a custom since my earliest days not to say anything which might offend somebody. But in regard to this statement (of the Schema)... I ought to state that it is not in accordance with the sane mind » (*ibid.*).

[66] *Ibid.*, 481.
[67] *Ibid.*

e. *Patriarchs and National Churches*

It is obvious that the Bishop wanted by all means not only to establish some sort of balance of power within the Church, but he struggled with the same vigor to reverse the Church's movement toward absolutism. He continually suggested that the Church should go back to the practice of her early centuries. In order to accomplish this, he reasoned without much ado, it would be necessary that a special decree be issued by the Council that vicar apostolics have the same rights and privileges as the ordinaries possess. (It is apparent that by this recommendation vicar apostolics would be placed on the same level with the rest of bishops, and as a result, they would be much less dependent upon the Holy See and freer in exercising their duties). His proposal that patriarchs instead of vicar apostolics should be instantly reinstaded in the cities of Costantinople and of Alexandria, was more farreaching than the previous one, and it at least symbolized some counteracting against the power of Rome.[68]

His advocacy of preserving the rights, customs and privileges of churches in various nations is congruous with his basic ideas on the structure of the Church. After having completely aligned himself with bishops Darboy of Paris and Dupanloup of Orleans on this matter,[69] he continued to elaborate on the rights and the customs of different churches which serve the spiritual welfare of various nations. These practices were to be preserved as long as they were in conformity to or did not violate the unity of the universal Church and in as far as they did not prejudice the rights of the Holy See. He rather pursued the topic along these lines. Strossmayer's awareness of psychological particularities of each nation prompts him to state: « regardless how all of us wish to see the unity in the Church, if this unity or rather uniformity goes to the extreme I am afraid that this severe and extravagant conformity will cause rebellion and create rebels within the Church ».[70] Besides

---

[68] *Ibid.*, 488.
[69] *Ibid.*, 484.
[70] *Ibid.*, 483-484. In his Pastoral of 1869 he said this on the rights of churches in various parts of the world: « There are indeed some churches in various parts in the world which have their specific customs and habits, but

this latent danger of potential revolt and defiance in the Church, this extreme uniformity was going to be in the way to the reunion of the Churches. During this discourse he brought in his impressions and experiences of his numerous encounters and debates with the separated bishops (Greek Orthodox). He claims that they were most fearful that in the case of reunion the rights, privileges and customs of their respective churches would be taken away or abolished by the Church of Rome.[71]

f. *Priests*

It is necessary to say a few words on his views on the position of a priest in the Church of God. This is warranted by his notion of freedom and his inimical attitude to any kind of arbitrariness regardless where it might occur or by whom it might be exercised. Most probably the problem of a priest was precipitated by Archbishop Pedicini's attack on some priests who wore a sign of distinction. (It occured to me », Strossmayer says, « against my own will, that is, I have expected from his (Pedicini's) zeal that he would subject to criticism the other signs of distinction, too, as those of color and titles since there is a great danger that these matters, which are a product of the human laws and of human institution, do not outweigh those which are of divine law and institution ». (Here he is referring to the college of cardinals).[72]

Prior to this retort he enumerated the ways how the priests were debased and humiliated in the Catholic Chuch. Some theologians even approached and begged him by invoking the names of all the saints to take the priests under his protection. « I asked them (theologians) to remain calm since I knew that the more erudite, more learned and more distinguished bishops would take them (the

---

nobody will touch them as long as they do not violate the unity in the Church and as long as they are of great benefit and consolation to the faithful. These customs and habits are under the immediate protection of the supreme power (papacy) as is the case with the privileges of our nation that in some parts of our country the divine mysteries and the holy sacrifice of the Mass are celebrated in the national language ». BS, *loc. cit.,* 13.

[71] Mansi 50, 485.
[72] *Ibid.,* 667.

priests) under protection; and I come to their defense with my whole heart ». [73]

He discussed the question of priests at some length, and brought out some of their plights. First of all, he says « It is right and just that we the bishops defend the priests of the second rank when they are discussed: they are our brothers, our co-priests, our cola-borators in the vineyard of the Lord; the main portion of our episco-pal cares they carry; without their love, confidence, affection, piety and zeal, all our strivings and our mission will be in vain ».[74] Se-condly, he proposed that the Church must provide ways and means to support of priests so as prevent their being engaged in marke-ting. If this should be done, then priests would be spared from de-basing themselves by resorting to begging alms from house to house or in the public places and by innundating like « grasshoppers » some richer dioceses in search of Mass stipends, which – in his mind – was in no way a solution to provide means for their li-ving.[75] Thirdly, he expressed his agreement with Msgr. Haynald that breviary for the clergy, engaged in the pastoral work, must be reformed and accommodated to their heavy and demanding daily duties.[76] Fourthly, he demanded that the arbitrariness in the case of an accused priest must be eliminated except in the extremely rare cases which might create a grave scandal. As a rule, in his judgment, courts and judicial procedures must be formed in such

----

[73]   Ibid., 663. The Bishop was in favor of freedom at any cost. When the Diocese of Zagreb had issued the order that no priest can belong to the Croatian Party of Right whose leader and founder was Dr. Ante Starčević, he said « that order is asinine ». Even though Starčević and his political party were the strongest opponents of Strossmayer in politics he came out with the statement that a priest can belong to any political party, and the church autho-rities have no right to tell the priests which political program to follow as long as that particular party is not banned or outlawed by the government. Cf. KRS, IV, 212.

[74]   Mansi 50, 661.

[75]   Ibid., 665-666.

[76]   Ibid., 665. He justifies his proposal with the following explanation: « Human nature by itself is prone to find excuses for its shortcomings, there-fore, there is nothing more common among men, than when they are fa-ced with the excessive demands of the law, that they do away with those things which are necessary and easy to be fulfilled, and all this is done under the pretense that too much is required from them » (ibid.). (It is apparent that he was in favor of making the breviary shorter for the clergy).

a way that each accused priest would have a fair and just trial.
If this were done, then no priest would be able to say that he was
a victim of bishop's whim and arbitrariness.[77]

g. Science, Scientific Institutions, their Freedom and Priests

No churchman of the past century was so deeply and unsparingly involved in promoting science and art as was Strossmayer.[78]
He kept pouring the funds of his diocese on schools on all levels
and on scientific institutions.[79] His diocese, one of the richest in
Europe, was wealthy in estates which he organized and moderni-
zed. Under excellent management the estates prospered.[80] All this
wealth he used for the betterment of his nation. In some instances
this was not solely limited to his native land Croatia, but it extended as far as Paris, France, where Louis Leger, professor at the
University of Sorbonne, was given unlimited funds by Strossmayer
for his publications dealing with South Slav problems.[81] His en-
dowments to various publications and scholarly institutions reached
such proportions that he became one of the most famous maecenas
in Europe and as such attracted the attention of the politico-Catholic newspaper L' Univers of Paris and became the most favorite
target of attacks launched by its editor, Louis Veuillot, in 1867.
In his speech on the occasion of the inauguration of the Yugoslav
Academy of Science and Art in Zagreb, delivered on July 28, 1867,
he made the following reference of this subject:

« Let us finish this part of my speech with one remark which

---

[77] Ibid., 663.

[78] Emil Ollivier, op. cit., II, 13.

[79] « There is no high school (gymnasium) », he claimed in his speech
delivered on the occasion of the opening of the Art Gallery in Zagreb, « in our
country which I did not (financially) support » (TS, p. 194). He also founded
a special school for higher education for girls in Djakovo, and contributed a
lot to the founding of the same kind of school in Osijek (ibid.).

[80] CP, pp. 847-935. Cepelić and Pavić have devoted hundred pages of
their book to his sector of the Bishop's activities.

[81] Luis Leger, loc. cit., 224. The Bishop said to Leger: « I place unlimited credit at your disposal for the works which are in the interest of our nation ». Luis Leger wrote the following works: Le Mond Slav (Paris, 1885),
La Save, le Danube et le Balkan (Paris, 1884), Etudes Slaves (Paris, year is
not indicated.

concerns my person. Recently, while I was in Paris, I came across a politico-Catholic newspaper L'Univers which is mercilessly attacking me for spending church money on secular matters. It is easy to guess the source and where these undignified attacks come from, and that these « secular matters » are our Academy and our University. Thanks to God, that I am not the only guilty person in this matter since our entire clergy – from the first to the last – are just as guilty; clergy knows that whatever is done for religion is also done for science, and whatever is done for the promotion of science it will eventually serve to the religion. Let everybody know that neither calumnies nor threats will prevent us to follow our chartered course, that is: while we are conscienciously performing the duties of our vocation, we will employ all our abilities to promote every cause which will be of benefit to the promotion of material and intellectual progress, and which will improve the future and the better living conditions of our people. I have to admit that the truth is gained by faith and science, and they are advantageous to each other ».[82]

On this topic of the role of science in the human race and its contributions to the improving of living conditions he became more specific when he stated that « the science has a sublime goal to penetrate deeper and deeper into divinely marvelous nature and from there to draw new resources for the benefit of mankind... ».[83]

Is there then any wonder that he discussed at Vatican I the role of modern sciences – which was also one of his favorite topics – within the context of the priestly education. First, he insisted that in these modern times a priest must be well trained to meet the needs of the contemporary society not only in strictly theological disciplines but also in modern sciences or as he says a priest « must devour holy and secular books as well ».[84] Secondly, he also re-

---

[82] TS, pp. 164-165.
[83] TS, p. 199. Cf. his Pastoral on the forthcoming council of 1869 (BS, loc. cit., 7).
[84] MANSi 50, 663-664. He addressed these words to his clergy on the occasion of his installation (Djakovo, 1850): « Priests are the interpretors of divine law, custodians of Tradition, teachers and spokesmen of their people, prophets of the coming divine judgments, medics of the soul, masters of life and death, by the power of their mission... In spite of all these splendid

commended the founding of Catholic universities in which lay professors « will participate since they are also invited to be participants in the royal priesthood, especially now when the faith is threatened so that they also may defend the walls of Israel with their genius and knowledge. Believe me, if the priests are not erudite and learned, if they are not the leaders and standard-bearers, if they are not only the salt to the earth but also the light to the world: light to the world, as some saint had said, during the day to spread the light of the divine doctrine everywhere, the light at night to disperse the darkness of errors in order to show the way to the people entrusted to their care, to the clearer day; if these re-quirements are not met, everything else will be in vain ».[85] Thirdly, he advocated that the intellectuals and their needs be taken into consideration since the present method of teaching and instructing the general public and the children in faith is not suitable « to the genius of the learned men »[86] Fourthly, in the same speech he re-fered to the secular newspapers and other secular publications and to their attacks on the Church of God. Not wishing to violate civil liberties, he came out with the concrete proposals how to counte-ract these calumnies against the Church. He indicated that the clergy of this time, due to the lack of proper training and education, was not able to cope with the secular writers, therefore the priests must study secular sciences in order to become advocates and protectors of the divine truth. What is more, clergy educated in various sciences would be apt to move into teaching positions at various universities, and thus would be enabled to be in touch with educated youth. He also reminded the council Fathers that once upon a time it was a priestly privilege to hold in their hands the educational institutions but that this was past; the only road was that the priests through their education obtain teaching positions.[87] He finished his reasoning with the following words:

« If this be realized then we can say with Tertullian what he

---

titles a priest cannot meet the responsabilities of his vocation without solid knowledge » (JJS-DK, I, 147) and passim. Cf. BS, *loc cit.,* 9-10.

[85] MANSI 50, 664.
[86] *Ibid.*
[87] *Ibid.*

had said in his Apologia 'We are since yesterday but we have already filled your cities, camps, senate etc.; only your temples are left to you'. Venerable Fathers, believe me, this is the day that we should recommend to the priests to study sciences most earnestly since it can happen that those (priests), who are expected to stand on the top of mountain and extend their visions to the extremities of the earth, remain at the foot of mountain, then they, in their obstinacy and haughtiness, either ignore or refute someone else's visions and ideas ».[88] It is not hard to see what the Bishop was after: he wished that the clergy step into all the fields of human activities and give them the flavor of the Gospel. Nobody will deny that his statement about the hierarchy and the clergy, who prefer to complain and criticise the ideas of other people instead of becoming progenitors of new ideas, is correct even in our own day.

This idea of providing Catholic clergy with good education did not leave him for a moment, nor did it die with the closing of Vatican I. It was constantly on his mind and extremely close to his heart and to his cultural undertakings. What is more, he wanted to see theological higher studies organized into theological faculties, which must be part of the local university, and he tried to have theological schools centralized, which again indicates that he planned to do away with religious and diocesan major seminaries. All these ideas of his are evidenced not only in his native Croatia but in Italy where he was an unofficial adviser to the Italian government.

Strossmayer in his « Pro memoria » of January 20, 1872, addressed to the Italian government, made the folloying recommendations on this topic of educating Catholic clergy in order to encourage leading Italian politicians to take the initiative on this issue in contrast to the inertia of the Holy See and its slowness in responding to current and urgent problems. In this document he proposed that a theological faculty be formed in each larger Italian city and be made part of the local university. Should the Italians not have enough first-class professors, they should bring some in from other countries. In this way, the Bishop reasoned, the junior clergy would be freed from the major seminaries which usually had an ill-qualified faculty, who were hostile to modern society and new

---

[88]   *Ibid.*, 664-665.

ideas. Pious and talented young clergy must be encouraged to also pursue other sciences besides theology. Furthermore, the Italian government was expected to unsparingly provide the means and ways for this purpose. Those clergymen who distinguished themselves in scholarship in various branches of science should be given professorships at the respective universities or elsewhere. In this way the young clergy would be well equipped to tackle the problems of modern society, and by way of contact with the laymen would be in position to perceive the needs of the nation.[89]

Let us return to his native land Croatia for a better look at this problem. The theological faculty of Zagreb, in his opinion, had to be an organic part of the University. For this reason he insisted in his speech of November 9, 1884, that theology professors must never sever themselves or their research from the Academy of Science and Art; they had to work hand in hand with their brothers, lay professors, in cultivating and promoting all sciences and exchanging their views with one another. He perceived a great danger if the theological faculty should ever attempt to separate itself from the other faculties.[90] All the faculties of the University « are sisters and the rays of the same sun ».[91]

It seems to us that the Bishop, since the very moment he envisioned the founding of the Academy of Science and Art and of the University in Zagreb, had in his mind to do away with diocesan major seminaries and to bring theology students from all other Croatian provinces (Bosnia included) to the University of Zagreb. The purpose of the centralized theological faculty would be to speed up the reunion in many and varied respects of all Croatian people into one entity; and naturally this school of higher learning would provide a better faculty and a better theological curriculum by offering an excellent library to the students.[92]

---

[89]   Carte Minghetti, cartone 84, fasc. III.
[90]   At present the Communist regime in Croatia has severed the Theological Shool from the University of Zagreb, which is to be deplored. Most certainly this act violated the wish of one of the prominent founders – Strossmayer. The same Shool still enjoys the right to confer degrees, but they are only valid *in foro ecclesiastico*.
[91]   TS, pp. 196-197.
[92]   Strossmayer writes to Rački (just a few months before the opening

One might get the impression that the Bishop was totally and exclusively devoted to promoting science; what is more, it almost seems that his absorption in the science borders on obsession. We may even add that this equally goes for the arts. Perhaps, this would not disturb anybody if one would not know what fantastic sums of money he spent on these two branches of human endeavors. Undoubtedly, as we have seen previously, he was critized for this « extravagance », « luxury ». Many a time the implications expressed in the accusations against him were that he had to use the wealth for the church or to give it to the poor. If anybody had the destitute at heart, it was the Bishop, who kept helping left and right. We do not maintain that we have given a satisfactory answer to the Bishop's attitude toward science, art, schools and scientific institutions.

This problem cannot be solved without inquiring into his general outlook on solving the problem of the poverty of his people. It is evident that it was odious to him to dissect man; he approached and treated man like a single entity, an entire man: body and soul. He could not have thought of helping one part of man and neglecting the other. Only in the light of this concept can one properly comprehend the actions and the enterprises of the Bishop. We believe that we are justified in assuming that this primary goal was not so much to help financially the poor as it was to eliminate the poverty and awaken man to his dignity by enabling him to stand on his own two feet. It was detestable to him to see either a man or a nation sitting and begging at the table of someone else. For this reason he time and again reminded his clergy that the su-

---

of the University of Zagreb): « Undoubtedly, you have noticed from my previous letters that I am strongly in favor of having theological studies centralized in Zagreb, namely, that all our students of theology may have opportunity to attend the university's theological curriculum » (KRS, I, 304). In the same letter he speaks of bringing Franciscan theological students from Bosnia to Zagreb, and these may reside in the nearby Franciscan monastery (*ibid.,* p 305). Cf. the articles of Dr. Antun Bauer (Archbishop of Zagreb) « Pokrovitelj o svom predšasniku » and of Dr. Stjepan Zimmerman « Strossmayer i Sveučilište » in *Josip Juraj Strossmayer (Spomen – spis prigodom otkrivenja spomenika hrvatskom rodoljubu i narodnom prosvjetitelju)*, edited by Dr. S. Rittig and Dr. R. Maixner (Zagreb, Tisak Tipografije D. D., 1926), pp. 7-9 and 17-21.

rest and the best road to the moral and spiritual revival of people and to the other human noble strivings is by way of enlightenment and material progress.[93] In his address « The Three Words to our University » he placed grave responsibility on the shoulders of those who were going to be educated in the University. It was their duty to descend to the common people and to tend to their needs. He called to their minds the unsurpassed example of Christ who had abandoned his divine qualities – so to speak – so that He could serve, and concluded with this reminder: « Every educated man must dive in his love and humility into the depths of his people and to become its servant ».[94] He seizes the chance to reproach the government for not taking this course in helping the people and alleviating their poverty and miseries.[95] Therefore, we may sum up his life-long program of science and his people « Through the enlightenment and knowledge to the material, spiritual, cultural advancement and to the national freedom ».

While we find the Bishop justified in investing fabulous amounts of money in schools, in scientific institutions, and in numerous and varied publications, we are a little apprehensive to ascertain the same thing concerning his interest in the art which he cherished and loved so intensely. In purchasing various pieces of art – especially paintings – all over Europe and spending a large amount of money on them, we do not believe that we would sin against charity in saying that in this particular case at the core stood his Croatian national pride. His native Croatia, on account of waging so many wars against the Turks, had been in no position to develop the arts as the other European countries had; furthermore, Napoleon's conquest of Dubrovnik had put an abrupt halt to the artistic creativity of that republic, which had been considered the Athens of Croatia. It was the Bishop's fond desire to bring his nation to the artistic level of the other European countries. To this end, in 1884, he donated to the Art Gallery of Zagreb

---

[93] In the Bishop's article « The Paintings in the Cathedral of Djakovo » (TS, p. 269). This lenghty article was originally published in GBBS in 1873, no. 18, in 1874 in nos. 1-2, and 19-23, and 1878 in nos. 1 and 3, and also in nos. 5-10. The entire study was reprinted by Tade Smičikals under TS.
[94] TS, p. 317.
[95] KRS, IV, 180.

over 300 pieces of art of the first class.[96] How many more pieces he later added to this collection we do not know.

Naturally, the Bishop in his other documents alleges other motives which prompted him to embark on procuring some masterpieces of the leading European artists. We should recall what has been said earlier on his concept of man and how man is prone to evil, and that this inner divisiveness of man has to be tamed by the principles of the Gospel and by means of art. In his firm conviction in every Christian soul must be developed and cherished not only religious sentiments but also esthetic ones.[97] This view inspired him to hire the leading European architects and artists to work in his cathedral in Djakovo.[98] He firmly believed that the purchased pieces of art would serve as an incentive to the youth

---

[96] R. W. Seton Watson, *The Southern Slav Question,* 121. The same historian says « ... Strossmayer devoted himself tirelessly to the task of fostering the tender plant of Croatian culture; and though in later life his politcal influence waned, his striking personality has impressed itself indelibly upon the ilfe of the nation. Almost all that is ideal in Croatia of today is his work » (*ibid.,* p. 52). According to Ben Hurst, Strossmayer is Croatia's « Moses and her Chrysostom, her Pericles and her Maecenas, her Thomas à Kempis and her Michelangelo » (« Founder of Modern Croatia » in *The Catholic World,* v 81 (1905), p. 775.

[97] In his article « The Cathedral of Djakovo » (TS, p. 213). This study was originally printed in GBBS in 1874, nos. 5-18, and in the same year it was published under the same title in Zagreb as a brochure.

In his letter to Rački of March 26, 1875, which is an official letter and addressed to the public, he explains his stand toward art and its role in human life:

« In our own days the Croatian people have succeeded to found two temples: The Yugoslav Academy of Science and Art and the University of Zagreb. It is now up to the vital energies of these institutions to develop and to perfect themselves and also to cultivate science not only for its own sake but its fruits must reach the general public.

« If we wish that our national abilities grow systematically and universally then it is not only necessary that the intellect of our people become enlightened but also its hearts and nature must be ennobled, the latter is accomplished by art. By observing human nature, the development of mankind and the growth of various nations I have learned that science and art complement each other. And for this reason I have considered it my duty to subsidize both, in our nation, according to my financial means. For many years I was engaged in collecting pieces of art, which demanded a lot of labor and money. This was done for the sole purpose that my art collection may become the property of our entire nation and as a basis for the Art Gallery which slowly and gradually can become completed » (KRS, I, 342-343).

[98] « The Cathedral of Djakovo » (TS, pp. 203-246).

of his country in becoming artistically creative. All the Croatian young artists found a great maecenas in the person of Strossmayer.[99]

Before we bring out what freedom and independence science and scientific institutions are predestined to enjoy in human society, we would like to see his stand on the relationship among science, faith and art:

« I am a priest and a bishop », he said to the university professors and students on Nov. 9, 1884, « and I was in position to contribute something to the founding of the (Yugoslav) Academy of Science and Art and of the University in order to prove to my people that there are no contradictions whatever between the holy faith on one side and the science and the art on the other. If from time to time some oppositions emerge among them, they are not caused by their natures but rather they are the results of human passion, weakness and fanaticism. Both the faith and the science are the offsprings of God and due to their common origin and to their very natures they are directed to each other for mutual love, harmony and support. Believe me, when God enabled man to strike the first spark of his thought out of his intellect, and when man elicited for the first time a sentiment out of his heart, and when God made man to pronounce the first word, at the same time the faith and the science were brought into existence by God, and they (faith and science) became the heritage of the human race of all ages ».[100]

After having taken several detours on this topic of science and of art and what position the Bishop took on them and their role in the Church in particular and in the human society in general, we must say a few words on how he felt about the relationship between science, art and scientific institutions on one side and free-

---

[99] Cf. CP, pp. 671-693. The Bishop's intention was not only to encourage young laymen to study art and to become artistically creative but he also wanted the young clergy to foster art. As a matter of fact, he was preoccupied with this thought since his early life. In his speech of July 21, 1861, in the Diet of Zagreb he tried to convince the Croatian leaders to reorganize the (Croatian) college of St. Jerome in Rome so that the young ecclesiastical students may study and devote themselves to art. (TS, pp. 80-81).

[100] TS, p. 199 (His address on the occasion of the opening of the Art Gallery in Zagreb). « Man, by being created into image of God, instantly in the irresistible way began to search for truth » (ibid., p. 304).

dom on the other. Needless to say, his championship of freedom
extended to all human endeavors. It is therefore no wonder that
he considered it his sacred duty to elaborate on academic freedom which must be alloted to the students and to the professors
as well. On this subject the English universities served him as an
excellent example. First of all, it was his firm conviction that the
English nation was the most pratical nation in the world, always
struggling to find a balance in solving its most vital problems.[101]
Such a balance he saw exemplified in the relationship between order and freedom on English campuses.[102] He preferred the English
academic freedom to that of Germany and Austria where it sometimes turned into rioting and disorders of great proportions. (Un-
doubty, he became acquainted with the English university system
through his intimate friend Lord Acton and some English bishops).
Strossmayer strongly implied that he wanted to see the University
of Zagreb follow the example of the English universities in this regard. In all probability he would have come out with much stronger recommandations had he not been afraid of repercussions from
Vienna and Budapest. Of course, he urged the students to attend
classes regularly and to devote themselves unsparingly to their studies, but he stressed his opinion that what is done on the private
initiative is more meritorious than what is accomplished by an order from above.[103]

Another problem, which confronted him in this respect, was
of a much more serious nature. This problem concerned choosing
and nominating faculty members. Naturally, it did not involve the
academic qualifications of the prospective professors, since this had
to be executed by another body, but it rather pertained to the inner formation and to general outlook on human life of the university personnel. In other words, what stand should be taken in case
a prospective professor happened to be an agnostic or an atheist,
or an anti-Christian? Might such an individual begin to propagate

---

[101] « Unity in the Church » his Pastoral of 1877 (TS, pp. 398-399).
He maintains, however, that the French are more spiritual and more talented
than the English. *Ibid.,* p. 399.

[102] *Ibid.,* p. 307.

[103] *Ibid.,* p. 308.

his beliefs and ideas to the students? First of all, the Bishop did
not intend to have in Zagreb a Catholic university but rather a
Christian university whose doors would be kept open to the Catholic and to the Greek Ortodox students as well. Secondly, he
brought out the fact that the parents of students expected their
sons to be educated in the Christian spirit and environment, and,
of course, he would give priority to the wishes and the expectations
of the university students' parents rather than to those of the
prospective professors. Finally, he resolved this problem in the
following manner:

« Our people wishes and requires that its youth be educated
in the Christian spirit and especially on the university level. If
someone does not intend to comply with the wishes of the people,
he does not have any right to come into possession of a university
chair. Cristianity is founded on free will and free decision; if someone does not have it, let him live peacefully in the vocation and
position he chose and let him perform his duties; such a one would
sin against the will of people, against the Holy Spirit, and against
the future of our nation, if he, as an unbeliever or as an apostle
of atheism, would ascend the podium of the university hall ».[104]

Finally, to do justice to the Bishop's idea on the freedom of
science and art and on that of those who are directely involved
in them, and because his concept is just as pertinent today as it was
a century ago, it is cited in its entirety:

« One more thing, which I wish to see from the bottom of
my heart to be realized, is that our Academy and our University
as well preserve always their intact independence and freedom.
After faith and conscience nothing else is more in need of freedom
and independence as it is the case with science and art. Science
and art are the rays of the eternal light. As the rays of the sun need

---

[104] *Ibid.*, p. 314. It is true, however, that Strossmayer through Francis
Rački wanted to exert influence so as to prevent the Jesuits from obtaining
any teaching post in the Theological School of Zagreb. He goes so far as to
state that « paganism » and « jesuitism » are equally dangerous to the people
and « a tout prix » – as he says -- are to be kept out of the school. Cf. KRS,
I, 285. His distrust and dislike for the Jesuits, in all probability, dates back
to Vatican I.

the entire atmosphere to warm up the earth and to awaken it to
bring forth the crops, by the same token the light of science and of art
is in need of freedom to enlighten human spirit and to enhance human hearts to the sublime enterprises; in other words: science, art
and faith can only properly and beneficially prosper under the protection of freedom and authonomy. May God forbid that I would like
to cut off the organic bond which exists and must exist between the
Academy and the University on one hand and the State authority
on the other. No, I am not after that, what I intend to say is that
whenever either State or other public authority whishes to approach
these sublime institutions, it has to be done in the name of truth, of
justice and of freedom which is guaranteed in their by-laws. This is
the foundation to life and to progress. Every attempt and illegal
interference in the conscience and in convictions of the priests of
science and of art ruins scientific institutions and at the same time it
undermines the foundation of every scientific and noble aspiration ».[105]

---

[105] TS, p. 197

IV

THEOLOGY AND PATRISTIC STUDIES

If we are to gain a complete picture of Strossmayer's role in the Catholic Church, of his activities and of his stand on certain issues, we must understand his theology and particularly his ecclesiology. This is related to what has been said earlier about his conceptions of some human basic problems. What is more, one cannot correctly comprehend either his speeches delivered at Vatican I or his actions and behavior during the Council unless one grasps the ecclesialogical concepts which he had developed, fostered, defended and pursued all his life. His ecclesiology was basic to his cultural and political undertakings in his native land (Croatia) and among the South Slavs; it also inspired his activities toward the reunion of the Eastern and Western Churches. In other words, it is our principal aim to discover the pivot of his motives: his theological conceptions are the foundation to all his endeavors.

By perusing his pastoral letters, his speeches, and correspondence one gets the impression that he was an extremely well-read and well-posted man on all current events and issues of his time not only on those pertinent either to his native land or to the Catholic Church but equally so with world affairs. All his leisure time was devoted to serious study which lasted until late at night. His curiosity to learn reached out in all directions from philosophy and literature to the Church Fathers whose were his daily bread. His abundant quoting their works confirms this. He very seldom made reference to the Scholastic theology. From his student's years when he plunged into the study of the Church Fathers he remained submerged in them until his last breath; he was not able to write or to say anything without referring to them.

His reading material was not solely limited to the Catholic writers like Bossuet, to Fenelon, or Pascal; he was almost equally attached to some Protestant scholars, including Leibnitz and F.

Guizot. For the latter he developed such a great esteem that in Vatican I he recommended Guizot's book « Les meditations sur l'essence de la religion chretienne » to the council Fathers for reading[1] which suggestion, of course, was not very appealing to the Prelates. What is more, he never ceased reading the Roman classical writers.

Naturally an exposition of someone's theology involves finding out who influenced that individual and to what theological school of thought he belonged. By reading Strossmayer's works and by noticing that he often quotes French writers, one is tempted to think that he was influenced primarily by the French thinkers. Undoubtedly, he imbibed some of their ideas, but his basic theological notions point in another direction, namely, to Johann Adam Möhler or to the Theological School of Tubingen. Strossmayer in his « Travelog » relates of his visit to the cemetery of Munich, Germany: « I would have looked for the grave of Johann Adam Möhler had I not been so exhausted. When I was young I read Möhler works with great enthusiasm and particulary his 'Symbolism', his patristic works 'Unity in the Church' which equals by its importance the work of St. Cyprian by the same name (Unity in the Church) »[2].

By a curious coincidence a circle of Strossmayer's friends were also the friends of I. Döllinger, for instance Lord Gladstone and Lord Acton, the latter being also a pupil of Döllinger. The young Johann Möhler, whom Srossmayer most probably had never met, was Döllinger's friend. (Möhler died in 1838 in Munich). It is doubtful if Strossmayer was personally acquainted with Döllinger prior to Vatican I, but thereafter he was his friend[3] with whom he used to keep company even after he was excomunicated by Rome, and from time to time he read some of Döllinger's lectures[4].

---

[1] MANSI 51, 75. On another occasion he praised very highly Leibnitz's book *Theodicea* (cf. TS, p. 159).

[2] TS, p. 357.

[3] C. Begouen was told by Strossmayer « Döllinger was my dear friend », *loc. cit*, p. 69.

[4] Francis Rački censored the part of the Bishop's « Travelogue » which dealt with his meeting with Döllinger (cf. KRS, I, 331). He reacted in this fashion to Rački's censorship: « I am so sorry », the Bishop wrote to Rački

All these striking personalities were interested in the reunion of the Churches[5] and were characterized by being strongly involved in studying patristic theology[6]. What is yet of greater interest is that all these famous individuals went their way in their theology and stuck to their religious convictions while the centre of this circle of friends – Döllinger – retrogressed, and in reality he was left alone to himself.

There are several facts which will aid us in appraising Strossmayer's theology and in particular his ecclesiolgy. First of all, in spite of his love for and understanding of Döllinger there is no indication in Strossmayer's writings and speeches that he was under Döllinger « ecclesiological spell ». They had some common thougths on certain ecclesiastical problems, but this is to be ascribed to a mere coincidence rather than to anything else. Secondly, it is obvious that Strossmayer followed the ecclesiology of Johann A. Möhler. This, however, did not preclude his developing some theological ideas of his own, as we shall see during this study. Thirdly, it is necessary to resort to quite a few documents of his to reconstruct his ecclesiology, for he did not write a systematic theological treatise on certain topics but merely Pastorals, speeches and memoranda, of which some are sizeable brochures. This indicates that his ecclesiological ideas warranted by the circumstan-

---

afterwards, « that you have omitted my observations on my visit to Döllinger. I put them purposely in 'Travelogue' in order to instruct our people on since·rety and genuine love. The whole matter was very carefully formulated. Can't you see in what sort of circumstances we live that an honest man must hide » (*ibid.*, p. 332). In another letter he wrote to Rački « I have read Döllinger's lectures. They are splendid ». KRS, I, 161.

[5] Herbert Paul in his « Introductory Memoir » writes: « Belonging to two different branches of the Christian Church, they both (Gladstone and Acton) desired the reunion of Christendom, and both held that religion was guiding star in public as in private life ». *Letters of Lord Acton to Mary Gladstone*, edited by H. Paul (London, 1904), pp. XXVI-XXVII. (Mary Gladstone is the daughter of W. Gladstone).

[6] « A further inspiration to Möhler in his work were a number of outstanding contemporary scholars including such men as Sailer, Gugler, Drey, Klee, Hirscher, and Döllonger... were characterized in varying degrees by the union of extensive patristic learning and high philosophical speculations », writes GUSTAV VOSS, S. J., « Johann Adam Möhler and the Development of Dogma », in *Theological Studies*, v. IV (1943), p. 425. Cf. also *History of Freedom*, Lord Acton's article « Döllinger's Historical Work », pp. 377-379.

ces, or as he felt at times that they should be communicated to the faithful. He also repeats some of his ideas time and again, and for this reason we shall simply choose those texts of his in which they are expressed best. His Postorals were of great interest to Rome, and Pope Leo XIII and Cardinal Rampolla praised them very highly[7]. Fourthly, it is impossible to exactly assess Strosmayer's dependence upon J. A. Möhler, because Strossmayer in his works also used the ideas of the Church Fathers as Möhler did. Nobody will question that this noble representative of the Tubingen Theological School was inspired to great extent in forming his ecclesiological concepts by the Church Fathers. On account of this it is difficult to state in each particular instance what the Bishop directly borrowed from J. A. Möhler and what he developed himself by reflecting on the works of Irenaeus, Athanasius, John Chrysostom, Jerome, and Augustin, whose works he also abundantly cited.

All the writers are agreed that Möhler's had shown a tremendous evolution as far as his ecclesiology is concerned[8]. This growth of Möhler can be divided in three stages: first, his doctrine found in his articles published in Theologische Quartalschrift prior to the publication of his famous work « Unity in the Church »[9]. This stage is characterized by his hostility to Rome and by his denial of papal infallibility; he asserts that the pope, as far as the faith is concerned, represents only the faith of his own diocese and not that of the universal Church. Furthermore, he opts for the « episcopal system » against the « papal system », and favored very strongly the replacement of Latin by German in liturgy[10]. The second stage comprises the time of the publication of « Unity in the Church »

---

    7   Dr. Andrija Spiletak, Strossmayer i Pape, III, 202.
    8   It is practically impossible to quote all the literature on J. A. Möhler which deals with this topic. An extensive bibliography by P. Riga's article « The Ecclesiology of Johann Adam Möhler », in Theological Studies, v. XXII (1961), p. 563, note 1.
    9   Original title Die Einheit in der Kirche oder das Prinzip des Catholicismus, dargestellt im Geiste der Kirchenväter der Erstern drei Jahrhunderte (Tübingen, 1825).
    10   Herve Savon (translated by Charles McGrath, PH. D.), Johann Adam Möhler the Father of Modern Theology (Glen Rock, N. J., Paulist Press, 1966), 24-33.

in 1825. It cannot be said yet that this sensational work was in line with the Roman doctrine even though he took in it a giant step toward it. At this stage he sees the Church as guided and united in the Holy Spirit; he overlooks Christ's founding of the Church and His presence in her. This book is full of romantic theology. What is more, he tries to establish the organic and living unity of the Church by commencing with the bishops through the metro-politans, finally arriving at St. Peter's successors who are the cen-tre of the Church unity[11]. In this work he abandons the « episcopal system » and attempts to find the balance between episcopacy and papacy with the following statement: « Two extremes, however, are possible in Church life and both are called egoism. Two extre-mes exist, namely when *everybody* or when *one individual* wants to be all. In the latter case the bond of unity becomes so tight that one cannot ward off suffocation; in the former case everything so falls apart and it becomes so cold that one freezes to death. One form of egoism generates the other. But neither *everybody* nor *one individual* should want to be all. Only all can be all, and the unity of all can only be an all-encompassing whole. This is the idea of the Catholic Chrurch »[12]. The third stage in Möhler growth was attained in his book « Symbolism »[13] in which his views on the ecclesiastical structure are well-balanced. In this work the Catholic Church is not the community of the believers who are in the full possesion of the Holy Spirit as it was the case in « Unity in the Church », but it is rather the body of believers founded by Christ;

---

[11] *Ibid.,* pp. 34-54.

[12] Quoted by HANS KÜNG, *Structures of the Church,* p. 319. Küng is using J. R. Geiselmann's edition, Darmstadt, 1957. He makes the following comment: « The overgrown function of an organ harms an organism no less than overgrowth itself. Too little is ascribed to the Petrine office when, at best, it is regarded as a human structure, as an establishment of human law, and the inner connection of the papacy with the Petrinist Church hierarchy groun-ded in Scripture is not fully valued. And too much is attributed to the Petrine office when full value is not given to its service character in the Church and it is regarded as an absolutist ruling power and the administration of the Church and initiative is reduced as much as possible to the direction and initiative of the Petrine office » (*ibid.*).

[13] German title *Symbolik oder Darstellung der dogmatischen Gegen-sätze der Katholiken und Protestanten, nach ihren öffentlichen Bekenntnis-schriften* (Mainz, 1832).

and the Church is a visible and invisible organism and at the same
time is the continuation of the Incarnation of the Son of God[14].

We feel justified in assuming that the Bishop accepted Möhler
more or less at his third stage of theological evolution as it occurred in his book « Symbolism ». In spite of this it seems to us that
the two principal ideas of Möhler « Unity in the Church » remained
with him all his life: the unity of the Church must be realized in
the pope, and a healthy balance must be found between the college
of bishops and the pontiff. It is interesting to note that one of
Strossmayer's dissertations – judging by the title – bears a great
similarity to Möhler's « Unity in the Church ». Besides, he wrote
a lengthy Pastoral letter in 1877 with the exactly same title « Unity in the Church », of which we cannot assert that it is in line with
Möhler's work. What is more, it is evident that he Bishop was
unable either to write or to deliver a sermon without touching
upon the subject of the ecclesiastical unity.

1. - Johann Adam Möhler (Tübingen Theological School) and J. G. Strossmayer vs. the Reunion of Christendom

The reunification of the Christian Churches was very close to
Möhler's neart. As a matter of fact, the very writing of « Symbolism » was motivated by this, and one can easily perceive in this
work that he felt a strong pain in his soul at seeing his nation torn
apart[15]. On this issue of the reunion Strossmayer was of the opinion that one has to work for its realisations as he wrote to Cardinal
Rampolla and on so many other occasions[16]. Furthermore, he was
more optimistic on this question than Möhler had been and pre-
dicted that the reunification of the Eastern and the Western Chur-

---

[14]   P. RIGA, *loc. cit.*, 576-578.
[15]   *Symbolism* (2nd edition) translated by James Burton Robertson
(London, 1847). Möhler writes in the Preface: « A real removal, therefore,
of the differences existing between the Christian communities, appears to me
to be still remote. But in the age in which we live, I flattered myself that I
might do something toward bringing about a religious peace, by revealing
a true knowledge of the great dispute ». *Ibid.*, I, p. XVI.
[16]   KRS, IV, 13.

ches might take place by either the middle or the end of the twentieth century[17] while Möhler stated « I did not, indeed, dream of any peace between the Churches, deserving the name of a true reunion, as being about to be established in the present time ».[18] The desire for the reconciliation of the Churches never left Möhler during the course of writing his masterpiece « Symbolism ». He was sincere and explicit in depicting the faults of both the Protestants and the Catholics as well, and believed that once the people in the both camps became cognizant of their shortcomings, then they might stretch a friendly hand to one another[19]. In his judgment, the sincere admission of mistakes on both sides would be the first step which might lead to the platform of reconciliation. All this he had expressed in the following words: « Both (the Protestants and the Catholics), conscious of guilt, must exclaim: 'We all have erred – it is the Church only which cannot err; we all have sinned – the Church only is spotless on earth'. This open confession of mutual guilt will be followed by the festival of reconciliation. Meanwhile, we still smart under the inexpressible pain of the wound which was then inflicted, a pain which can be alleviated only by the consciousness that the wound has become an issue, through which all the impurities have flowed off, that men had introduced into the wide compass of the dominations of the Church; for she herself is ever pure and eternally undefiled ».[20] He mentioned the strivings of the Church in obtaining the unity and her candid and extreme joy over it should it become a reality. He gave free reins to his sentiments when he described the incident of the reunion of the Western and the Eastern Churches which had taken place at the Council of Florence by quoting Pope Eugene IV at length « Rejoyce ye heavens, and exult, o earth: the wall of separation is pulled down, which divided the Eastern and Westen Churches; peace and concord have returned...[21] ».

At this place we have to say that there was a difference bet-

---

[17] Ibid., p. 245. Cf. the Preface to the 4th volume by Dr. F. Šišić, p. VII.
[18] Möhler's Preface to Symbolism, I, p. XV.
[19] Symbolism, II, 31.
[20] Ibid., p. 32.
[21] Ibid., p. 13.

ween Möhler and Strossmayer on this issue to some extent: while the former tried to pave the way for the reunion in the scholarly and theoretical fashion, the latter being a man of action – or as he calls himself a « pratical man » – became more active in the practical sense by establishing contacts with the leading Christians of the Eastern Church as for example Vladimir Soloviev and by initiating the dialogue between the Rome and various Greek Orthodox nations as for instance Russia, Montenegro and Serbia. Naturally, Strossmayer concentrated his talents, his repute, his connections and energies on the Eastern Church in whose immediate vicinity he lived and worked. Regardless of how both of them might have looked in the eyes of their contemporaries, history has vindicated both of them. It looks to us as if their correctness and farsightedness are not so much mirrored in their respective ecumenism as they are in their immediate approach to the problem of the division of the Churches.

The approach to the problem of the reunification of the Churches of both of them is identical. It is true, however, that Strossmayer's approach is more explicit and evident than Möhler's due to his renown and to his position. Christian love ought to be the point of departure in dealing with this question of the reunion and the basis of the conduct of Catholics toward ununited brothers. Möhler in his Preface to « Symbolism » states that the differences between Protestants and Catholics « must be imparted with the utmost charity, conciliation, and mildness, with a sincere love of truth and without any exaggeration... yet we are required by our Church to embrace all men with love, for Christ's sake, and to evince in their regard all the abundance of Christian virtues »[22]. Strossmayer in one of his conferences (and in so many other instances) to the theological students of the Augustineum College in Vienna, Austria, delivered in 1848, followed the same thread of thought of Möhler when he said: « The Catholic Church does not recommend anything else so ardently to her children in communicating with the ununited brothers as to be tolerant and always ready to perform toward them every humanitarian and charitable

---

[22] *Symbolism*, I, pp. XII-XIII.

work. The Catholic Church knows very well that the greatest and best virtue of the Christian faith is to practice love, charitable works, clemency, benevolence, patience; and besides, to promote in every Christian individual desire for peace and reconciliation regardless of one's personality and faith »[23]. Furthermore, the Bishop considered Möhler one of the greatest champions in the modern times in furthering the reunion of Christendom. He placed his name next to that of Leibnitz[24].

Strossmayer was more eloquent than Möhler on this question of the reunion, for he considered it his duty to work for reunion of the Churches – the Eastern and Western – and also to find the ways how to achieve it. The basis for his conviction is the mission of the Catholic Church. First of all, he thought of the Church as a living organic entity, the heir not only of Christ's ruling power, but of His heart, His love and benignity toward the entire world[25]; thus the Church in her divine mission is expected to equally exercise her power and her love. This was one of his favorite refrains at Vatican I[26]. On account of this he on numerous occasions referred to the pope not only as he head or the centre of the Catholic Church and of all Christians, but as the father and the teacher of all races and nations, whose love must encompass the entire human race.[27] He praised or paid homage to either Pius IX[28] or to

---

[23] Dr. ANDRIJA SPILETAK, « Tres casus a J. G. Strossmayer propositi ac soluti », in BS, XXII (1934), p. 286.

[24] « The reply to the Greek Orthodox Bishops » (KRS, IV, 472).

[25] BS, XXII (1934), 9. Cf. also Strossmayer's article « O slobodnim zidarima », in BS, XX (1932), p. 310. This Pastoral is found in the article of Dr. Andrija Spiletak under the title « Strossmayer o slobodnim zidarima ». The above mentioned Pastoral was published in 1885.

[26] MANSI 50, 141 and passim.

[27] This he bases on the fact that the Church of God « is the genuine and true mother of all nations... and she will never change into a stepmother ». Cf. ANDRIJA SPILETAK's article « Je li biskup Strossmayer bio liberalni katolik i pobornik pokreta za osnivanje narodne Crkve? », in BS, XIX (1931), pp. 326 and 329. This quotation is taken out of Strossmayer's Pastoral of 1888 (cf. ibid., p. 317). In his long letter to his clergy (1859) upon his return from Rome he writes: « ... go to the supreme shepherd of the Church and to the common father of all believers: go to your father and shepherd who is not only a vicar and heir of the power of Jesus Christ but also of his love which encompasses all men » (JJS-DK, I, 424).

[28] JJ-DK, I, 431.

pope Leo XIII[29] for exhibiting and practicing this universal love and for their noble endeavors to bring other Christians into the unity with the Catholic Church. This particularly gained its momentum when the said Pontiffs did something for the Slav race.

There is hardly a speech or a document of Strossmayer's which does not deal with or touch upon either the unity of the Church or of mankind. Naturally, the unity of the Churches must be realized first, and then the unity of mankind will necessarilly follow. The initiative, in his opinion, lay with the Catholic Church, and especially the popes, the bishops, the priests who were expected to take the lead in this sacred matter, as he used to so often call it. He reminded his clergy of this duty by pointing to the prayer, which are recited immediately before receiving holy communion, and in which every Mass celebrant offers supplications to God to unite the Church and to preserve peace and tranquility within her[30]. In his debate with the three Greek Orthodox bishops he suggested that the clergy on the both sides of the fence should commit themselves unsparingly to this holy cause to bring about the unity of the Church[31]. Equally emphatic was his letter to Cardinal Rampolla on this issue in which he claimed that not only in the Church of Rome but also in the Russian Church religious societies existed which continuously offered their prayers to God for the achievment of the Church unity[32].

He did not limit himself to the realm of prayer and to the expectations that God like « Deus ex machina » would bring his dreams and desires to a happy end. Most of all, he believed in making contacts and establishing dialogue or as he said repeatedly: « Once this problem of the reunion (of the Eastern and Western Churches) is begun to be discussed calmly and scholarly on the both sides, half of it is already accomplished and solved »[33]. Since the time he began to think of the reunion – and this was before

---

[29] Strossmayer's letter to Cardinal Nina, Secretary of State (KRS, II, 328-329).
[30] Pastoral of 1891 (KRS, IV, 246-247).
[31] KRS, IV, pp. 474-475.
[32] KRS, IV, p. 13.
[33] KRS, III, p. 202 (Strossmayer's letter to Rački of January 1, 1886).

he became Bishop of Djakovo – his eyes were turned to Russia. He always thought that the Russians would be the first of all Slav nations to leave the schism and to enter into the Catholic Church[34]. Undoubtedly, he had his own reasons for thinking this way. First of all, the Russians as a group were very religious people; secondly, as he wrote to Cardinal Rampolla, at that time there was a bishop of Kiev – a very learned man – by name Platon who happened to be interested in the reunion. What is more, he strongly indicated to the same Cardinal that at least that portion of Russia was still in the union with the chair of St. Peter since the Council of Florence. At this Council Bishop Isidore of Kiev in company with Bishop Bessarion entered the Church of Rome, and both of them died in the union with the Roman Church. The Prelate of Djakovo was of the opinion that this unity between Kiev and Rome was never juridically or otherwise rescinded, which meant that the faithful of Kiev region were still in the union with the Church[35]. What is more, he was well acquainted through his intimate friend Vladimir Soloviev with the movement among the Russian intellectuals of whom some thought of themselves as still being in the union with the Rome. This he also communicated to Rampolla and notified him about his connections with some Russian personalities[36]. In his idealistic mind he also held that once the Russians – as the most numerous Slav nation – entered the Catholic Church, the other Slav national groups would follow their example[37].

Soloviev's correspondence and visits to Strossmayer and to Francis Rački and their debates conducted either in Rogaška Sla-

---

[34] JJS-DK, p. 45. In the same letter of June 23, 1849 Strossmayer wrote to Andrija T. Brlić that the Russians will do it before « our neighbors — the Serbs » (ibid.).

[35] KRS, IV, 15. Cf. also ibid., p. 245.

[36] KRS, IV, p. 13. In the same letter Strossmayer expresses that the eternal judge will be merciful to him for associating with the « sinners » since He did the same thing while on this earth. Ibid., p. 15. Vladimir Soloviev wrote to Rački in June, 1886 that he had been invited by the Petersburg's Theological Academy to expound his views on the reconciliation of the Churches. And according to Soloviev's report the outcome was very satisfactory. What is more, this matter was debated in the Russian press. Cf. KRS, IV, 448.

[37] KRS, IV, p. 14. In the same letter to Rampolla he did not omit to quote St. Augustine « errant materialiter certe, sed formaliter non errant » (ibid.).

tina or Djakovo or Zagreb on this matter of the reunion were not fruitless, for under Strossmayer's influence and encouragement Soloviev wrote his famous book « Russia and the Universal Church »[38] which was a great sensation in all Europe. The relationship and correspondence between Strossmayer and Soloviev have been thoroughly treated by scholars in Russia, France and Croatia[39].

At present we would like to make one remark in regard to Soloviev and Strossmayer, namely, Soloviev did not become involved either in ecumenism and in the irenic movement through either Strossmayer and Francis Rački but on his own initiative and through his own reasoning and personal convictions. The similarity or the sameness of the ideas is purely coincidental.[40]

What Strossmayer wanted to accomplish in Russia by inaugurating the dialogue between the Russians and the Holy See, he attempted with the two neighboring nations of the Eastern Church: Serbia and Montenegro. He was a Vicar Apostolic of Serbia from 1851 until November 26, 1896, when he gave up this position and handed his resignation to the Propagation of Faith in Rome. During this period of time he visited Serbia seven times, was on cordial terms with the Serbian Dynasty, and corresponded with quite a few Serbian leading politicians, including Ristić, Mijatović, Novaković, and Nikolić. At first he wished to accomplish two things in Serbia: to provide priests for the spiritual needs of Catholics who happened to be either permanent residents or migratory workers from various European countries. This was a very touchy problem, since the Serbs were extremely intolerant of the Catholic Church and did not allow Catholic services to be conducted on their territory. Secondly, he thought that the first step to be untertaken in order to introduce friendly relations between Serbia and the Holy See was a concordat.[41] While the former was to some

---

[38] KRS, IV, p. 248.
[39] Cf. ANTE KADIĆ, « Vladimir Soloviev and Bishop Strossmayer », in *The American Slavic and East European Review,* v. 20 (1961), p. 164, note 6.
[40] Dr. F. Šišić's Preface (KRS, IV, pp. V-VI).
[41] Cf. CP, pp. 759-768. A great number of documents and quite a few letters between Strossmayer and the Serbian leading personalities is brought by Dr. Andrija Spiletak in his articles « Strossmayer i Pravoslavlje » in BS, XXIII (1935), pp. 121-144 and 277-304, and « Neke i danas savremene Stros-

extent realized, the latter attempt fell through and was not realized until August 24, 1914, nine years after the Bishop's death. This failure can be attributed partly to the inner political disorders in Serbia and partly to the intrigues of the governments of Vienna and Budapest.[42]

Strossmayer had better luck with the Prince Nicholas of Montenegro who after the Congress of Berlin decided to enter into a concordat with the Holy See. The Prince actually asked the Bishop in his letter of December 30, 1878, to help him in accomplishing his goal, to which the Bishop wholeheartedly responded. In this matter Strossmayer was strongly supported by Canon Nicholas Voršak and Fr. Cesare Tondini who also acted as a missionary priest in Serbia. At last the concordat was signed by the Holy See and Montenegro August 18, 1886,[43] and Fr. Simon Milinović, O.F.M. was the first Catholic Bishop in Montenegro.

It would take us too far away from the subject to explore everything the Bishop did in this direction toward the other Slav nations as for instance for the Bulgarians (who belong to the Eastern

---

smayerove misli », in BS, XXV (1937), pp. 161-172 and 291-300). These documents are the greatest testimony to the Bishop's benevolence towards the brethren of the Eastern Church. In one istance he even helped a Greek Orthodox pastor in Gračac to build a church.

[42] Cf. Dr. VJEKOSLAV WAGNER, « Povijest katoličke Crkve u Srbiji u 19. vijeku (od 1800 do konkordata 1914 godine) », in BS, XXI (1933), pp. 1-16, 140-153, 225-235, 297-307 and in BS, XXII (1934), pp. 20-46 and 124-140. Cf. also the article of IVAN VITEZIĆ, « Počeci organizacije katoličke Crkve u modernoj Srbiji i talijanski barnabita Cesare Tondini », in Mandičev Zbornik (Roma, Hrvatski Povijesni Institut, 1965), pp. 275-307. Vitezić gives credit to Strossmayer and to Fr. Tondini for achievements in Serbia (ibid.I p. 302), but on the preceding page he holds Strossmayer and his cooperator Fr. Tondini responsible for not accomplishing more in this respect. He finds the causes for this failure in Strossmayer's « irenic movement » and also in the intensive animosity of the Governments of Vienna and Budapest toward the Bishop. Ibid., p. 301. Cf. also VLADIMIR SOLOVIEV, Russia and the Universal Church (London, Geoffrey Bles. The Centenary Press, 1948), pp. 68-72. Soloviev accuses the Serbian government for using their Church as a political tool.

[43] Strossmayer was authorized by Cardinal Jacobini to regulate the status of the Catholic Church in Montenegro with Prince Nicholas. The Bishop intended to go himself to Montenegro to speed up the negotiations but Rački suggested that Fr. Tondini go instead, and he complied with the wish of Rački. Rački's letter to Strossmayer of February 12, 1886 (KRS, IV, 443. Cf. also CP, pp. 769-770).

Church), whose students he put through schools by giving them scholarship and by subsidizing literary publications such as those of the Miladinov brothers.[44]

These incidents, mentioned only in passing, testify to his deep involvement in bringing the Catholic and the other Slav nations of the Eastern Church closer to one another. Adrian Fortescue in the article on the Bishop of Djakovo, which is full of historical and geographical inaccuracies and abounds with derogatory remarks against the Prelate, has this to say « What remains of Strossmayer's life, after those controversies (at Vatican I) are forgotten, is his work for the reunion of Christendom, and for his people... If a still more sacred cause prevails, if the day comes when the Church of God no longer has to mourn the loss of the Eastern children, then in the feast of reunion the memory of the Catholic and patriot Bishop must have a place too ».[45] According to Emil de Laveley the Prelate of Djakovo is a « Christian according to the Gospel, and he is against any sort of intolerance »,[46] while Ben Hurst describes him as a strong adherent « to the Croatian proverb: a brother is a brother, of whatever creed ».[47] Often he wrote or said that he would never hurt either religious or national feelings of anybody for anything in the world, and he tried in every way to remain faithful to his program of his.[48] He was so steeped in the idea of the reunion of the Eastern and Western Churches, which had to be realized by practicing love, that he never bore any resentment toward those who either misinterpreted his plans or wanted to get rid of him as was the case with the Serbs, who did not want him any more to be a Vicar Apostolic for the Catholics on the territory of Serbia.[49]

---

[44] Cf. CP, pp. 770-778. ANTE KADIĆ, *Strossmayer and Bulgarians,* in *East European Quaterly,* vol. V. n. 2, pp. 134-151.

[45] ADRIAN FORTESCUE, « A Slav Bishop: Joseph George Strossmayer », in *The Dublin Review,* v. 163 (1918), pp. 256-257. Fortescue goes so far as to state: « He (Strossmayer) loved his Church too well to confuse her cause with things of earth, and he loved his people too well not to wish to see them Catholics » (*ibid.,* p. 257). This is a grotesque exaggeration.

[46] LUIS LEGER, *loc. cit.,* p. 217.

[47] BEN HURST, *loc. cit.,* p. 773.

[48] Cf. KRS, IV, 251 and also *ibid.,* p. 475.

[49] He wrote to his friend Matija Ban (Febraury 19, 1886) « I am a bone in the Serbian throat » (TS, p. 84). There is no vestige of resentment or bitterness on his side toward the Serbs in this lengthy letter.

Undoubtedly, on many occasions he felt hurt when he was ignored or dispised by the ununited brethren[50] but this did not prevent his holding fast to the basic governing Christian principle of love nor did it deter his following the path toward the reunion. His attitude can be understood solely under two perspectives: first of all, that the Catholic Church must search for the suitable means and recruit all her forces to achieve the unity, and secondly, that he thought of himself as an exponent of the Church in those regions, and consequently he took upon himself this obligation of furthering the idea of ecumenism. Since he held that one of the basic missions of the Church is to obtain the reunion of Christendom, he would never undertake anything which might become detrimental to this sublime cause. Regardless of how ardently he loved his nation and what sacrifices he performed for it, the welfare of the Church and the realization of her mission in world had the priority over that of his nation[51]. It is true that he, like nobody

---

[50] He wrote to Rački from Rogaška Slatina (August 1, 1893): « There are a lot of our Serbs here and the Serbs from Serbia. They are drifting away from us further and further. Petranović (Greek Orthodox Bishop) and I were like bread and salt last year – this year he will not even look at me » (KRS, IV, 383). In his Pastoral of 1891 he wrote: « I recall very well when once I preached at Dalj in the presence of the Greek Orthodox patriarch, who was a bishop of Temisvar at that time, on love, harmony and unity among the brethren and between the Churches (Eastern and Western), later on at dinner he told me, 'Brother, I approve every word, from the first to the last, of what you said in your sermon today' » (KRS, IV, 251).

[51] After having received the political program of the People's Party from Zagreb – drafted and signed by Šime Mazzura, Dr. Blaž Lorković, Dr. Luka Marjanović, Fran Folnegović, Dr. Fran Vrbanić and Dr. Ivan Zahar – which was in its basic ideas very close to the Croatian Party of Right whose program was « neither with Vienna nor with Budapest but Croatia for herself » (KRS, II, 201-204). Strossmayer wrote to Rački (March 11, 1879) « If the Opposition wishes to have my support... then they ought to leave each religion free and everything must be in conformity with my conscience and convictions » (ibid., II, p. 207). In other words, there should not be anything in the program that might hinder the mission of the Church. Nothing must be found in it which might be in the way of reunion. Cf. VATROSLAV MURVAR, Hrvatska i Hrvati (Chicago, « Croatia » Hrv. Izdavalački Zavod, 1953), 240-242. Therefore, we believe that F. Šišić is correct in his appraisal of Strossmayer when he wrote that « the main goal of the life of the Bishop was to reconcile the Eastern and Western Church, and all the other ideas and undertakings of his (political included) are intimately connected with the former one » (Šišić's Preface to KRS, IV, p. VII).

else of his time, placed the firm boundaries between religion and politics, and he never confounded these matters[52]. However, in spite of his acumen and of his clear-cut views, he did experience a conflict – even anguish – within himself which was brought upon him by the constantly increasing antagonism between the Serbs and the Croats: the former belonging to the Eastern Church and the latter to the Church of Rome. This was particularly evident toward the end of his life when it seemed that he would be deserted by his fellow Croats and when the Serbs interpreted all his undertakings as being hostile to them[53]. In all this clamor he remained faithful in promoting the reunion by way of practicing love[54].

The ideas that he worked for may sound unrealistic and unfeasible but since he was a pupil and adherent of the Romantic theology, as we shall see later on, he carried this spirit of romanticism into the realms of practical life. He could not have behaved differently. Perhaps no human soul except Francis Rački's and that of Vladimir Solovies's was so akin to his; and perhaps nobody except these individuals was able to penetrate deep enough into the most inner crevices of his soul and to fully appreciate his ideas. Most probably it was Vladimir Soloviev who had formulated best the conceptions of Strossmayer: « A whole world full of energies and yearnings but with no clear consciousness of its destiny knocks at the door of universal history. What is your road, ye people of the world? The multitude knows it not yet, but powerful voices issuing from your midst have already disclosed it. Two centuries ago a Croatian priest announced it with prophetic tongue, and in our own days a bishop of the same nation has more than once proclaimed it with superb eloquence. The utterance of the spokesmen

---

[52] ADRIAN FORTESCUE, *loc. cit.*, 234-235 and passim.

[53] « Strossmayer, during the last years of his life, saw the intentions of the Serbian politicians but he either did not have the courage or he did not wish to face them firmly », writes te Croatian publicist and politician VLAHO A. RAIĆ, *Hrvatska i Srbija* (Buenos Aires, 1953), 39. What is more he holds Strossmayer ecclesiastical ideas « well-intentioned dreams » (*ibid.*) and accuses him of not knowing « the pulse of his nations » (*ibid.*, p. 38); and this « dream » of Strossmayer cost a great deal of miseries to his own nation (*ibid.*).

[54] Pastoral of 1895 on « Neighborly Love » (GBBS, p. 29 and passim).

of the Western Slavs, the great Križanić and the great Strossmayer, needs only a simple *Amen* from the Eastern Slavs. It is this *Amen* that I come to speak in the name of a hundred million Russian Christians, in full and firm confidence that they will not repudiate me.

« Your word, o peoples of the word, is free and universal Theocracy, the true solidarity of all nations and classes, the application of Christianity to public life, the Christianizing of politics; freedom for all the oppressed, protection for all the weak; social justice and good Christian peace... »[55].

What would have happened in Russia and in the Church of Rome in particular and in Europe in general, had those in Petersburg and those in Rome listened to Strossmayer's and Soloviev's suggestions; Strossmayer continuously advocating the internationalization of the Roman Curia and his urging the Church officials in taking initiative in promoting the reunion of the Churches and both of them, Strossmayer and Soloviev, pleading that the Church of Russia should free herself from the state tutorship if she wished to fulfill her divine mission. Therefore there is no wonder that Soloviev toward the end of his life in 1894 was very skeptical about the future of Russia: « Once upon a time I thought that the reunion of Russia with Rome was possible, and now it looks to me that the public is not yet prepared. In my opinion Russia as one entity will never unite with Rome. This (reunion) could save her (Russia). Isn't it, perhaps, somewhat too late? I am hearing the echoes of thundering. A great evil is in store for Russia – the time is coming when neither of our authorities will be given a chance to be preoccupied with religious matters any more »[56].

Furthermore, from his early years the Prelate preached the universal brotherhood and fellowship. This idea was expressed best in his sermon, delivered on the occasion of his installation in Djakovo, in which he stated that all men are the children of the same Creator, and consequently we are bound to love one another regardless of one's origin and creed.[57] He went still further in this

---

[55]   Vladimir Soloviev, *op. cit.*, 35.
[56]   P(etar) G(rgec), « Prorok ruskih nevolja », in *Hrvatska Straža* (1931).
[57]   JJS-DK, pp. 160-161.

respect when he wrote in his Pastoral of 1877 that « Religion, which is able to disseminate dissensions among men, is not a religion at all but rather a mere superstition; that sort of religion does not contain the truth of God but the human error »[58].

His constant insistence that the reunion of the Churches must be realized in papacy, which he underscored so often in his writings and speeches and also in dedicating the Cathedral of Djakovo to the Prince of the Apostles, St. Peter, and at the same time by inscribing on its walls « To the glory of God, to the reunion of the Churches, and to the love and harmony among our people »[59] does not intrude upon Christian love which must be universal and all-embracing – otherwise it is not genuine[60]. It is precisely for this reason that his conception of the universal brotherhood is so pregnant that in his judgment – as he said so often – the Church of God has received by inheritance from Christ not solely His power to govern but more so to exercise His love toward everybody[51]. The latter clearly indicates that the Church of God is the continuation of the work of her bridegroom and founder, Jesus Christ, and also she is the bearer of the universal brotherhood among men. This is manifested best in his words, addressed to his clergy and faithful, delineating what attitude to take toward the members of the Eastern Church:

« We live side by side with brothers of the Easten Church. Let us therefore be full of charity and kindness toward them. Let us remember that the most convincing proof of the true faith is pure and benevolent charity. Remember that love is the dominating force that no one can resist. Let us love the brothers among whom we live wholeheartedly, not only because they are of our blood and of our nation, or because their liturgy is beautiful and majestic, given to them by St. Basil and St. John Chrysostom, whom we also honor and invoke as great saints of God. Let us love our brothers because on their altars, as on ours, the living God is present, because in their sacred chants the voice of the East sounds no less

---

58   TS, p. 398.
59   CP, p. 378.
60   Pastoral « Unity in the Church » (TS, p. 401).
61   Pastoral « Sts. Cyril and Methodius » (TS, p. 442. Cf. also *ibid.*, p. 401).

beautiful than the voice of the West in ours. Never listen to those who would excite you against neighbors, these are obviously the enemies of both Churches. We all honor and invoke St. Cyril and St. Methodius, and in doing so we all serve God. May these two holy names unite us in brotherly love »[62].

One might think that the Bishop completely lost sight of and excluded from his concern the nations of other creeds, or that perhaps he was merely preoccupied with the reunion of the Slavs of the Eastern Church with the Church of Rome. Undoubtedly, the latter held the predominance in his undertakings and activities, but it never assumed the form of exclusiveness. He implicitly relegated the duty of working on the reunion between the Protestant Churches and the papacy to those Catholic bishops and the clergy who lived in their immediate midst or were in the close contact with them. Regardless of how ardently he wished to see the Christendom to be united in the successor of St. Peter, he never wanted to see either Christianity or Christian nations function for themselves without extending and offering their spiritual benefits and material achivements to the less fortunate races and nations of other creeds. This particular trait of his conception of Christianity and its mission in the world is especially manifested in his correspondence with Lord Gladstone, who most certainly shared the Bishop's views[63]. On March 13, 1879 he wrote to the British Prime Minister: « We also put our cause into your hands for the future, and undertake most solemnly to prove ourselves always worthy of our English friends and protectors by our truth, justice, love and good-will towards all men. In my pastoral letters I preach (the doctrine) over and over again that we can only become worthy of freedom and culture by extending the same freedom to all with whom we come into contact, of whatever faith or race they may be, and by letting them partake equally with ourselves of the

---

[62] TS, pp. 442-443.

[63] Lord Gladstone wrote to the Bishop December 15, 1876: « I should like to serve my country and humanity till death. But this service can be rendered in more than one way. If I ask myself where in our days most is done for the good of humanity, I answer that it is not in sphere of ordinary politics » (CBSG, p. 427).

benefits of freedom and civilization. This is the teaching of the Cross and the law of every community which wishes to be worthy of the fruits of the Redemption »[64].

It was in the spirit of the universalism, but above all else it was in his correct notion of the Redemption, that he pleaded with Gladostone for the cause of Ireland[65], nor did he hesitate to remind his distinguished English friend of the ravages of famine in India and to ask him if anything had been done by the Government of England to prevent such terrible disasters or at least to mitigate them[66]. Having all this in mind, it should not be a surprise to anybody to read the following lines in the Bishop's letter (addressed to Gladstone): « Great people possessing culture and the Divine favour (and to these England especially belongs) are called before all others to represent truth, justice and liberty in the world: otherwise they are untrue to themselves and to God ».[67]

2. - Redemption and Sin

It is evident from what has been said so far that Strossmayer held that one of the essential missions and duties of the Church of Rome was and is to bring about the reunion of the Churches. As mentioned, this reunification of the Eastern and the Western Churches was his daily preoccupation. Several times in Vatican I he pleaded with council Fathers for the cause of the Eastern Church. He even exclaimed on one occasion that « the Eastern schism cannot be called Greek any more but rather Slavic since there are 80 million Slavs who are outside of the Catholic Church »[68].

One can justifiably pose a question: was he solely motivated by the love toward the Slavs and by his ardent desire to see the Slavs united with the chair of St. Peter, or was he also guided in all this by his theological concepts and by his unreserved love

---

[64] CBSG, p. 438.
[65] *Ibid.*, p. 444.
[66] *Ibid.*, pp. 432-433.
[67] *Ibid.*, pp. 433-434.
[68] MANSI 52, 403.

for the Church? He gave the best answer himself when he wrote to his friend Andrija T. Brlić: « The love for my country and to further its welfare is my supreme law; if I had millions of lives, I would sacrifice them for the Church and for the salvation of human souls »[69]. His episcopal motto « all for faith and fatherland » also underscored the program of his life[70]. It is apparent that his activities toward the reunion of the Churches were inspired by his love toward the Church and toward the Slavic race but the other much deeper and more significant underlying reasons were present all the time. These reasons, undoubtedly, were of a theological nature.

In order to understand Strossmayer and his theological ideas one must constantly keep in mind that he belonged to the Theological Romanticism in Germany of which Johann A. Möhler had been one of the principal protagonists. For the adherents of this theological school there was nothing static, everything is in becoming. They love a mystic thought and interpret everything under the aspect of historical continuity and whatever is human under organic growth. Thus, according to his concept of historical development, man is not severed either from history or from the previous generations since he is in them; or as P. Riga says « Romanticism may be compared to the continous flow of a river in which continuous generation plunges, takes part, and is by that very fact a continuous unity or reunion of those who are contemporary with those in the past... it is conferred on him (man) the harmonious realization that he was a part of mankind – in union with all men »[71].

This trait of Romanticism is extremely evident in Strossmayer, and it was much more intensive in him than, for instance, in Möhler. All his writings and speeches are permeated with it. His constant refrain « everything and everybody tends toward the unity » is applied to the Catholic Church in a special manner that through her and in her the unity of mankind will eventually be realized. His point of departure was the Roman Empire with its excellent

---

[69]   Letter of August 20, 1849 (JJS-DK, p. 61).
[70]   CP, p. 417.
[71]   P. RIGA, *loc. cit.*, 569. Cf. also G. VOSS, *loc cit.*, 423-424.

roads which God provided that they might serve as means of easy
and secure travel to the apostles to spread Christianity[72]. In the
Vatican Council, while advocating the necessity of holding ecumenical councils more often, he underscored the previous thought
and added that God in his infinite mercy and love has provided
mankind with modern means of transportation so that we may
more easily gather around the head of the Church in order to discuss current problems and to discover solutions to them.[73] In his
numerous Pastorals he treated the problem of unity in the Church,
and in two or three letters to Gladstone he touched once more
upon this subject. This letter to the British statesman sets forth his
view that unity in the Church is a preface to the unity of mankind:

« For some time my mind has specially busied itself with the Unity
of Faith and of the Church, which is at once the most precious
fruit of our redemption and its final aim. I have indeed chosen this
as the subject of this year's pastoral to my clergy. It seems to me
that mankind, despite its errors and numerous frailties, is tending
toward this unity. God formerly converted the great Roman Empire into a preface and a true introduction to Christianity; today I
think that God whishes to make those wonderful instruments of
communication and traffic between the most distant parts of our
globe, which steam and electricity offer, into a preface and introduction to that ideal unity which our Lord made the subject of his
noblest prayer to His Eternal Father before his death (St. John
XVII). How gladly I shall some day discuss these lofty subjects
with you, if God will! It is true that for this to be done successfully,
Bossuet would have to arise in the Bishop (Strossmayer), just as

---

[72]   Pastoral on the eve of Vatican I (BS, *loc. cit.,* 10).

[73]   « If I am a right interpreter of God's mysterious plans, the course
of human events points to the more frequent holding of ecumenical councils.
As God has open the roads to the apostles – to the first heralds of the word
of God – all over the vast Roman Empire, at the very outset of the Church
to shed the divine light of the Gospel on all nations and tribes, thus I believe
that God in our own days – through the easy means of communications, invented to promote material welfare of nations – offers them to the Church,
that the nations may cherish their hopes, that various churches can easier
get united with the Holy See whenever they hear the voice of the supreme
shepherd, inviting them to come to an ecumenical council and to gather
around and with him » (Mansi 50, 482).

the famous Leibnitz has arisen in my dear and valued friend (Glad-stone) ».[74]

It appears that Strossmayer was in possession of a certain amount of the spirit and of the vision of Teilhard de Chardin. It also becomes obviuos that in the mind of the Bishop mankind is heading toward the union in itself and ultimately with its Creator. This is precisely what we wish to express by stating that he was an ardent follower of Romanistic Revival.

His romanticism was founded upon his conception of the redemption of mankind. One might rightly expect from him that he would begin firstly to talk about Christ but he took a different approach to this subject. Whether he followed on this topic the example of J. A. Möhler, or perhaps he wanted to dramatize it as was appropriate to his rhetorical genius, we do not know. At any rate, there is a resemblance on this approach between him and Möhler.

The latter in « Symbolism » begins with a sin in order to illustrate and to develop the concept of the Church and so does Strossmayer in quite a few instances. Both Möhler and Strossmayer were preoccupied with the distinction between our being « image » of God and our being created into « likeness » of God, and both attempted to prove that we have only lost « likeness » (holiness and justice) through the original sin, but we have still remained « image » of God, namely, capable of searching for and of loving God[75]. Besides, Strossmayer's other purpose was to em-

---

[74] CBSG, pp. 430-431. Cf. also Strossmayer's letter to Gladstone of April 11, 1878 (*ibid.,* p. 438), his Pastoral of 1891 (KRS, IV, 244) and in so many other places.

[75] *Symbolism,* I, 1-67. According to Möhler to lose « likeness » means to cease to be holy, just and acceptable to God. *Ibid.,* pp. 34-35.. Strossmayer in his Pastoral « Jesus Christ » of 1893 treats the same problem on several pages. In his judgment, in spite of Original Sin and its consequences, man feels the burden of sin and seeks to reconcile himself with God. He points out that this is especially manifested in the books of the Old Testament: the Jewish nation was in costant search to reconcile itself with God (GBBS, pp. 10-12 and 14-15). « Man, by losing the supernatural gifts, has lost the link with God and with eternal life... but his nature has remained intact: his mind, conscience, and will... man remained the image of God... The Fallen man still feels God in his being and his soul: he is ashamed of sin, he fears God whom he offended... he confesses his sin » (*ibid.,* p. 13).

phasize the wickedness of sin and to point out its sources, namely, that a sin is man's wish to be totally indipendent of God and his laws, to be his own law-maker, self-sufficient, « to be his own God », and to hold himself as his own final aim. What is more, human society – in his judgment – as such is sinful and responsible for its miseries[76]. The way he describes sin and its consequences. it almost assumes the cosmic dimensions and implications. He portrays the sin and its relations with the Incarnation and the redemption in this manner:

« ... the primary goal of our holy redemption is the unity of the human race. Through sin and wickedness we have not only set ourselves against God, our eternal source, but we have set ourselves against one another. Sin and wickedness have poisoned us, separated us and crushed us in such a measure that there is no doubt tha without higher help we would annihilate ourselves and push ourselves into eternal grave. The holiest and the most natural ties were destroyed by sin and evil. This was and still is the consequence of sin and wickedness. The eternal Word of God had become man that, first of all, He reconciles us with His eternal Father, and thereafter us with one another in order to return us to fraternal love and harmony in striving toward our eternal destiny. Through Christ we have become one holy family to which He, as the first-born, placed Himself at the head. He, through His blood and passion, has freed us from sin and its consequences and transformed us into the sons of God and His own brothers that we may become among ourselves genuine brothers and the members of that holy mystical body of which He himself through His holy and glorious resurrection has become the eternal and living head. This is the nature and the goal of that holy mystery which was initiated in the stable in Bethlehem and was consummated on Calvary »[77].

---

[76] Quoted by A. SPILETAK, op. cit., 242-243. This Pastoral on « Sin » was published first in GBBS, no. 2, pp. 9-40. Cf. also his Pastoral « The Church of God », GBBS, XXVI (1898), 26-27.

[77] Strossmayer's sermon delivered in Rome on May 61, 1877 (CP, p. 133). Man by committing a sin, according to Möhler, also alieneates himself from God and himself. Cf. Symbolism, I, 33-34. In order to prove the necessity

There are certain matters in the previous text which must be cleared up. First of all, sin is a failure in fellowship with men. It causes separation where there should be togetherness. It is also evident that sin creates a breach not only between man and man, but also between God and man. No man can be at peace with God when he is not at peace with men. It almost looks that a man must be in fellowship with men before he can find the fellowship of God. In other words, sin affects God and men as well which again indicates that sin is failure in love. What is more, one of the greatest effects of sin is the disturbance in personal relationship. The Bishop's conception of sin is the creation of disunity, and due to this it almost appears that men have become fragments, scattered all over the globe. Under this aspect he views the Incarnation and the redemption, namely, the Word of God – by assuming human nature upon Himself – has actually taken to Himself and upon Himself all these fragments, and thus He has established the unity of mankind by uniting it to Himself. And on account of this reality he so repetitiously says in his speeches and pastorals that Christ « has offered us as a sacrifice on the cross to His heavenly Father »[78]. Besides, through the realization of the unity of mankind in the divine person of Christ, and since the Church of God is the being of Christ then consequently this unity of human race must be achieved in her and through her.[79]

After having returned from Rome, he wrote to his clergy June 3, 1859: « If the great and holy minds were preoccupied in the past with the thoughts of reconciliation and reunion (of Christendom), then most certainly the illustrious soul of the Holy Father Pius IX is also imbued with the same thoughts and intentions who has not only the supreme power in the Church but also the heart which, following the example of Christ, loves equally all the races and all

---

of the Incarnation and Redemption, Strossmayer maintains, that man – provided he is forgiven his sin – is not yet able, on account of his natural limitations, to bring himself to God and attain eternal life without help from the outside: and this help had been given by the Incarnation and Christ's sacrifice on the cross. Cf. GBBS, XXVI (1898), 21-22.

[78] « The Reply to the Three Greek Orthodox Bishops » (KRS, IV, 480) and passim.

[79] *Ibid.*, p. 223 and passim.

the nations; he (Pous IX) has the heart which equally desires to make all men the participantes of the divine redemption... he is eagerly waiting to embrace all new-comers... ».[80]

The Incarnation and the redemption were not solely the means to reconcile us with God and to unite us with one another and finally with God Himself, but the Incarnation also served that the Word of God might communicate to us « God's inner life, His power and glory »[81]. In other words, Christ is also the revealer of God. (What is more, one – by perusing his speeches and his other documents – must necessarily perceive that he must have been constantly reading the holy Bible not only of the New Testament but also of the Old Testament). It becomes apparent that he tried by all means to establish the continuation from one to the other. He was very familiar with the concepts of the Old Testament; this is strikingly evident in his conception of *corporate personality,* namely, that a group is incorporated in the personality of its leader, be it a Jewish king or a patriarch. And as a rule the Jewish people identified itself with its king or patriarch, and considered their successes as its own. No wonder then that the Word of God, in the mind of the Bishop, by becoming man, has assumed a corporate personality. This conception of his is expressed in some places implicitly, in some explicitly, as for instance, when he says: « The aim of our holy faith is to unite men into one entity through the holiest and most tender bonds, as the eternal Anointed One of God has done through His holy sacrifice by connecting heaven and earth and by transforming the human race into one living being »[82]. This thought runs through his allocutions and writings as to stress this sublime reality and to become cognizant of its significance.

Furthermore, in order to emphasize the ardent desire of Christ that this unity and oneness may be realized among us in the same hope, faith and love on numerous occasions he quoted St. John: « I pray not only for these, but for those also who through their words will believe in me. May they all be one. Father, may they be

---

80 JJS-DK, p. 431.
81 Bishop's sermon in Rome (CP, p. 137).
82 The Pastoral « The Unity in the Church » (TS, p. 398).

one in us, as you are in me and I in you, so that the world may believe it was you who sent me » (John XVII, 20-22). He suggested that this prayer of Our Lord is so important that every Christian should know it by heart and recite it every day[83]. Thus the whole world would recognize the divine mission of Christ and strive towards it[84].

We would like to add one or two more things to his conception of the redemption which might help us grasp better some of this ecclesiological ideas. Our redemption was motivated by love and humility, and these virtues were manifested in the highest degree in Jesus Christ. He, being extremely aware of this actuality, on the occasion of the solemn opening of the Yugoslav Academy in Zagreb on July 28, 1867, delivered his address to the academics by holding in his hand a crucifix which had been donated to him by Pius IX. The theme of his allocution was love and humility, and both these virtues had been exemplified by Christ, beginning with His birth in the stable of Bethlehem and culminating in their supreme realization on the cross. In this address he mentioned and quoted men of great distinction who were inspired by the idea of the cross among them: Blaise Pascal, St. Augustine, Daniel O'Connell, Gottfried Leibnitz, François Guizot, Jacques Bossuet. His whole idea was to make the academics aware of their mission in their respective nation that they, like Christ, might practice love toward « the poor and the unfortunates » and with humility lower themselves to the needs of the neglected because « Christ especially had the poor at His heart »[85].

His favorite Biblical text, on the significance of love and humility in the person of Christ, was the epistle of St. Paul to the

---

[83] KRS, IV, 246. See also Strossmayer's letter to Gladstone of April 11, 1878 (CBSG, p. 438) and TS, p. 420.

[84] KRS, IV, 247. This argumentation of the Bishop bears a great similarity to that of Möhler. Cf. *Symbolism*, II, 25-27. In this instance both Möhler and Strossmayer are in accordance with St. Cyprian. Cf. Ancient Christian Writers, St. Cyprian: *The Lapsed and the Unity of the Catholic Church* (translated by M. Bévenot, S.J.). (Westminster, Md., the Newman Press, 1957), p. 49.

[85] TS, pp. 157-170.

Philippians 2, 6-11: « His state was divine, yet he did not cling to his equality with God but emptied himself to assume the condition of a slave, and became as men are; and being as all men are, he was humbler yet, even to accepting death, death on a cross. But God raised him high and gave him the name which is above all other names so that all beings in the heavens, on earth and in the underworld should bend the knee at the name of Jesus and that every tongue should acclaim Jesus Christ as Lord, to the glory of God the Father ».

In the conclusion of his last speech in Vatican I, after having exhausted all his arguments against defining the dogma of papal infallibility, he cited the above text of St. Paul and begged the Pontiff to practice the virtue of humility and desist from proclaiming this dogma since « the mystery of greatness is hidden in humility and selfdenial »[86]. In one of his conferences, most probably delivered to the theological students in Vienna in 1848, he reminded them that it is not advisable to preach on sin and vices often because in this manner « the clergy might infuriate the sinners and scandalize the good », but rather let the themes of your sermons be more concentrated on the love and mercy of God[87]. In the Preface to the New Ritual he advised the clergy that the best material for their sermons could be found in the mysteries of the incarnation and redemption, and this could be easily obtained by reflecting on the goodness, love, mercy and humility of Christ[88].

When he discussed the problem of our own salvation, and what we are expected to do in order to gain it, he connected it with the mystery of the incarnation and redemption on the cross. The qualities of the Redeemer (Jesus Christ) are just the opposite of ours: man displays pride and disobedience in sinning, and consequently the Redeemer had to be humble and obedient, so every individual

---

[86] Mansi 52, 404. In one place of his address « Three Words to the University » he prayerfully expressed himself in this fashion: « O Lord, since you have humbled Yourself to the death on the cross because of me, I beg You for the grace that I may remain humble like you and that I may recall the words of St. Augustine 'whoever wishes to erect a big building of knowledge and virtue, let him dig deep foundations of humility' » (TS, p. 311).

[87] BS, XXIII (1935), 81-92.

[88] TS, p. 367.

on the path to his salvation has to be obedient and humble[89]. In short, the requirements of salvation are the reversal of those traits manifested in perpetrating sin.

3. - The Church

It was earlier mentioned several times that the Bishop had not written theological treatises ex professo. However, his Reply of February 4, 1882, to the Greek Orthodox Bishops can be considered a treatise on the Church. Had it be put in the form of a book, it would be a tractate of over 100 pages. This reply was originally published in several instalments in GBBS in 1882. The three Greek Orthodox Bishops: Stefan Knežević of Zadar, Gerasim Petranović of Kotor and Teofan Živković of Karlovci[90] had attacked Strossmayer and his Pastoral letter of 1881 on Sts. Cyril and Methodius. We almost feel grateful to the above mentioned bishops that they, with their respective Pastoral letters, prompted him to develop more elaborately his conception of the Church of God. There is no doubt that the Bishop in his other writings has elaborated on the mission and the structures of the Church, but in no other document was he so precise and prolific as he was in this instance.

Not only was the corporate personality of the human race realized in the person of Christ, by the same token the Church of God, in his judgment, is the corporate entity, too. What he wanted to imply was that all mankind should be united in and through the Church. Due to the redemption of Jesus Christ, which comprises the whole human race, and whose fruits are deposited in the Church, and subsequently she « is expected to bring along with her (the entire human race) into the presence and glory of the Triune God, and thus she will make whole mankind the participants and sharers of God's bliss »[91]. In a word, the mission of the Church of God

---

[89]   KRS, IV, 223-224. « As we were not able to be redeemed without Christ's humility and obedience, so we cannot be saved without (our own) humility and obedience. The source of Original Sin and of every other sin was and is pride and disobedience » (ibid.).
[90]   Cf. CP, pp. 305-306.
[91]   KRS, IV, 495.

was and still is to embrace into her arms and bosom all races and nations and to deposit them in front of the majesty of the Almighty.

Naturally, this concept of the Church evoked in him on numerous occasions a question: how about those who are not in the Church – what is their destiny in this ecclesiological context. To this question he often attempted to give an answer. In order to solve this problem he resorted to make a sharp distinction between those who belong to the Mystical Body of Christ and those who merely appertain to the soul of it. All those who are in search of truth, who are willing to accept it and who follow the voice of their conscience, belong to the soul of the Mystical Body of Christ[92]. On this point he was very consistent: in Christ just as well as in the Church all men should find unity, and logically the Church does not stand in any real opposition to men of good will outside the inmost circle of her mystical body. In other words, the nature of the Church must be explained in the light of Christ's Incarnation and His redemptive work since both these realities are universal – all-encompassing. He did not want to judge the Church and her relations to the whole world on the empirical or human basis, but he rather wanted to see her under the perspective of Christ's supplication « Father, that all may be one » as he either said or wrote tens of times. What is more, that opinion is based on St. Augustine's theology[93].

We do not doubt that Strossmayer had a well developed conception of the Church during the session of Vatican I even though he did not give the precise definition of it. Most probably the reason why he refrained from doing it was that he did not wish to appear as a lecturer. However, at one point he said in the Council that « the Church – in my judgment – besides being made the heir by Christ of His power and his rights, she is also made a mediatrix between God and men, and she is the continuation (continuatrix)

---

[92] *Ibid.* See also his Pastoral « Sts Cyril and Methodius » (TS, p. 438), his Pastoral of 1888 in BS, XIX (1931), p. 326 and A. Spiletak, *op. cit.,* (Pastoral of 1894), p. 242.

[93] KRS, IV, 495.

of the redemption (of Christ) in order to be constantly eternal organism of life and strength »[94]. One can readily perceive that he abstained from giving legalistic and juridical appearance. The Church is the ever-living organism and the extension of Christ's redemption, and this is his perennial refrain.

His starting point in developing his concept of the Church is that « in her the mystery of the Incarnation and that of the sacrifice on the cross is continued, and thereby she unites in her being and in her structure both divine (which is invisible) and human (which is visible) elements, and whoever would dare separate or divide one from the other he would necessarily weaken and destroy her own being and her work ».[95] Under the aspect of the Incarnation he looked upon the visibility and invisibility of the Church: Christ's humanity stands for the visible Church while His divinity stands for the divine element in her. Furthermore, according to him some Church Fathers and some modern theologians « had rightly compared the Church of God to Jeus Christ, her eternal bridegroom, who had united in His person divinity and humanity, and whoever would attempt to disunite these elements, he would violate and destroy His own being and the entire mystery of His redemption would be rendered nil »[96]. Undoubtedly, this reasoning resembles that of J. A. Möhler who had also found the justification for the visibility of the Church « in the Incarnation of the divine Word »[97]. At this place it remains to us to remark that the Bishop gave the implicit definition of the Church, by underscoring the visibility of the Church, while Möhler had been more specific in his definition of the Church by stating that she is « the visible community of believers, founded by Christ... and appointed to conduct all nations, in the course of ages, back to God », and Christ's redemptive work is continued in her « to the end of the world under her guidance of the spirit »[98]. Needless to say this Möhler's definition

---

[94]   MANSI 50, 142.
[95]   KRS., IV, 495.
[96]   *Ibid.* Undoubtedly he has understood « under modern theologians » Johann Adam Möhler since in this document he referred once or twice to the mentioned theologian.
[97]   *Symbolism,* II, 5.
[98]   *Ibid.*

bears resemblance to that of St. Cyprian that the Church is « the new community of the believers »[99]. Of course, the Bishop also had Cyprian's definition in mind, but Möhler had developed it to a much greater degree.

Having in mind what concept of the Church the Bishop had and where he found the basis for her visibility and invisibility, namely, in the Incarnation itself, will make it easier for us to grasp some of the other statements which pertain to the nature of the Church: « Christ is the mystical (invisible) head of the Church »[100], « the Church is God's institution and through her and in her Christ lives and works among us »[101], « she continues the work of our redemption in the visible manner here on earth »[102], « Christ, our God and redeemer, has deposited all his being and His power in the Church and also all the merits and fruits of His passion and death »[103], « the holy Church in her being, her teaching and her functioning is the very same Jesus Christ »,[104] « as Jesus Christ has carried and carries in His being and in His divine heart whole human race, in the same fashion the Church of God, the eternal heir and vicar of Christ's love and mercy, carries in her soul and heart all mankind »[105], « the Church of God... is the being of the being of Christ. Jesus is the eternal source of all holiness, and the holy mother Church through the mystery of her altars is also the source of it »[106].

The latter statements of the Prelate undoubtedly prove in what sense the Church is compared to the Incarnation of the Son of God or why she is called « Christ Himself », namely, he simply wanted to emphasize that Christ lives and works in the Church. In other

---

99   Ancient Christian Writers, *op. cit.,* 66.

100   KRS, IV, 493.

101   *Ibid.,* p. 492. Cf. also Strossmayer's Pastoral of 1890 in A. Spiletak, *op. cit.,* 195-196.

102   KRS, IV, 493. See also his Pastoral of 1892 in A. Spiletak, *op. cit.,* p. 207.

103   KRS, IV, 470.

104   *Ibid.,* p. 233.

105   *Ibid.*

106   His Pastoral of 1893 in GBBS, XXI (1893), p. 45. Cf. A. Spiletak, *op. cit.,* 221.

words, he intended to underscore the continuous efficacy of Christ within the Church in a visible way and with visible means, or as Möhler said « the Redeemer not merely lived eighteen hundred years ago, so that he has since disappeared, and we retain but a historical remembrance of him, as of a deceased man: but he is, on the contrary, eternally living in his Church... »[107].

a. *Visibility of the Church*

The Bishop wanted to emphasize in his debate with the three Orthodox Bishops the visibility of the Church. The latter element is particulary manifested in the seven sacraments: « Jesus continues not only His redemptive work at the right of His eternal Father, but also in the visible fashion in the seven sacraments through which in every situation of our life the fruits of His passion and death are imparted to us »[108]. Of course, Christ is the source of every grace which is given to us in the sacraments, but it is so constituted that our priestly presence and activity is also essential[109].

In order to corroborate and to strenghten his position on the necessity of the visible Church he borrowed from the Eastern Church the concept of a bishop and the allotted role to him in his respective diocese, and therefrom he continued to construe his argumentation. He argued in this fashion: « Christ governs His Church through the genuine, living and visible college of bishops; since there should be besides Christ – whom the mortal eyes cannot see – a genuine and living bishop through whom Christ works and governs the diocese; by the same token – and even more so – there should be, besides Jesus Christ, a true and living vicar through whom and in whom He governs the entire body of Christ – the Church[110]. In favor of his argumentation for the necessity of the visible head in the Church he alleged the results of the analysis and research of Augustin J. Gratry contained in his book « La morale

---

[107] *Symbolism*, I, 335.
[108] KRS, IV, 494.
[109] *Ibid.*
[110] *Ibid.*, 495.

et la loi de l'histoire » according to which no society can either exist or function without having a visible authority[111].

In his Pastoral of 1898 on « The Church of God » (which is actually a brochure of 60 pages) he has developed more subtly his concept on the visibility of the Church of God. Once again he states that « the Church is the being (of the being) of Christ » and that « Christ is in the Church with His doctrine and His divine authority »[112]. His Pastoral (Jesus Christ) of 1893 was more specific on this point when he compared the kingdom of God (the Church) to the Incarnate Word composed of divine (invisible) and human (visible) elements, and consequently both factors are to be found in the Church[113].

Where does he find this visibility of the Church and how is it manifested in the human society that anybody can perceive it? As he said so many times elsewhere so does he in these mentioned Pastorals that Christ has deposited his redemptive work in the Church, and the fruits of the mystery of redemption are to be distributed by the Church. Moreover, the Bishop's second premise is intimately bound up with the previous one, namely, that Christ has placed Himself in the Church, and logically « being the crown and the head of the apostleship » the popes and the bishops « whatever they have and whatever they can perform, they have it and they do it in Him and through Him ».[114] Since « they are links in the chain which reaches to heaven – to Jeus Christ who sits at the right hand of the eternal Father », the power of hierarchy comes directly to them from Christ[115]. Because of this intimate and organic closeness between Christ and the Church officeholders and because of the fact that the Church is in possession of Christ's redemptive work[116], which is intended to be offered to the entire hu-

---

111   *Ibid ,* 496.
112   GBBS, XXVI (1898), p. 29.
113   *Ibid.,* XXI (1893), 45. Möhler reasons in the same fashion when he states that « the blame of this formal difference arises from overlooking the fact, that Christ was God-man, and wished to continue working in a manner, conformable to his two-fold nature » (*Symbolism,* II, 52).
114   GBBS, XXI (1893), 45.
115   *Ibid.*
116   GBBS, XXVI (1898), 29.

man race, then « Christ had instituted the holy and visible magisterium which is to take His place in the Church of God ».[117]

Christ's reason for establishing a living and visible magisterium in the Church were many. First of all, this teaching institution is predestined to administer the mysteries of the redemption by way of the holy sacraments and also by celebrating the holy Eucharist in the visible manner[118]; secondly, this visible magisterium has to preserve « the Christian doctrine and the holy faith in its original purity, clearness and completeness... »[119] « as it came out of the mouth of Jesus Christ, attested by his miracls, and handed down to us by the tradition ».[120] The Church magisterium is the extension and continuation of Jesus Christ, therefore, there is no wonder that Strossmayer insists that we have to listen to the Church of God as to Christ Himself[121]. Furthermore, the magisterium is in the Church that it may discern what is true and what is false, and that it may also reestablish peace and tranquility within the Church of God if dissensions arise[122].

b. *Unity in the Church*

This topic is very closely tied up with the former one. The unity of the Church cannot be imagined without the central and visible head[123] which must be realized in the papacy as he said so many times, beginning with his first letter to Pope Pius IX until his death[124]. It would take us too long to enumerate all his arguments be they biblical or traditional: St. Irenaeus (Contra Hereses), St. Cyprian (The Unity of the Catholic Church), St. Jerome (his epistle to Pope Damasus), St. Ambrose, Leo the Great and so on[125]

---

[117] GBBS, XXI (1893), 34.
[118] *Ibid.*, XXVI (1898), 54.
[119] *Ibid.*, p. 43.
[120] *Ibid.*, p. 32.
[121] *Ibid.*, p. 43. « Let us, therefore, revere, listen to and follow holy mother Church as Christ Himself » (*ibid.*, p. 42).
[122] *Ibid.*, XXI (1893), 48. Cf. also *ibid.*, XXVI (1898), 35 and see also Möhler's view in *Symbolism*, II, 53-54.
[123] KRS, IV, 492.
[124] JJS-DK, p. 165. Cf. also his Pastoral « The Church of God » in GBBS, XXVI (1898), pp. 47-48.
[125] KRS, IV, 497-501.

to prove the primacy of the Roman bishop. Once the primacy of the Roman pontiff is proven, then it logically follows that the unity of Christendom must be realized in him.

Since his biblical and patristic arguments are very common, we would rather busy ourselves with some other aspects which have a great bearing on this topic of the Church unity, and which are specifically his. This specificity comes to the fore particularly in the holy Eucharist as he looked upon it in his writings.

First of all, holy Eucharist is our spiritual food in the eschatological sense. Christ in the sacrament of altar offers Himself to His Father but at the same time, by His total presence in it, He communicates Himself and His life to us that we may live in Him, and He in us. Due to this reality « we are transformed into a new man... and thus eternal life is already inaugurated within us ».[126] His other aspect of holy Eucharist, however, is even more forceful than the one already mentioned. Whenever he discussed holy Eucharist and its role in the spiritual life of a Christian, he drew a parallel between Christ's presence in the Church and that in holy Eucharist. This conception is best expressed in the following text: « The Catholic Church by her very name refuses the doctrine of a national church because the Catholic Church maintains and believes that Jesus also died on the cross for us all that He may remain and live in His entirety under the species of bread and wine in every corner of the world in order to unite human race into one and single holy family and also to aggregate all particular national churches into one holy Church, and thus to enable and make each of these churches to enjoy not only their proper life but also the universal life... ».[127] By this « universal life » ought to be understood from the context the life of Christ which he perpetually communicates to the mankind; or as he says « the mystery of the body and blood (of Jesus Christ) means the unity of human race; Jesus in this holy mystery... also dwells that He may unite to Himself and transform all of us into one holy family ».[128]

---

126 CP, p. 143 and passim.
127 KRS, IV, 502.
128 CP, p. 133 (His sermon delivered in Rome).

From all this what has been said so far one can easily perceive that there was a logical chain in the mind of the Bishop: first, the entire human race was united in the « corporate personality » of Jesus; secondly, Christ as such has deposited « His entire being into the Church »; thirdly, He did the same thing in holy Eucharist which was and is destined to embrace in itself the whole mankind[129]. At lenght, all this indicates that the unity of mankind has to be realized: first, in Christ then in the Church and finally in holy Eucharist as a prelude to the eternal union.

Therefore, there is no wonder that in his mind holy Eucharist is the eternal source and pledge of the « holy love, harmony and unity to which all of us are invited by Christ through the Church »[130]. Through and in the celebration of holy Eucharist in any nation, and especially in England and Germany religious and national unity sooner or later will be achieved[131].

Because of this conception of the Church of God which is almost an enduring incarnation of the Son of God (understood in the sense of Christ's efficacy in the Church) and on account of his firm conviction that the « unity in itself is the holiest matter after which every noble human heart should yearn[132], he very often speaks or refers to papacy as 'being a sacrament' ».[133] This appellation is attributed to the papacy on account of its position and relationship to Christ on one side and to its role in the visible Church on the other; and naturally, because of its divine origin.

He, being a « practical man », in his correspondence with various individuals of the Eastern Church underscored the essential requirements in achieving unity, not only within the Catholic Church but also with the Eastern Church. The main prerequisite for any

---

[129] Strossmayer once again draws a parallel between the Incarnation of the Son of God and the holy Eucharist. This is done under the aspect that Christ's divinity and humanity are present under the species of bread and wine, and Christ as such gives Himself – divine and human – to a Christian. Besides, this indicates in what sense he applies the expression « Incarnation » to the Church and the holy Eucharist – it is simply Christ's efficacy in both instances. Cf. his Pastoral of 1898 in GBBS, XXVI, 35.

[130] KRS, IV, 247.
[131] Ibid.
[132] Ibid , p. 470.
[133] CP, p. 142.

kind of the ecclesial unity is the independence of the church in her operation and mission. A church deprived of this privilege can have neither life nor genuine fruitfulness.[134] He wanted with this to ascertain that there was no unity in the Eastern Church, and consequently there is no manifestation of it in her.

He genuinely rejoiced over the fact that patriarchates of Bucharest, Sofia and Belgrade became independent from the Patriarch of Constantinople, and that these churches finally freed themselves from the corruption and simony of the Phanariot bishops,[135] but he persisted in asking where was the solidarity of the Eastern Church if each of these churches lives separately and independently[136]. He deplored the position of the Russian Eastern Church that she had become a state institution ever since the Patriarch of Moscow was replaced by the Petersburg synod. What is more, he added that the Church of Russia, even prior to that, used to live under state tutorship, and allegedly could not have lived and functioned otherwise.[137]

It was not his intention so much to point to the disunity of the Eastern Church, by bringing out the sad occurrences, as it was to deplore the sad situation in it. Not only did he desire to see solidarity within the Eastern Church, but he equally wanted the Church of the East to free herself of her servitude to her respective governments. Once she became free of the state fetters, she would instantly regain much desirable freedom, but her vitality would be able to find a cure to her ills and to stop the spread of the nihilistic doctrines which were so rampant and rapidly growing[138]. This once realized would be a prelude to her reunion with the Church of Rome, and also would enable her to reflect upon herself and her mission in the world. His idealistic mind reasoned further: suppose this were a reality, then her joining the Western Church would au-

---

134   KRS, IV, 482.
135   Phanar is the residence of the Greek Patriarch in Istanbul. During the centuries, the Greek Orthodox bishops used to purchase their bishoprics from the Patriarch of Phanar with cash. Cf. Strossmayer's letter to Gladstone in CBSG, p. 437.
136   Cf. KRS, IV, 502 and 506.
137   *Ibid.*, pp. 482-483.
138   *Ibid.*, p. 508.

tomatically purge the Church of Rome of many anomalies and would also bring into her a new elan and vigor with her strong religiosity[139]. In order to support his stand on this issue he resorted to the practical cases as for istance in the USA where the Church really displays her efficacy, growth and prosperity, for she enjoys full freedom from the state authorities[140]. While he kept giving these suggestions to the Eastern Church to inspire her to throw off the fetters of slavery, he unceasingly kept repeating that the Church of Rome must be magnanimous vis à vis the Eastern Church in respecting and preserving her particular rights and customs, and to insist only on the essentials.[141]

c. *Ecumenical Councils*

Whoever reads the pronouncements and the writings of the Bishop from the time the Vatican Council was announced will notice that he placed great hopes in ecumenical councils. As a matter of fact, ecumenical councils are the living manifestation of the ecclesial unity, her life and vitality. The reason that in the Eastern Church ecumenical councils had not been held since she separated herself from the Church of Rome, he finds in the lack of the inner cohesion[142]. Before we bring out his reasons for advocating frequent ecumenical councils and national and diocesan synods, we would like to stress the fact that he never held that convoking and hol-

---

[139] This idea was expressed by Strossmayer so many times. « If I am not mistaken », he writes to Rački, « a great role is in store for the Russian nation, that is, to free the Western Church from the fetters through which she is chained to the States and to bring her (the Church of Rome) to her universal nature and mission. This must be considered the primary goal of the keener and more erudite Russian; they must free themselves of the State yoke and then enter into a union... This is going to be the aim of the next century of both Churches (Eastern and Western) ». (KRS, III, 145).

[140] KRS, IV, 472 and 236.

[141] *Ibid.*, p. 223.

[142] *Ibid.*, IV, p. 492. Strossmayer's intimate friend, Vladimir Soloviev, is in the full agreement on this topic with the Bishop of Djakovo. Soloviev almost accuses and challenges the Eastern Church for not holding ecumenical councils with these words: « otherwise, if apart from Peter the universal Church can expressly declare the truth, how are we to explain the remar-

ding these councils is a divine institution; he often said, however, that the apostolic council of Jerusalem served as an example and should be emulated. In addition, he never stated explicitly that the decrees of an ecumenical council are invalid unless they are accepted by the whole of the episcopal body. It is true, however, that in Vatican I he vigorously insisted on « moral episcopal unanimity » in deciding on the dogmatical decrees, but we do not know for certain whether he refused to sign the decrees of this Council because of the lack of moral unanimity of the college of bishops on those decisions, or because of some theological reasons of much more serious nature. In any case, this problem will be tackeled later on.

In his Pastoral on the eve of Vatican I he writes: « ... from now on most probably the Church will gather more often not only in the ecumenical councils due to the modern means of transportation but also in the provincial and diocesan synods which will bind together more closely all the members of the Church with one another in order to fortify the ecclesiastical unity and thus to bring a new life in the entire Church ».[143] What is more, the holding of ecumenical councils should be prompted and greatly enhanced by the trend in the world. « If it is approved and praised », he says, « that men, elected by their citizens, meet to discuss the matters of the world, why shouldn't we praise and admire the meeting of mankind, and who are not only representatives of their people but also of the Holy Spirit... ».[144]

In Vatican I he spoke on the significance of ecumenical coun-

---

kable silence of the Eastern episcopate... since their separation from the Chair of St. Peter? Can it be merely an accident? An accident lasting for a thousand years! To those anti-Catholics who will not see that their particularism cuts them off from the life of the universal Church, we have only one suggestion to make: Let them summon, without the concurrence of the successor of St. Peter, a council which they themselves can recognise as ecumenical! Then only will there be an opportunity of discovering whether they are right » (Vladimir Soloviev, op. cit., 88-89. Strossmayer and V. Soloviev are under the influence of Johann A. Möhler. Soloviev is very explicit on this point – Möhler is his ideal theologian. Ibid., p. 56.

[143]   BS, XXII, 13.
[144]   Ibid., p. 7.

cils several times. His frequent reference to them indicates that he was well acquainted with them and their procedures; this especially goes for the Councils of Chalcedon, Costance, Florence and Trent. The following portion, taken out of his last speech in Vatican I, will illustrate best what he thought of them and what purpose they might serve in the Church:

« Venerable Fathers, ecumenical councils are of great benefit, they are even sometimes of the utmost necessity. The spirit of the Church is the spirit of peace and harmony for which our Lord Jesus Christ had prayed so heartedly to His eternal Father in the last moments of His earthly life. The spirit of the Church is also the spirit of mutual counseling and fraternal understanding of which the Apostles had left us an example in Jerusalem, that is, the spirit of discipline and required obedience, but at the same time it is the spirit of the holy freedom – of that freedom – of which St. Paul made use in repremending St. Peter (Gal. 2, 11); it served to the glory of St. Paul, but it did more so to Peter who knew how to take this reproach in humility.

« I maintain, however, that there is nothing more beautiful and greater in the Church of God than to watch the scene when all the bishops from all over the world are gathered around the head (the pope) in the ecumenical councils in order to promote the glory of God and the salvation of souls of the faithful. For this reason, Venerable Fathers, at the very beginning of the Church the apostles had held the council of Jerusalem, wishing to give an example to the posterity which is to be imitated in the Church in the times to come; on account of this reason St. Gregory the Great compares the first four ecumenical councils to the four gospels; Durandus, the greatest theologian and canonist at the Viennese Council, was asked what would be the best remedy to the evils in the Christian society of that time, he replied: there is no better remedy than the frequent holding of ecumenical councils; the Council of Costance (1414-1418), inspired by the same ideas, had not only praised to heavens ecumenical councils and their fruitful effects but it had also enacted a law according to which an ecumenical council has to be convoked every tenth year. It was said that this law was never practiced; had they (ecumenical councils) been held, in my opinion and conviction, many evils would have been prevented, and perhaps the Reformation would never have come into existence ».[145]

d. *Episcopal System vs. Papal System*

In order to grasp the Bishop's conception of the structure of the Church it is absolutely necessary to cite a few texts that he quoted so often. At present we shall cite only three of them since they serve in many respects as a basis to many of his ecclesiological deductions. The first one is chapter 17 of St. John in which Christ prays to His Father that He may preserve the unity among the apostles and also among those who accept their preaching. Secondly, he quotes St. Cyprian:

« The authority of the bishops forms a unity of which each holds his part in its totality. And the Church forms a unity, however far she spreads and multiplies by the progeny of her fecundity; just as the sun's rays are many, yet the light is one, and a tree's branches are many, yet the strenght deriving from its sturdy root is one. So too, though many streams flow from a single spring, though its multiplicity seems scattered abroad by the copiousness of its welling waters, yet their oneness abides by reason of their starting point. Cut off one of the sun's rays – the unity of that body permits no (such) division of its light; break off a branch from the tree, it can bud no more; dam off a stream from its source, it dries up below the cut. So too Our Lord's Church is radiant with light and pours her rays over the whole world; but it is one and the same light which is spread everywhere, and the unity of her body suffers no division. She spreads her branches in generous growth over all the earth, she extends abundant streams ever further; yet one is the head-spring, one the source, one the mother who is prolific in her offspring, gene-

---

[145] MANSI 52, 396-397. Cf. also his introductory speech in Vatican I (Mansi 50, 483): « I am convinced that, had the ecumenical councils been held frequently, many evils within the Church would have been prevented: perhaps the Reformation, which has separated so many faithful and nations from the faith and the unity of the Church, would never have materialized ».

ration after generation; of her womb are we born, of her milk are we fed, of the Spirit our souls draw their life-breath ».[146]

The third one is of St. Ignatius who frequently in his epistles used to compare the relationship of a bishop with his flock with that of Christ and His Father; and consequently the Saint says that one has to be obedient to a bishop as one should be to Christ[147].

These quotations offer the evidence that in his mind the organic unity between the bishops on one hand and the faithful on the other should prevail in the entire Church at all times. Neither did he want to see the Roman pontiff either separated from the bishops or from the faithful; the pontiff should be looked upon within the Church. In his first speech in the Council he had already outlined the unity between the college of bishops and the pope with these words:

« As all of you are of the opinion – so am I – that the Church derives her strenghth and integrity from those of the head (of the Church). Therefore, before anything else the rights of the holy See are to be guaranteed if we wish that everything in the Church of God and this Council takes its proper and correct course... It is not less important that the role of the other membres of the mystical Body of Christ is to be established and to the college of bishops those rights are to be given which belong to them due to their office and character in order that the head (pope) himself can retain his office and dignity, using them for the salvation of all. These two factors (papacy and episcopacy) in my humble belief, are intimately connected and inseparably united by the plan of God... This unity and relationship – if I am not mistaken – Lord Christ, the author and consumator of our faith, had in mind – before ascending into heaven – when he ardently prayed that as He and the eternal Father are one so they remain one – those who are appointed by Him to be ministers of His divine work, the heirs and vicars of His love and mercy toward human race »[148]. In this same speech he was prompted by

---

146 The Ancient Christian Writers, St. Cyprian, op. cit., 47-48.
147 Mansi 52, 392.
148 Mansi 50, 140.

the idea already quoted and equally so by the trend among the nations for democratic governments[149] to come out with the proposal that all decisions, agreed upon in the Council, should be published in the name of the entire Council and not in the name of one even though he holds the highest authority.[150]

In his subsequent speech once again he advocated that the decrees be published in the name of the Council. In this instance he amplified his position and became more specific when he introduced another proposal that, while the council Fathers sign the decrees of the Council, « defining I sign » should be inserted. The reason for this insertion he finds in the fact that lately some theologians of a certain school had so weakened the verb to « judge », which the Fathers were ordered to use in this ecumenical Council, that its worth was reduced to the mere power of approving, and also because in the previous councils the bishops used to sign « defining I sign ». And finally, to insure the rights of bishops he proposed that all decrees should be signed by the bishops in this « judging and defining I sign »[151] Naturally, he did have in mind that both the pontiff and the bishops employ the same vocabulary, otherwise they would be separated and the unity would be disjointed. However, he did state that the bishops and the pontiff do not sign with equal rights.[152]

He wanted by all means to see the Church function in all her aspects and activities as one indivisible entity and organism. It is possible that on this issue he was under the influence of J. A. Möhler who wrote: « The dogmatic decrees of the episcopacy (united with the general head and centre) are infallible, for it represents the universal Church... Hence, as the institution (the Church) which Christ has established for the preservation and the explanation of His doctrines, is subject, in this its function, to no error; so the

---

149   « Nobody can deny that in our own days there is a movement among the cultural nations and peoples to define and determine their own common interests and rights with mutual agreement » (Mansi 50, 141).

150   *Ibid.*

151   Mansi 51, 73.

152   *Ibid.*, 72.

organ, through which the Church speaks, is also exempt from error »[153].

It seems to us that this Möhler's text and that of St. Cyprian constantly hovered before his eyes. This is particularly expressed in the following words: « In the divine formation of the Church all her constitutive parts are intimately and undividedly united among themselves; and in this unity they mutually complement one another and perfect themselves; and in the marvelous manner they tend to the goal which is confided to them by God. If this inner cohesion is upset in any way, then everything else is necessarily upset, and consequently some members of the divine body of the Church will be deprived of the innate life-giving power and significance »[154]. Therefore there is no wonder that he urged the Council to discuss both objects (papacy and episcopacy) « ex professo » and simultaneously.[155] Hereafter, in order to corroborate his contention he quotes St. Matthew 28: « He said: 'All authority in heaven and on earth has been given to me. Go, therefore, make disciples of all nations; baptize them... and know that I am with you always; yes, to the end of the world, » and concludes that Christ had transferred his power to all the apostles as a group or as he says « in solidum »; then he adds: « If these words are true, then we are protected by the assistance of the Holy Spirit from any error as long as we are united with our head (the pope) either being dispersed over the world or congregated in a council... »[156]. Furthermore, on this topic of the Church unity he followed the footsteps of St. Cyprian who had claimed that « there is one and undivided episcopate all over the word », and consequently Strossmayer made a claim that « in my judgment beside the ordinary jurisdiction (of the bishops in their respective dioceses) the bishops are endowed with the virtual right over the rest of the Church due to their episcopal character and ordination »[157]. To substantiate his opinion

---

[153] *Symbolism*, II, 77-78.
[154] MANSI 52, 392.
[155] *Ibid.*
[156] *Ibid.*
[157] *Ibid.*, 393. On one occasion during Vatican I when patience ran low,

he quoted St. Gregory of Nissa who had praised St. Cyprian for his fruitful influence not only on the Church of Africa but on the universal Church[158].

If we wish to appraise correctly Strossmayer's stand ond the structures of the Church and especially his position on the relationship between the pontiff and the college of bishops in governing the Church of God, it is necessary to make several remarks. First of all, he felt – and he had said so in the Council – that every bishops has a virtual influence in the universal Church; secondly, the Church ought to be governed by the spirit of « mutual counseling and fraternal understanding »; (Here he refers, most certainly, to the cooperation which must exist between the head of the Church and the college of bishops); thirdly, it must be mentioned that he had undergone a development on the issue of the structures of the Church. This revision had taken place in him along with his change on the papal infallibility which he unequivocally accepted in 1881. On account of this, he has to be studied at two stages: one prior to and during Vatican I and second after Vatican I when he gave his consent to the dogma of papal infallibility.

It appears that his most forceful arguments in defence of bishop's rights were proferred in his last speech: first, the rights of bishops are to be insured as well as those of the Roman pontiff; otherwise if the bishops surrender their rights in ecumenical councils, the freedom in ecumenical councils and otherwise will be abrogated; second, he contended that bishops had exercised their rights in the former ecumenical councils and no limitations on the freedom of bishops were imposed « except those which are found in holy Scripture and Tradition »; third, he mentioned the Council of Chalcedon in which the Epistle to Flavian of Pope Leo the Great was first examined – bishops of Illyric and Palestine even expressed their doubts about its orthodoxy but they were given time, means and opportunity to examine it – and finally it was una-

---

Mgr. Ketteler reproached Strossmayer for « having exceeded the limits or episcopal power » (Tkalac's report of March 12, 1870, RSCV, p. 241).
[158] MANSI 52, 394.

nimously accepted by the entire body of the bishops in the said Council (this opinion was also shared by Msgr. Karl Hefele); fourth, he also asserted that the Council af Chalcedon had given the priority to the See of Rome, but at the same time the council Fathers had found pope Leo's doctrine to be in conformity with Holy Scripture and Tradition; fifth, Cyril of Alexandria was also acclaimed by the Council of Ephesus as pope Leo the Great was in Chalcedon even though Cyril was not the bishop of Rome; and this was done to Cyril because his doctrine was in accordance with holy Scripture and Tradition and also because Cyril's doctrine expressed the faith of the universal Church; sixth, he alleged Robert Bellarmine who had said that pope Leo's Epistle did not have « definitive but instructive character ».[159]

The whole tendency of the Prelate was to stress that the bishops in the former ecumenical councils had exercised their freedom in deliberating and examining the documents proposed to them by the Roman pontiffs indicating that the bishops had the right not only to judge but also to define a certain doctrine. One can hardly conceive that an ecumenical council would be merely convoked for the sake of approving. It is more appropriate to state that the ecumenical councils are held to hear the witnesses (bishops) to the Tradition of the Church. In addition, Strossmayer quoted pope Leo the Great saying « the sacerdotal office is exercised best when the authority of a superior is preserved and the freedom of subjects remained intact ».[160] The Bishop of Djakovo even went a little further by asserting that the bishops – if conscience so dictates – can also reject proposals in the council[161].

In his proposal, issued on the eve of the First Vatican Council, he touched on the problem of episcopacy within the Church, and he was very cautious in formulating the rights of bishops. He wholeheartedly admitted that the bishops's rights are « holy and purchased by the blood of the Lord, (but) if you sever them

---

[159] *Ibid*, 397-399. Cf. JANKO OBERŠKI, *Govori Strossmayera, op. cit.*, p. 120, note 15. Oberški, in the case of Pope Leo's Dogmatic Epistle to Flavian, maintains just the opposite of what Hefele and Strossmayer had asserted.
[160] MANSI 52, 398.
[161] *Ibid*.

from the supreme power (papacy) of the Church, at the same time they are cut off from their eternal source – you tear off the branch from the vine »[162]. In the same document he cautioned against the false advocates of the bishop's rights with these words « Indeed the advocates of bishops' rights are crafty when they defend them (the rights) in such a manner that they become detrimental to the unity of the Church and to her supreme power from which the bishops receive their strength and freedom, and without which (papacy) they always wither and sooner or later they become victims to the devious intentions of the enemies »[163].

He could not imagine a bishop and his office functioning without being in the living union with the Roman pontiff, but on the other hand he found extremely difficult to discover a right place for a bishop within the Church. It is also obvious that he believed that in the Church all the major problems should be solved by consultation between the bishop of Rome and the college of bishops. Here he stood during Vatican I. However, later on when he accepted the dogma of papal infallibility and came out in defense of it, he explained in what sense all the apostles were given power « in solidum » or « loosing and binding ». He stated that « what Christ has given to Peter alone and individually, He has never given anything to the rest of the apostles without Peter; therefore, Christ – by commisioning the apostles to 'loose and bind' -- did not take them from under Peter's jurisdiction under which He placed them earlier. The power of the rest of the apostles (bishops), even though it was entrusted to them in solidum, is limited, ... while the power, once given to Peter, remains the same all the time, it remains complete (plenitudo potestatis) and unlimited... »[164]. Most certainly, the text cited does not leave much room for « mutual counseling and fraternal understanding » in governing the Church as he has envisioned earlier. However, it must be noted that he did not abandon it all together since he constantly kept insisting that the Church should be internationalized, and thus

---

[162] BS, XXI (1934), *loc. cit.,* 12.
[163] *Ibid.*
[164] « The Reply to the Ttree Greek Orthodox Bishops » (KRS, IV, 507).

at least in the central Church government in Rome the above recommendation would be put in practice.

Let us return once again to the Vatican Council and to Strossmayer's struggle against its basic proposals. In all fairness to him, to his acumen and eloquence we must state that he was at pains to reconcile the episcopal system with the papal system within the Church and to establish a well-balanced exercise of power of both parties. In his argumentation he was continuously preoccupied with clarifying his position and simultaneously producing objections to the proposals of the Deputation on Faith. First of all, the object of his criticism was the Canon on the Primacy of the Roman Pontiff which said: « And so, if anyone says that the Roman Pontiff has only the office of inspection or direction, but not the full and supreme power of jurisdiction over the whole Church, not only in matters that pertain to faith and morals, but also in matters that pertain to the discipline and government of the Church throughout the whole world; or if anyone says that he has only a more important part and not the complete fullness of this power; or if anyone says that this power is not ordinary and immediate either over each and every church or over each and every shepherd and faithful member: let him be anathema ».[165]

It seems to us that he found the crux of difficulty in the words of said Canon where it stated that the pontiff's episcopal power of jurisdiction is « ordinary and immediate... over each and every bishop »; this he attempted to discredit with the following reasoning: « If the two (pontiff's and bishop's) juridical powers are exercised in the same place and under the same aspect (sub eodem respectu) they are in the way to each other; therefore, according to the very nature of their function... they exclude each other which is of great detriment to the common good (of the Church) »[166]. The Bishop purposely inserted the expression « sub

---

[165]   *The Church Teaches – Documents of the Church in English Translation,* translated and prepared for publication by: John F. Clarkson, S. J., John H. Edwards, S. J., William Kelly, S. J., John J. Welch, S. J. (St. Louis B. Herder Book Co., 1955), p. 99.

[166]   Mansi 52, 393. Cf. the study on his topic of P. Umberto Betti,

eodem respectu » since some bishops of the majority, and especially Bishop Pie, had quoted Thomas Aquinas who had discussed the
same topic — the relationship of pope and bishop in exercising
the power of jurisdiction in the same diocese. According to Aquinas the pope's and local bishop's power would cancel each other
if their jurisdiction should be used « sub eodem respectu » and
if there were not one sphere of jurisdiction subordinated to the
other.[167]

From the way he intended to present his objection it
looks as if the jurisdiction of the local bishops would be absorbed
by that of the pontiff. Almost immediately hereafter he added that
according to the mind of St. Cyprian « the Church is so constituted and so organized from diverse elements to serve the same purpose that there is in her not only correct order and subordination...
but she enjoys holy and indivisible unity, and she also provides
moderate liberty and special rights for particular churches and
bishops; therefore, in my opinion, there is no place in the Church
of God for anything absolute or to call anything absolute »[168].

Here we would like to underline, since Strossmayer quite a
few times in the Council referred to the Petrine office as « absolute », that he did not mean that the office of the pope has appropriated to itself either the powers or prerogatives of God or of
Christ, but he rather called the papal authority « absolute » since
the pontiff is given the prerogatives to operate separately from
the rest of the episcopate and the Church. It looks to us that he
remained faithful to himself as far as his concept of the Church

---

O.F.M. « Natura e Portata del Primato del Romano Pontefice secondo il Concilio Vaticano », in *Antonianum,* XXXIV (1959), pp. 161-244 and 369-408.
Betti has summarized the position of the opposing bishops in regard to this
point in these words: « Com'è facile vedere, tutti questi interventi di vario
genere alla formula 'ordinaria e immediata' o da essa occasionata hanno un
elemento in comune: quello di mettere al sicuro l'autorità dei vescovi nei
confronti di quella del Papa, in modo che da questi non ne sia né diminuita
né, molto meno, assorbita » (*loc. cit.,* p. 185) and also R. Aubert, « L'éccle-
siologie au Concile du Vatican », in *Le Concile et les Conciles* (editions de
Chevetogne / editions du Cerf, 1960), pp. 254-284.

    167 Mansi 52, 33. (St. Thomas: in IV. Sent. dist. 17-47). Cf. J. Oberški,
op. cit., 118, note 2.
    168 Mansi 52, 393.

was concerned, namely, that the Church is the community of believers in which there is « subordination and order » but not to such a degree that the Petrine office could be looked upon as something totally isolated from the Church or as lording over the entire body of the Church. Besides, he could not have reconciled his thesis that the Church should be ruled through « mutual counseling and fraternal understanding » with the way the prerogatives of the Roman pontiff were about to be defined; nor was he able in this context of papal prerogatives to find the room for the bishops and other churches to bear witness to the holy Tradition. His refrain, that the voice of the other churches along with the principal church of Rome should be heard and taken into consideration, did not have much value any more. It seemed to him that these voices were suffocated in that of Rome.

The Bishop and his ecclesiology can be comprehended only in view of the Tubingen School and of the patristic theology. Due to the influence of that School, he had been since his student years preoccupied with the ecclesiastical thoughts of the early Christian writers. The question why he did not quote the theologians of the Tubingen School — and especially J. A. Möhler — in his speech in the the Council cannot be answered with absolute certainty, but we believe that this omission can be attributed to the fact that he thought that the council Fathers were not acquainted with them, their writings and ideas, and that besides, their authority would not make any impact on the present.

In truth, J. A. Möhler had tackled the problem of papal system and episcopal system in his Symbolism. However, the latter was not confronted with how to solve the relationship between these two systems in pratical life; therefore it was easy for him to state that episcopal system and papal system and their constant « opposition (to each other) are very beneficial to ecclesiastical life »[169], but to establish the practical balance of power between these two forces was not and is not an easy job unless one is willing to accept papal total absolutism or to erase completely or diminish considerably episcopal divine rights, or to accept Episcopalianism.

---

[169] *Symbolism*, II, 77.

Let us make it clear here that his unyielding resistance to the extreme proposal of the majority in their formulating the prerogatives of the primacy of the pope and his infallibility must be attributed to a great extent to his being steeped in the Tradition of the early Church. This immersion in the Tradition did prevent his being susceptible to the new formulations and made him react toward them the way he did. What is more, he was very decisive and definite on this issue when he said: « ... here we are discussing the positive matter – the structure of the Church is being discussed among us how she has come out of the hands of her Bridegroom, our Lord Jesus Christ; no other arguments have any validity except those taken out of the treasury of the holy Tradition; only these arguments can convince us, and we are willing to be convinced »[170]. This patristic carryover was so strongly imbedded in him that it remained with him though somewhat diminished, until his death.

The loyalty and the firm adherence of the Bishop to the chair of St. Peter are unquestionable. He professed his loyalty to the Roman pontiff hundreds of times, and there was no force in the world which would separate them. On numerous occasions he said that he would rather see his tongue and arm withered then to speak against or violate the rights of St. Peter's succesors. (Of course, we know that this had been originally said Bossuet). On several occasions in his speeches at Vatican I, when he was either interrupted by the chairman or indirectly accused of disregarding the papal rights, he used to say that he was willing to sacrifice his own life in defense of them[171]. Now and then he used to remind the neo-Ultramontanes that, « while we express our loyaltly and benevolence in the just manner toward the pontiff, we should

---

[170] MANSI 52, 396. In his previous speech he stated: « I affirm that we must follow and remain on the path chartered by the Council of Trent. It is known that the Council of Trent, without any doubt, wanted the authority and rights of the supreme pontiff to remain intact, and this is correct; but the same Council of Trent with equal firmness and decisiveness saved the divine rights of bishops... Had I had a chance to defend this proposal of mine in the midst of the council Fathers at Trent, I am convinced that all of them – perhaps except a few – would approve it by applause » (MANSI 51, 74).

[171] MANSI 50, 667.

not violate the law of love and justice toward our brethren (bishops). Let us keep in mind », he continued to say, « that among the principal duties of love and respect toward great men and institutions the truth occupies the first place; the truth – pronounced with holy intention – never did any harm either to the person or his dignity; it was always of advantage ».[172] These words were aimed at the Pontiff himself who wanted to have his prerogatives defined, and the Bishop tried to persuade him to abandon that course. It is equally true that he was sincere in his search for the balance of power between the papal and episcopal systems. There are also strong indications in his speeches that he intended to halt the growth of the papal system which might become eventually detrimental to that of the episcopate. This endeavor gained momentum in his fight against definition of papal infallibility.

He did, however, attribute certain rights to the papacy. Naturally, we shall limit ourselves at present solely to his position vis à vis papacy during Vatican I, for he underwent a certain growth on that issue in the years thereafter. First of all, we have to underscore that the entire Church, in his opinion, derives her strenght and completeness from the papacy which is a divine institution[173]. In his first allocution he outlined the rights of the Roman pontiff by stating that « the first and principal place occupies the head of the Church and whatever is decided in the Council it is his to confirm, publish, execute and put it in practice; this belongs to the head by right and custom »[174].

It looks to us, however, that during the course of the Council, perhaps due to his reflection on the position of the pope within the Church, he did make some progress in this respect. What is more, it almost seems as if he were using some kind of strategic bargaining vis à vis the papacy and its prerogatives so as to find a happy medium between these two forces (papacy and episcopacy) or to engage the Council in discussing the rights of bishops « ex professo ». From the very opening of the Council until its closing

---

[172]   *Ibid.*
[173]   *Ibid.,* 140.
[174]   *Ibid.*

he kept insisting that it is the sacred duty of the supreme pontiff to convoke a council, preside over it and ratify its decisions. Besides he held that it is also the pontiff's duty to preserve peace and tranquility in the council and in the Church as well for the salvation of souls; the bishops, congregated in the ecumenical council, ought to help him in reestablishing peace within the Church and in solving newly arisen controversies.[175]

The implication is clear: the controversy came into existence in the Council over defining papal prerogatives, and consequently something must be done to terminate it. Toward the end of his last speech in the Council he professed: « Therefore, we admit that the plenitude of power is given to Peter and his successors... This fulness of power is exercized by the supreme pontiff in various manners: he exercises it most solemny when convokes ecumenical councils, he also does it when he presides over them and confirms their decisions and canons which, by this very fact, become divine and irrevocable ».[176] In other words, he admitted the papal infallibility but only while in the union with the college of bishops as their spokesman. Moreover, it is evident that this kind of infallibility is rather embedded in the universal episcopacy than in the pontiff's person.

For the sake of better undestanding of the Bishop's stand, which he expressed in his speech on June 2, 1870, in the Council, we cite the famous speech of Cardinal Guidi, pronounced on June 18, which carries a few ideas similar to those of Strossmayer. In his speech the Cardinal proposed that « the correct title of the chapter would be, not 'the infallibility of the Roman Pontiff', but 'the infallibility of his dogmatic definitions' »[177]. In the same speech he also added that « the Pope is bound to use ordinary human diligence in arriving at a right judgment, as prayer, consultation, study; and that the normal means is consultation with a greater or less number of bishops... the bishops being the witnesses to the belief of their churches. Therefore, it should be made clear in the

---

[175]   Mansi 52, 397.
[176]   *Ibid*, 396.
[177]   Quoted by D. Butler, *op. cit.*, 353.

decree that not the Pape alone issues a definition; but the Pope with the bishops consenting to...».[178] The Cardinal, while speaking, was interrupted once or twice by murmuring of the Ultramontanes; but when he descended from the podium, he was embraced by Strossmayer[179].

At the end of this portion of our study we would like to add that, in our judgment, it is extremely difficult to classify Strossmayer either as a Gallican or as an adherent of Episcopalianism or of Febronianism. It is true, however, that the Church historians, as a rule, place the bishops of the opposition into the said theological movements. It seems to us — at least in the case of Strossmayer who was most radical opponent to the papal infallibility and who held the farthest flank of the opposition — that he was preoccupied with finding a happy balance between the episcopal power and that of the Roman pontiff. As far as Gallicanism is concerned, on one occasion during the Council he said that Gallicanism is « of vague and unqualified name »[180]; and this seems to point out in the context that he did not want to align himself with it. Later on in the same speech, while interpreting Irenaeus, Tertullian and Cyprian, he almost spoke in the terms of Gallicanism when he stated:

« The tradition of the Roman Church looked to these men (Irenaeus, Tertullian and Cyprian) like a huge river which has to irrigate and make fruitful the entire Catholic Church. Of equal importance seemed to these men the tradition of the other apostolic churches which, like tributaries, unceasingly feed and nurse this larger river (the Roman Church) that she never goes

---

[178] D. BUTLER, op. cit., 353-357. Guidi was called by Pius IX to give an account of why he opposed him. Pius upbraided him severely. During the ensuing conversation Guidi stated that the bishops are witnesses of Tradition, too, but the Pontiff retorted « There is only one (witness of Tradition) — that's me ». Ibid., p. 355. (Naturally, the Pope's statement is theologically wrong). Tkalac brings the same incident in detail in his dispatch of June 21, 1870 (cf. RSCV, pp. 313-314). What is more. according to Tkalac's report, Cardinal Guidi was placed, by Pius IX, under house arrest and was kept incommunicado after having refused to recant his speech of June 18 (ibid., pp. 316-317).

[179] D. BUTLER, op. cit., 355.

[180] MANSI 52, 395.

dry and disappears... All these great men knew that the testimony of the first apostolic See was of the utmost significance and authority in matters of faith. However, these men insisted if the testimony (of the Roman Church) should manifest divine power and authority, then the consensus of the other apostolic churches and bishops should be added to it; St. Cyprian – as I have said so many times already - had called the whole Church one flock which is to be led by the unanimious and common consensus of all the bishops ».[181]

At this place it ought to be remarked that he unequivocally expressed himself that, in defining a certain doctrine, all the churches have to be not only consulted but their consent obtained. This way of reasoning might place him among the Gallicans, but on the other hand since he threw all the weight of his argumentation on St. Cyprian's ecclesiology it looks as though he did not want to be indentified with them.

For the sake of clarification of Strossmayer's dependence on St. Cyprian's theology let us make a short digression. Whoever reads carefully St. Cyprian's « The Unity of the Catholic Church », will notice that this great Saint was at pains with himself when he wrote on the structures of the Church. We do not intend to go into details on his views on this topic, but we do allege « that unity, in his (Cyprian's) theory, was constituted simply by the union of the bishops among themselves. Actually, Cyprian recognized the Bishop of Rome's special position in the Church in many practical ways. But he never formulated this to himself as implying a real authority over the whole Church »[182]. « He had never held that the Pope possessed universal jurisdiction. But he had never denied it either; in truth he had never asked himself the question where the final authority in the Church might be. The 'union of bishops' sufficed for all practical purposes – so he thought, at least until the baptismal controversy ». [183]

Since we plan to say more later on how Strossmayer considered

---

[181] MANSI 52, 400. On account of this statement J. OBERŠKI, *op. cit.*, 120, note 19 accuses Strossmayer of being « heterodox and Gallican ».

[182] Maurice Bévenot, S. J., in his Preface to Ancient Christian Writers, *op. cit.*, 6-7.

[183] *Ibid.*, 7-8.

the development of the dogma, it remains to us here to mention that the Papal Primacy in the early Church was « implicit », and also how Strossmayer interpreted the ecclesiology of St. Cyprian. First of all, he was well acquainted with Cyprian's basic ideas; and most probably his vehement opposition to the papal infallibility arose from his reliance on the Saint and his writings. It is unfortunate that his dissertions are not preserved because the writings of his early years would offer us a better insight into his understanding of St. Cyprian. They would furnish us with the facts so that we would be more capable of discerning what should be attributed to or caused by the heated controversy in Vatican I and what were his original and genuine convictions.. At any rate, it can be safely stated that he did not remain at the stage where the African Bishop had left off; Strossmayer in many respects greatly progressed. When he gives the interpretation to the comparisons of St. Cyprian « tree's branches and (its) sturdy root », or « the sun's rays... and the light is one », or « many streams flow from a single spring », in his Pastoral of 1869 he expounds them in the sense that a « single spring », « one light », and « one root » is the pontiff from whom all bishops receive their « life, power and strenght ». In the Vatican Council he looks upon St. Cyprian's comparisons and especially on the « tributaries » under the perspective of Christ who is the « root », the « light », and « one spring » and from whom the pope and bishops receive their divine rights; and consequently the « tributaries » – the bishops – have to « feed » the papal office with their testimonies; they all, as a group, were commissioned to « teach and preach ». By this he was motivated to insist on the consensus of all the churches and bishops in defining Church doctrine. This indicates that his theological reasoning was rather influenced by the theology of the African Doctor than by Gallicanism. Finally, he was greatly engrossed in the theology of the Tubingen Theological School. Strossmayer's basic dogmatic ideas are based on the Church Fathers just as well as those of J. A. Möhler. In adition, Möhler had wanted to discover the connection between the history and theological speculation[184], and so did Strossmayer.

---

[184] ERGAR HOCEDEZ, S. J., *Histoire de la Théologie au XIX Siècle* (Paris, Desclee de Brouwer, 1948), I, pp. 231-232.

His above two-fold commentary on St. Cyprian's comparisons does not contradict itself, but it rather convinces us of his two-fold viewing of the Church of God. In his first interpretation (in his Pastoral of 1869) he viewed the Church as a visible, independent and hierarchical society which is so constituted that all bishops receive « their life and strenght » from pontiff while in the second interpretation the Church is spiritual and invisible institution, and as such she derives her power from Christ. Whether or not within this context there is any room left for him to be an adherent of Episcopalianism or Febronianism, the reader must decide. Finally, pope and bishops alone are of divine origin, they are constituted in the Church to govern the faithful by the direct command of Christ; and their commission to rule comes from above and not from below, from the community.

Within this framework falls his continuous urgency in the Council that all decrees and definitions must be reached by moral unanimity of the council Fathers and not by a numerical majority of votes as it was introduced and approved in the same Council. Once again he resorts to the history and to what happened in the former ecumenical councils in order to refute the newly-introduced rule of numerical majority. He praised very highly the practice of the Council of Trent and the recommendation to the same by Pope Pius IV with these words: « Indeed one of the rules of freedom and wisdom had been given to the papal legates by Pope Pius IV – influenced by the spirit of Charles Boromeo – that nothing should be decided without a general or quasi general agreement of the Fathers »[185]. Strossmayer's whole goal was to prove that « moral unanimity » is postulated by historical practice, and that the general concurrence of the entire episcopate is also needed in formutaling a dogma. Naturally, this suggestion is ideal, but it is another question if it is feasible in practice.

e. Ecclesiastical Office and Ministry

Strossmayer's idea of the redemptive work of Christ based on love and humility, his firm conviction that we can only obtain our

---

[185] Mansi 52, 399-400.

personal salvation by exercising love and humility, his costant teaching that the Church of God did not only inherit the power of her Founder, but she has also received the mandate to love all races and nations, give us a strong inkling what he thought of the office holders within the Catholic Church and under what perspective they are expected to function. A part of his conception of office holders was his conviction that the Church – even though the divine institution – should be continuously in the process of reforming and improving. This idea « ecclesia semper reformanda » he expressed in Vatican I with these words: « ... regardless of who we are and how holy and perfect we might be, as long as we live in this mortal body of ours, as long as we dwell in this life of mortality, everyone of us – every moment of our mortal existence and until our last breath – is in need of reformation; and if I am not mistaken, our humble and sincere acceptance of this reality is our salvation and the pivot of our hope »[186].

His concepts on the ministerial work of the Church office holders were developed and well formulated a long time before the convocation of Vatican I. No doubt his ideas in this sense are the result of his laborious studies of the Church Fathers. In his first lettere to his diocese from Vienna (dated August 24, 1850) he quoted St. John Chrysostom: « In as far as we are Christians, it is because of us; as far as we are your bishops, it is because of you. As Christians we are concerned with our own salvation, as your bishops we are at your service and for the salvation of your souls ». (Sermon 165). Commenting on Chrysostom's words he says that Christ has instituted the eternal priesthood that He may continue to exercise His love toward mankind through clergy. Therefore, he concludes, whatever we have received through the imposition of hands it is unmerited grace of God and « it is property of the faithful ».[187] He ennunciated the practically same idea in Vatican I when he spoke on the rights and duties of bishops and when he declared that « whatever rights and duties we have received from God, they were not given to us as to make us boastful and elated, but we have

---

[186] Mansi 50, 478. Cf. also *ibid.*, 667.
[187] JJS-DK, p. 111.

received them with the most sacred obligation on our part to make them available to the faithful ».[188] Furthermore, « the rights of bishops are of divine origin: they are not our property », he emphasized, since « they are given to us by God to use them for the welfare and glory of the Council and of the Church and also for the benefit of our flock. Therefore, none of us can renounce them: we would rather give up our own lives... than our rights which are given to us in divine manner so that we may, on the day of judgment when the Lord would require them back, return them to Him intact and complete, and if possible with great profit »[189].

These statements strongly indicate that his notion of the hierarchical function in the Church was not to lord it over the faithful but to be of service to the people. This goes along with his conviction that the Church of God is not only an heir of Christ's power but that she is predestined and commanded to continue the work of love of her divine Founder which is found in Christ's service toward mankind.

In his Pastoral of June 4, 1859 (written in Latin) to his clergy, in which he describes his impression of his first visit to Rome, once again he reminds them of their principal duty – to be of service to their faithful, or as he says that « priests must place all their abilities and talents into the service of Christ and into that of the Church »[190]. The said Pastoral is flowing with praises to the then Pope Pius IX and the papacy, but in the midle of it he stops to reflect « on the genuine concept of authority and dignity » in the Church. Since this visit to Rome took place during Holy Week, he was induced to meditate that since the redemption was executed by love and humility, the Church as the Bride of Christ must also be permeated and animated by the same qualities. He refers to the Roman pontifi « vicar of Christ here on earth, he is the visible head of the Church and her supreme shepherd, he is the centre of Catholic unity, he is the rock upon which the Church of God is built, but he is also a servant of servants of God – not only in

188   Mansi 50, 477.
189   Mansi 51, 73.
190   JJS-DK, p. 430.

name but in reality, too ».[191] All the Church offices – from the first to the last – according to him are gratuitous gifts of God and merited by Christ. Therefore, these legacies are not subject to our arbitrariness but are rather freely given to us that we may use them for the glory of God and for welfare of the faithful, for they are the property of the Christians. What is more, he says, whoever is a minister of Christ in any capacity, is expected to emulate Christ's virtues: he ought to be benign, patient, understanding, merciful, zealous, and humble. Then he concludes « this is a genuine notion of dignity and authority which by way of humility goes back to their very source, God Himself, and they (dignity and authority) must be channelled through lavish and pious love toward the promotion of the welfare of our fellow-men »[192].

In no way can he separate clergy and hierarchy from the faithful; their living together and function are intertwined; hierarchy operates within the Christian community. In this instance, too, he brings in again as a basis his concept of the Church, namely, that « Christ in His infinite mercy has donated Himself and His properties to the faithful and He has made us priests by the holy Orders, that is, the heirs of His power and the vicars of His love: we do not belong to ourselves, we are with all our abilities, our life and health, with our erudition and holiness, with our supernatural gifts and virtue the property of the faithful »[193].

Some other aspects are to be brought in, too, in order to understand him fully. Time and again he repeats that according to Sts. Ignatius and Polycarp Christ resides mysteriously in each diocese through a bishop. He does not confine Christ's presence to the instance of a bishop, but – consistent to himself – he extends this charisma to a local pastor, since he is the miniature of the Church of God in which Christ eternally dwells and since the merits of Christ are placed at his disposal to be administered to the flock.[194] Whenever he turned and fixed his gaze within the Church, he saw

---

[191]   Ibid., pp. 426-427.
[192]   Ibid., p. 427.
[193]   His Pastoral « The Unity in the Church » (TS, p. 391).
[194]   Ibid., p. 390.

the unity between Christ and Church manifested in one form or another. No wonder then that he could not conceive of the hierachy and clergy otherwise but within the Church, in the community.

It has been said on the preceding pages that Strossmayer believed that priests should be well educated in order to meet the needs of the souls entrusted to their spiritual care in particular and also to cope with the newly arisen problems in the world in general. Priests, in his mind, are not only the « second rank bishops » as he expressed so eloquently in the Vatican Council or as J. A. Möhler had so beautifully writen: « the priests... are... a multiplication of the bishop »[195], but they are − so to speak − tentacles of the Church of God in every respect. « Therefore, God cannot show greater benevolence to a certain nation », he writes on the eve of Vatican I, « than by giving the priests who are according to God's heart and who are employing all their talents in practicing their love toward their nation and the faithful as our Lord had done toward us. The clergy is expected in performing their vocation to feel in their hearts every pain and misery of the entrusted people to their care as the Lord had wept over the fate of Jerusalem. Through this kind of priests God will shower earthly and heavenly blessings upon their respective nations ».[196]

When in Vatican I the civil rights of bishops and priests were debated, he rose up very energetically, stating that neither the bishops nor the priests should be forbidden to exercise their rights toward their respective nations. On the contrary, he forcibly urged that both bishops and priests should employ their energies in promoting the welfare of their nations. « Let not the Vatican Council diminish », he warned the council Fathers, « the civil rights (and their use) of the priests and bishops since I am afraid that the time is almost upon us that we shall be deprived of our civil rights (against our own wish) ».[197]

This confirms once again that he was unable to view either a bishop or a priest as alienated not only from his faithful but

---

195   *Symbolism*, II, 78.
196   BS, XXI (1934), *loc. cit.*, 9-10. Cf. his Pastoral of 1893 in GBBS, XXI (1893), 46-47.
197   MANSI 50, 485-486.

from his nation and its material progress. Priest and bishop by their very vocation must be in midst of their people and to be constantly of service to them. He did not believe in keeping himself in the « sacristy », nor did he advise his clergy to do it. Priest and bishop, in his belief, are expected to be in the forefront in every respect in their respective nations: the realm of their activities, naturally, must primarily comprise the spiritual needs of their flocks, but this should not prevent them from occupying university's cathedras and from the involvement in the civil rights if they possess talents. He candidly admitted several times that the Gospel is neither political nor social nor international code but he believed that the spirit of the Gospel is destined to permeate all of those spheres. Furthermore, he thought that if evangelical priciples were implemented in the various human intercourses in dealing with one another or in the intercourses of a nation with a nation, the wars, hatreds and jealousies would be utterly eliminated and universal brotherhood reestablished; if human abilities, and resources are properly channelled and used for the betterment of a man, the human miseries, illnesses, poverty would be reduced to a minimum. He even expressed hope that a day might come when « the liberty of strong nations, which serves to keep smaller and less fortunate nations in slavery, will not be called liberty any more, and when all significant national and international affairs will be solved not with brutal force and bloody wars but rather with rational means and with holy justice ».[198] In this context of wordly affairs he envisioned a priest and a bishop working toward the already chartered goal.

In depicting a ministerial work of the Church office holders he goes so far as to suggest that they have to sacrifice their own lives for the benefit of mankind. On one occasion Strossmayer disguised himself as Christ and on Christ's behalf addressed the following words to St. Peter and his successors: « Peter, know and remember that the holy mission which I perform and which I have confided to you and to your successors should never be defended with swords but with spiritual means. The mystery of my religion

---

[198]   His article « The Cathedral of Djakovo » (TS, p. 221).

ought to be guarded always with truth, God's justice, love, holiness, patience and honesty. I did not come into the world to lose it but rather to save it. My Peter, the cross and my death are my only weapons which I use to win the world. In my death and my resurrection lies the pledge of life and eternal glory. In these two instances I am leaving to you and to your successors an eternal example which you are to imitate. It is not your duty to inflict wounds or to shed blood, but rather it is your business and duty (if necessary) to shed willingly your own blood for your adversaries and enemies. This is the inheritance left to the Church by Christ... ».[199]

Within this scope falls his understanding of the « motherhood » of the Church. He often applied the name « mother » to the Church of God, but this « motherhood » is not limited to the Church office holders; it is to be understood as a « corporate motherhood » of the entire Christian community which comprises all her members as one living organic entity and which grows, widens and encompasses with its love new nations. The « motherhood » of the Church is found in the fruitfulness of the activities of her members first among themselves then toward the outsiders[200]. In the organic closeness of clergy and faithful and their productiveness in practicing their Christiantiy the Church deserves this title « mother », and not in the kindness and understanding of the office holders as we usually believe. Time and again he warned his clergy to display love and understanding toward their parishioners that they may truly feel at home whenever they entered into a rectory.

Whenever he was offered a chance to underscore the communal intercourse within the Church of God between the clergy and the faithful, he did not fail to do it. Most probably this was manifested best in the Cathedral which he built in Djakovo. He had done something unusual in his Cathedral, namely, he eliminated the rail between the presbytery and the naves which is intended to separate the clergy and faithful from one another. When he was asked by his friends for the explanation, he offered two principal reasons

---

[199] His article « The Paintings in the Cathedral of Djakovo » (TS, pp. 298-299).
[200] His Pastoral « Sts. Cyril and Methodius » (TS, pp. 408-409).

why he did not want to partition the sanctuary from the rest of the Cathedral. « It is true », he said, « that the clergy occupies more dignified place in the community of the faithful, but it is equally true that the clergy is essentially united to the faithful, and therefore, there is no reason in the world why the clergy should separate themselves from the rest of the people. Every need and misery of people must be felt in the heart of a priest; every people's illness must find its medic in a priest... Priest's duty is to live with his people and dedicate all his life, his time, and even if it is necessary to sacrifice his own life for the welfare of his people. Since there is such a union between a priest and faithful, why then to separate them from one another with the rail? ».[201] His second reason was more of a social nature. On this issue he dwelt for awhile. His starting point was that people, as a rule, are poor, they are even despised in their homes, then he remarked:

« It finally even happens that in the Church we deny them the equality which we must share with them by the order of God and His Anointed One. We wish to detach ourselves from them in the Church by reserving for ourselves more dignified place. We are building a very spacious church, and we wish to decorate it as beautifully as possible, that our good people may move freely in it... At least in this church they will be able to say: thanks to God, nobody here can despise me since the One, who is being sacrificed and offered in here, was pauper like myself... The One, who resides in here, is not concerned with someone's honor, dignity, and attire but with the people of good and honest heart... I won't give a chance to anybody », he continued to say, « in this church as to say: I am not like the rest »[202].

Let us make a short digression at his place in regard to building new churches and the faithful. Montalembert and Strossmayer became intimate friends in 1867 when the Bishop spent several months in Paris in self-imposed exile. It is evident from Strossmayer's writing and his citing of the speech of Montalembert that these two

---

[201] « The Cathedral of Djakovo » (TS, 225).
[202] *Ibid.,* p. 213.

striking personalities had discussed between themselves the problem of erecting new churches. As early as of 1847 Montalembert had subjected to severe criticism the way new churches were constructed and the special target of his criticism were the churches of Ste. Magdalene and Notre Dame in Paris which are loaded with gold and marble. He objected to this practice on the grounds that the poor people could not feel at home in such churches on account of their wealth which is alien to the poor. He advocated that the churches should be vast and simple in structure that the poor could feel in them at home.[203] Both Montalembert and Strossmayer had in mind the poor, and wanted to build churches which would correspond to the mentality and position of the ordinary faithful. The latter differed from the former by insisting that the art must be brought in so that the poor might benefit religiously and aesthetically[204].

At the end of this topic we would like to bring the most significant text of the Bishop which sums up the concept of honor, dignity and position of the office holders and on what basis they are founded and by what motives they should be motivated. In his Pastoral « The Unity in the Church » of 1877 he addressed the following to his clergy:

« In this way, my brethren, I understand my position toward you: it is my ardent wish to be of service to everyone of you. It is true, however, that a bishop is father, brother and friend to his priests, but at the same time he is their servant. This is ordained

---

[203] Quoted according to Strossmayer (TS, pp. 214-215). Montalembert had delivered this speech on July 26, 1847. When he died on March 13, 1870, a Requiem Mass was forbidden by Pope Pius IX because he was against papal infallibility being defined. See D. Butler, op. cit., 252-253. According to M. Cepelić, plans were made that Dupanloup was to celebrate a Requiem Mass while Strossmayer would deliver a eulogy. Cf. M. Cepelić, « Josip Juraj Strossmayer », in GBBS, XXVI (1898), p. 27a. Most probably M. Cepelić was told about this incident by Strossmayer himself.

[204] TS, p. 215. It seems to us that Strossmayer spent most of his time with Montalembert while he was in Paris. Montalembert begged the Bishop to go with him on a two months vacation in Belgium. Strossmayer did not accept this friendly gesture on account of his plans to open the Yugoslav Academy in Zagreb in July, 1867. We mention this incident, for the Prelate greatly regretted later on this refusal of his. Montalembert had in mind to write a book on the Croats (ibid.).

by God Himself and by our redemption. Jesus is true God of true God, the light of light, the source of life, and He had renounced all these properties in order to make us participantes of His being and grace... He renounced His glory and became not only man and our brother but also our servant, God's debtor..., in order to free us from our sins and death... Indeed our eternal Teacher has pronounced the eternal truth when He said: 'I did not come into this world to be served but to serve'... This is, my dear brethren, the meaning of honor and dignity in the Christian community. Whatever we have received through the holy Orders and from the higher power, it is not ours to boast about it; it belongs to Christ; since Christ has donated all His properties and even Himself to the faithful which means that He has given us these honors to be of service to the faithful. Whoever, He (Christ) says, wishes to be the first in the kingdom of God let him be the last. And indeed, we, who are at the head of the Church of God, have a sacred duty according to the example of Jesus to go down to the lowest needs of the Church and to dedicate all our abilities to the welfare of the people of God. This is the basic meaning of the mystery of our redemption on the cross... »[205].

f. *People of God and General Priesthood*

In view of what has been said so far on the topic of the ministerial functions of the office holders within the Church of God and on their intimate relationship with the faithful, it should not be a surprise to anybody that the Prelate had spoken from time to time on the subject of the general priesthood of the people of God. Both J. A. Möhler and Strossmayer speak of general priesthood but somewhat under different aspect: while the former treats general priesthood within the context of a visible and invisible Church and while he points out that a general priesthood has its

---

[205] TS, p. 385. In another letter to his clergy of August 8, 1875 he wrote « I beg you, brethren, to bear in patience with me and my shortcomings; please, substitute my failings with your virtues and your holy lives and, please, consider me worthy of your fraternal love and confidence » (CP, p. 172).

place predominantly in an invisible Church in which an « inward purely spiritual sacrifice » is offered and while, according to Möhler, « the authorization for the public exercise of ecclesiastical functions is imparted by a sacrament -- an outward act to be performed by men according to the commission of Christ, and which partly denotes, partly conveys an inward and divine grace ».[206]

Strossmayer's eyes are totally fixed and turned – leaving out completely Möhler's distinction -- to the practical side of the faithful and to their role within the Church of God; and in what fashion this mission is executed by them. It is true that he did not elaborate on this idea in one single document but the fragments of it are found in his numerous writings. What is more, he quoted quite often St. Peter « but you are chosen race, a royal priesthood »... (I Peter 2, 9), and on this text he developed the idea of general priesthood[207].

He attributed the title of a « royal priesthood » to the faithful for the variety of reasons. In Vatican I he applied this appellation, first of all, to the Catholic intellectuals and especially to those who are involved in teaching and educating the university youth and thus defending the Christian truths along with the clergy, or as he has said « those (Catholic educators) who defend the walls of the new Jerusalem ». Secondly, on account of the indivisible unity which prevails between the hierarchy and the faithful and also because of the fact that the Church of God as a one entity possesses the complete « deposit of faith », and that consequently it is a sacred duty of the entire body of the Church to preserve the teachings of Christ in their original purity, the faithful are called « regale sacerdotium, gens sancta, populus acquisitionis ». In other words, in the judgment of the Bishop, the people of God are priests in as much as they are also the bearers of the holy Tradition. Furthermore, he goes as far as to say that even a school child is entitled to this privilege, since he studies his catechism and realizes that its

---

[206] *Symbolism,* II, 72. « Hence », Möhler writes, « in an invisible Church only the invisible forgiveness of sins and confession before God are necessary; but it is otherwise in the visible Church » (*ibid.,* p. 73 in the note).
[207] « The Cathedral in Djakovo » (TS, 225).

contents derive from Christ Himself; and what is more, this child feels obligation to defend it, profess it and transmit it to the others[208]. Of course, at this juncture he states that the hierarchy is the principal carrier of the holy Tradition but the laity has its share in it, and that the people of God justifiably consider themselves to some extent proprietors of the « deposit of faith »[209]. This also is the way he used to view the Tradition of the Church.

Thirdly, parents also perform priestly duties in their domestic life when they instruct their children and the entire household in faith, or when they set a good example, or when they educate them to live in honesty and justice and in another Christian virtues, and especially when they take care that their offsprings often go to confession and recieve holy communion.[210] In this instance the parents are referred to a « royal priesthood » on account of their close cooperation with the clergy in transmitting the sacred teaching of Christ.

Fourthly, « St. Peter calls the laity 'gens sancta, regale sacerdotium', that is, holy people and royal priesthood. At present our faith and Christian virtues are attacked «, he continues to say, « therefore whoever carries holy faith in his heart, he is invited to become a priest, protector and advocate of the holy faith within the domain of his vocation. This can be accomplished with good word, advice, and admonition but above all else with one's own holy and irreproachable life he can defend Christian virtue and become a shield and a herald of the holy faith »[211].

Fifthly, the faithful are called a « royal priesthood » because they, united so intimately with clergy, are invited to offer the holy sacrifice of Mass along with the priest; he, the priest, functions on behalf of and within the community of the faithful.[212] In relation to this we must underscore once again that the holy Eucharist − according to him − is the realization of our unity with Christ, therefore the active participation of the people of God in the celebration

[208] « The Reply to the Three Greek Orthodox Bishops » (KRS, IV, 509).
[209] Ibid.
[210] His Pastoral « The Church of God », in GBBS, XXVI (1898), 34.
[211] Bishop's sermon in Rome (CP, p. 146).
[212] « The Cathedral of Djakovo » (TS, p. 225).

of the same is required: in and through Christ to the Father. In addition, the priestly vocation in the strict sense is not solely confined to the spiritual needs but it comprises those of their material welfare so does follow the general priesthood the same pattern; and thus both run parallel to each other.

Strossmayer's explanation in what sense Christians may « offer spiritual sacrifices » of which St. Peter had spoken (I Peter 2, 4-5) and why the faithful are referred to a « royal priesthood » will shed more light on the interrelationship of the narrow and official priesthood and that of general priesthood. At this juncture he becomes very specific and concrete by introducing into his theological reasoning once again the basis for our redemption which is Christ's love and humility or as he said that « the rulers and the other potentates ought to recall that Christ has renounced his divine qualities and has assumed upon Himself our infirmities in order that He may exercise His immense love and mercy toward us ».[213] Therefore, there is no wonder that he insists that even the rulers must leave their thrones and must come down in humility to the needs and miseries of their people in order to be of service to them and that all this must be done in love and benevolence. Hereafter he says that a lawyer exercises his priesthood when he defends truth and justice; this priesthood is practiced by a physician when he hurries to be of help to the poor as well as to those who are of wealth; a judge carries on his priesthood when « he would rather lose his right hand than sanction something which might be against his conscience and the law »; finally, every Christian exercises his priesthood if « he consciously performs his vocational duties toward the people »[214].

At the end of this chapter we would like to reiterate that unfortunately Strossmayer did not systematize his theological and ecclesiological ideas but rather left them scattered all through his writings. Nobody, however, can assert that his theology and ecclesiology do not possess freshness and originality. This especially

---

213 *Ibid.*
214 *Ibid.*, pp. 225-226.

becomes apparent if all this theological reasoning of the Bishop is considered in the light of modern theology. First of all, the Church – in his opinion – is the living body of Christ, or as he sometimes states she « is Christ Himself »; secondly, all the members of the body of Christ are important, and each is assigned by the divine plan to play his role; thirdly, his concept of the Church was different from that of the past: the Church, according to him, is made up of believers and not only of the governing official body, and consequently she is not any more a strict juridical institution but rather she is composed of believers who are in possession of priesthood; fifthly, the hierarchy is divinely instituted to govern the Church, but it is to be looked upon within the Christian community, and the basic, essential function of the hierarchy is to be of ministry to the faithful; sixthly, he attempted to revive the idea of a general priesthood in the Church which had been defunct in her for so many centuries. Most certainly on this issue of a general priesthood of the faithful he preceded by several decades the Encyclical « Mediator Dei » of Pius XII of 1947 on the priesthood of laity[215].

Undoubtedly, these ecclesiastical conceptions of his, plus others which we shall bring out on the subsequent pages, greatly contributed to his firm and sometimes even unyielding opposition to the plans and the procedures of Vatican I. It is deplorable that he was interrupted so many times during the course of the Council and was called to order on account of « straying away from the chartered procedures » of the Council since we believe that many more ecclesiological conceptions have gotten lost in his notes.

---

[215] *The Church Teaches, op. cit.*, 298-299. Pope Pius XII in « Mediator Dei » states « thus they (the faithful) participate, according to their state, in the priesthood of Christ » (*ibid.*, p. 299). Cf. also H. Küng, *The Church*, 363-480.

AT THE FIRST VATICAN COUNCIL

> « There is neither freedom nor truth nor honesty in this Council ». Strossmayer wrote this to Dr. F. Rački from Rome on April 20, 1870[1].

This topic deserves our attention for the variety of reasons. Undoubtedly no other prelate in the Church had created so much commotion as he, nor was there any bishop who was so radical and bold in his proposals as he. In view of what has been written so far in regard to his various ideological and theological concepts it was typical of him that he studied the matter thoroughly, and then he would have chartered the course of his actions accordingly. All his plans and undertakings in Vatican I must be viewed in the light of his general outlook on the Church and her mission in the world.

It is outside our present scope to go into details of the history of the Council. Many books have been already written on this subject; therefore, we shall rather limit ourselves to the incidents and facts which have a direct bearing on the Bishop and his role in the Council. This will help us to see him in better light vis à vis the Council itself. It is imperative, however, to disclose some incidents and the contents of some documents which had preceded Vatican I. These occurrences will show whether the Bishop was justified in insisting on what should be discussed in the Council. This particularly deserves our consideration, for it seems to us that the entire Council and its agenda were sidetracked from the original projects.

Pope Pius IX already on December 6, 1864, had held a secret meeting with the twenty-one cardinals, and had asked them for their

---

[1] KRS, I, 102.

opinion on the expediency of convoking an ecumenical council in order « to remedy by an extra-ordinary means, that is, by means of a council, the extra-ordinary distress of the Church ». The majority were in favor[2]. Following year on March 9, 1865, the Pope appointed the commission of five cardinals to make the preparations for the forthcoming council. By the end of April, 1865, thirty-six bishops from different European countries were asked by the Pontiff for their opinion on holding a council. They replied favorably. All these plans were covered with the veil of utmost secrecy for over two years until June, 1867, when 500 bishops from every corner of the world came to Rome to commemorate the eighteenth centennial of the martyrdom of Sts. Peter and Paul. On June 26, 1867, Pius IX revealed his plans and addressed the following words to the gathered prelates that « a holy, ecumenical and general council of all the bishops of the Catholic world will be held. Its object would be, by means of joint discussions and united efforts, to discover with God's help the necessary remedies against the many evils which opress the Church »[3].

On this occasion five hundred bishops signed the address which was presented to the Pontiff on July 1. On account of its significance we would like to quote some excerpts from it:

« We profess that our great concern and desire is that we may believe and teach what You do believe and teach, and that the errors You do reject, we also may reject; that under Your leadership we may walk with one accord in the ways of the Lord, and that we may follow You and work with You... You have deemed it to belong to Your supreme office to proclaim the eternal truths, to smite with the sword of apostolic speech the errors of the age, to dissipate the fogs of novel doctrine, and intrepidly to utter, to persuade, to enjoin what is necessary alike for individual men, for the Christian family, and for civil society: so that at lenght all may know what it is that a Catholic should hold, retain, and profess.

« Believing that Peter speaks by the mouth of Pius, what You have said, confirmed, uttered for the safeguarding of the deposit,

---

2 H. JEDIN, op. cit., 190-191.
3 Quoted by H. JEDIN, op. cit., 193-194.

we also say, confirm, proclaim; and with one voice and sould we reject all that You have judged to be reprobated and rejected. For we fully accept what the Fathers of the Council of Florence defined in the decree of Union: That the Roman Pontiff is the Vicar of Christ and Head of the whole Church, and Father and Teacher of all Christians, and to him in Blessed Peter has been given by Jesus Christ full power of feeding, ruling, and governing the universal Church »[4].

It is interesting to know that these lines were mostly drafted by Haynald and Dupanloup, and the signatories among others were: Matthieu, Darboy, Ginoulhiac, Simor, Melchers, Ketteler, Strossmayer, Kenrick, Clifford. The Address is almost « an implicit recognition of the Pope's infallibility », as D. C. Butler claims[5]. Can we not interpret that they, by offering an unreserved loyalty to the Pontiff, wanted to take the papal prerogatives off the agenda of the forthcoming council? In any case, the Pope replied to this Address by stating that the council would be convoked, but he did not set the date.

A year later, June 29, 1868, the Pontiff issued the Bull « Aeterni Patris » in which the date for the opening of the council was fixed for December 8, 1869, the sessions to be held in the Basilica of St. Peter in Rome. The voting would be the same as it had been at Trent. Since this Encyclical – addressed to all bishops, including titular bishops, to the monastic congregations, and the generals of Orders – gives the outlines and program for the agenda of the forthcoming council, we quote it:

« It is at this time evident and manifest to all men in how horrible a tempest the Church is now tossed, and with what vast evils civil society is afflicted... So that not only our holy religion but human society itself is plunged in an unspeakable state of disorder and suffering.

« Wherefore we have judged it to be opportune to bring together into a General Council all our venerable brethren of the whole Catholic world, who have been called to share our solicitude. In

---

4   Cited by D. Butler, op. cit., 68.
5   Ibid., pp. 68-69.

this ecumenical Council must be examined with the greatest accucy, and decreed, all things which in these difficult times relate to the greater glory of God, the integrity of faith, the gravity of divine worship, the eternal salvation of men, the discipline of the secular and regular clergy and its wholesome and solid culture, the observance of ecclesiastical laws, the amendment of manners, and the instruction of Christian youth. And with most intent study, care must be taken that all evils may be averted from the Church and from civil society »[6].

The Address of the five hundred bishops of July 1, 1867, and the Pope's Bull « Aeterni Patris » of June 29, 1868, have some matters in common. Both documents are not only concerned with the welfare of the Church but also with that of human society; both are designed to search for and discover remedies to the ills in the Church and to those of human society; they unequivocally recognize the supreme power of the Roman Pontiff, and they make a promise to search for the means to fortify the Church in her present instability.

Let us make one more remark in relation to these two Documents and especially in regard to the Bull « Aeterni Patris ». This concerns the Bishop himself and his approach to the matters discussed in Vatican I. In this instance we have in mind, what has been already treated earlier and what has been discussed under the title « Thoughts and Proposals », namely, that he was against defining any dogma, and that he advocated the topics, for instance, of human conscience, of individual and national freedom, education of clergy, reformation of the central government of the Church, how the Church can obtain and enjoy her freedom in society and state, frequent holding of all kinds of councils and synods. This confirms that he remained more or less – at least in his first speech – within the confines of the outlined program of the Bull « Aeterni Patris », and that he earnestly searched for the wholesome solutions to the Church problems and to those of human society as well.

Before we take into consideration his approach to the newly arisen problems in the Church, it is appropriate to mention that

---

6   Quoted by D. Butler, op. cit., 69-70.

his correspondence with Francis Rački prior to Vatican I is completely devoid of any reference to it. The correspondence concerned the internal problems of their native land, Croatia. The only thing that is obvious from his letter of October 28, 1869, is that he left Djakovo on October 29 for Budapest, where he stayed until November 3. From Budapest he went to Vienna and from there to Venice and then to Rome[7]. Finally, we find him in Rome on November 8, 1869, when he wrote a letter to F. Rački[8]. There is no indication that anybody was with him. In his next letter from Rome (dated November 23, 1869) he delineated the situation in Rome in a few lines: « As far as the situation here is concerned, everything is still uncertain. The party of the (Roman) Curia has at its disposal a great number of monastic bishops. We the liberal men do not know one another, and it is feared that we will not agree, and that we will not have the necessary courage without which nothing can be accomplished and especially here. In the meantime it looks to me that the so called 'Infallibilists' should not have much hope that their labor and intentions will bear fruit. We shall see! »[9].

Strossmayer from November 23, 1869, until March 9, 1870, did not write any letters to Fr. Rački. By the explicit order of the Bishop Canon N. Voršak was in charge of corresponding with Rački. What is more, N. Voršak was instructed by Strossmayer to keep Rački posted on all major happenings in the Council[10]. Voršak

---

[7] KRS, I, 98.

[8] *Ibid.,* pp. 98-99. Cf. AJA, XII A 810/20 (N. Voršak's letter to Rački from Rome, dated November 9, 1869).

[9] KRS, I, 100. Almost a year later Lord Acton in his article « The Vatican Council » wrote the same thing about the members of the minority: « The bishops had not yet learned to know each other » (*History of Freedom, op. cit.,* 527). Cf. also AJA XII A 810/20 and 21. These two letters of N. Voršak to F. Rački of November 9 and December 1, 1869 strongly indicate the solidarity of the opposition. He (Voršak) highly praises the attitude of the North American bishops for « their practicallity, humility and determination ». Furthermore, he foresees « the failure of the Jesuits' schemes of pushing through 'personal infallibility' of the Roman pontiff ». *Ibid.*

[10] AJA XII A 810/20. Strossmayer through N. Voršak excused himself to Rački for not writing directly to him on account of pressing chores that he had to perform either writing speeches, studying the schemas and attending various meeting. Cf. AJA XII A 810/23 (Voršak's letter to Rački, dated January 9, 1870).

was very faithful in fulfilling his duty for about three months. His reports to Rački were quite comprehensive and accurate, and bore some resemblance to those of Imbro I. Tkalac. Unfortunately, since February 9, 1870, until June 23 of the same year there are no reports from Voršak whatever in the Archives of the Yugoslav Academy.

According to Granderath and Oberški, Voršak was relieved of his duties of being a « scrutator votorum et assignator locorum » in the Council, for being involved in divulging the secrets of the Council's proceedings and for communicating its documents to some Austrian newspapers[11]. There is no documentary evidence either to confirm or to deny this contention. It is possible, however, that Voršak had been « fired » by the Vatican officials on the insistence of the Nuncio of Vienna, Austria, but was later reinstated after Strossmayer and he had energically protested[12]. In any case, the absence from the Archives of the Yugoslav Academy of Voršak's reports to Rački is a puzzle. Even if we suppose that Voršak had been discharged, we cannot account for why he should have ceased sending his reports to Rački (for over four months) since he was still acquainted with the occurrences in the Council through Strossmayer whom he saw every day. Are we assuming too much if we suppose that someone, in the immediate vicinity of Rački (after Rački died) destroyed these reports on account of their touchy and unpleasant nature as to prevent their getting into undesirable hands. The reports, writings and other deeds of Strossmayer's friends will help us in reconstructing his role in the Council and his activities behind the scenes.

---

11 Cf. on this point J. Oberški, *Hrvati...*, *op. cit.*, 39. It is obvious from Voršak's correspondence with Rački that he was not « innocent ». Several time Voršak keeps reminding Rački which European newspaper he can use as reliable sources for the happenings in the Council. Cf. the above cited letter. In his report to Rački Voršak explicitly claims that « there are quite a few of his lines in Dupanloup's newspaper ». Cf. AJA XII A 810/23 – letter dated January 9, 1870. In his dispatch of February 9, 1870 to Rački he already expresses that the Vatican people maintain that he is one of those who divulge the Council's secrets. Cf. AJA XII 810/24. It is certain from Voršak's letters that in some instances he knew the names of the divulgers and in other cases he was the source himself.

12 Cf. J. Oberški, *Hrvati...*, *op. cit.*, 39.

1 - Strossmayer's Circle of Friends during the Vatican Cauncil: Imbro I. Tkalac

First of all, we have at our disposal the dispatches of Stross-mayer's friend and conationalist, Imbro I. Tkalac, representative and correspondent for the Italian government of Florence in Rome during the Vatican Council[13]. Under orders from Venosta, the Ita-lian foreign minister, Tkalac contacted Strossmayer immediately on arrival in Rome. The reports of Tkalac on the developements of the Vatican Council were held in the Italian archives of the fo-

---

[13] Imbro I. Tkalac was born in Karlovac (Croatia) May 6, 1824. At the age of nine he, in addition to the Croatian language, spoke French and Italian fluently. He graduated from high school and college in Graz, Austria. Unlike the other young Croatian students who pursued their higher education at the University of Vienna, Austria, he matriculated first in the University of Berlin and from there he went to the University of Heidelberg, Germa-ny, where he obtained a doctor's degree by presenting in 1848 the dis-sertation in Latin *De religione Christiana in Slavis introducta, propagata, re-formata. Commentatio historico-philosophica* (Christian Religion among the Slavs as it was Introduced, Propagated and Reformed. Historico-philosophical Commentary). The dissertation was published in Leipzig, Germany and de-dicated to the great Croatian hero, Ban Joseph Jelačić. In the meantime, he also attended lectures at the French College, Paris, France, given by Adam Mickiewicz, a famous Polish poet. From 1851 to 1861 we find him in Zagreb where he was secretary of Commerce. In 1861 he became the editor of the weekly newspaper *Ost und West* in Vienna, Austria. By the end of 1863 he was incarcerated by the Austrian government because of his writings; and the rumor reached Strossmayer that he had commited suicide which greatly saddened the Bishop. Cf. KRS, I, 18. Strossmayer thought of him as an « extraordinary talent ». *Ibid.* Finally, Imbro I. Tkalac was expelled from Austria, and he set-tled in Italy, whose citizenship he was granted and financial support was gi-ven to him by the Italian government. He was employed by the Italian King's government in one capacity or another until he died in Rome in 1912.

He was a prolific writer, and his literary contributions are found in all the European leading newspaper and reviews and especially in those in Ger-many, as for instance *National Zeitung* of Berlin. In signing his various ar-ticles he used the pseudonim Hector Frank in order to protect his identity, so that he would not have to compromise his position as an Italian diplomat. Pope Pius IX and the Secretary of State Cardinal Antonelli were targets of his journalistic attacks from time to time.

He supplied Emil Zola with the material for the novel *Rome.* Naturally, Tkalac sold « all this dirt » to the French novelist for cold cash. Cf. A. Tam-borra, *op. cit.,* 7-30 and passim. See also Tkalac's book *Jugenderinnerungen aus Croatien,* Leipzig, Germany, 1894. Almost immeditely this book was trans-lated into French. In 1945 it was finally translated into his native (Croatian) language by Dr. Sv. Rittig, published by Matica Hrvathka, Zagreb, under the title *Uspomene iz Hrvatske.*

reign ministry until 1966, when they were published by A. Tamborra in his book « Imbro I. Tkalac ».

Tkalac shared quite a few views with the Bishop. Both were in favor of obtaining the reunification of each nation – Italian included – and of granting a national independence to every nationality; and personal liberty must be guaranteed by way of democracy[14]. Tkalac did not believe either that the modern society, which was in making, was in need of any new dogmas, or as he said in his doctoral dissertation « tempus autem nostrum dogmata non fert ». In addition, he was preoccupied, too, with the reunion of Christendom, and strongly advocated that the human society can be ruled by the Christian love « Unicum hominum ligamen (est) amor christianus »[15].

Furthermore, he was anti-clerical, and yet all the time he was in their company. He criticised the Catholic Church, and yet had a great admiration for her of which (the Church) he said that she contains within herself such energies that she is constantly in the process of rejuvenation from one pontiff to another, from one council to another; but she remains the same[16]. However, in his dissertation he favored the decentralization of the Church government and advocated such unorthodox ideas as the separation from hierarchical authority – at least for the Slavs. For this reason he glorified John Huss who was his ideal, and Huss ideas so far were only realized by the Bogomils of Bosnia and Herzegovina[17].

Why was Tkalac chosen by the Italian government of Florence to be its unaccredited representative in Rome during the session of Vatican I? This was done for many reasons. First of all, he was known to Visconti Venosta and the other Italian leading politicans of that time as a strong opponent to the papal temporal power which Tkalac had manifested on the pages of « Ost und West ». Secondly, he was a man « of independent judgments » and also a man of « grandissima cultura » with the knowledge of many

---

[14] A. TAMBORRA, op. cit., 127-128.
[15] Quoted by A. TAMBORRA, op. cit., 31.
[16] Ibid., p. 213 and passim.
[17] Ibid., p. 31.

languages. Thirdly, he was deeply involved in Italian diplomacy and in its rebellion against the Austrian empire[18]. What is more, in the judgment of the Italian foreign minister, Visconti Venosta, there were very few men in the whole of Europe like Tkalac, who would be so competent in religious and theological matters and who would be more capable of moving around in the cosmopolitan society of Rome during the time of Vatican I as Tkalac was[19]. His friendship and acquaintance with the European leading politicians and intellectuals in Paris, Vienna and Berlin as for instance with Thiers, Migne, Mgr. Felix Dupanloup, Jesuit theologian and one of the principal architects of papal infallibility Clement Schrader and many other churchmen also contributed to his appointement[20]. Of course he was a friend of J. G. Strossmayer who promised him to supply him with the information about social and political matters that might be discussed in the Council. What is more, the Bishop of Djakovo had expressed his willingness to place him in contact with personalities who might be in possession of vital information[21].

At this point it is not ours to pass judgment on Strossmayer's violation or non-violation of the secrecy imposed on the council Fathers. On the other hand, it is a historical fact that Archbishop Manning was dispensed from the obligation of keeping secrecy by the Pope himself in order to supply Odo Russell (who was dear to Pius IX) with all information to forward to the British government whose official Agent in Rome he was[22]. Almost certainly that Tkalac's Reports to Venosta are the expression of the Bishop's mind to a great extent.

An Italian historian Angelo Tamborra opines that Tkalac's Reports are « precise and informative »[23]. Tkalac even boasted to the Italian Foreign Minister that within an hour he would learn whatever had taken place either in the congregations of the Council or

---

18 *Ibid.*, p. 127.
19 *Ibid.*, p. 129.
20 *Ibid.*, pp. 32-33 and passim.
21 *Ibid.*, pp. 129-130. Cf. also RSCV, p. 228.
22 D. BUTLER, *op. cit.*, 270.
23 A. TAMBORRA, *op. cit.*, 133.

at the various national and international meetings of the council Fathers. The web of his informants extended to both minority and majority parties. His free access to cardinals and bishops enabled him to come into possession of valuable information[24]. In addition, it is of great interest to know that both Pope Pius IX and the Secretary of State Cardinal Antonelli had issued inofficial orders that neither the police of the Vatican nor anybody else should disturb or prevent from browsing around him whose « barbarian » name they did not even bother to pronounce. The Pontiff referred to him as an « ambasciatore in partibus infidelium ».[25] It is hardly believable that either the Pope or the Secretary of State knew for what government he worked.

2. - Lord John Emerich E. Acton

Perhaps, there were no two men so akin to each other in their views and ideas as Lord Acton (1834-1902) and Strossmayer. Most probably these two great intelects became acquainted and eventually became the most intimate friends during Vatican I. Were they brought into a cordial and lasting friendship by the sheer coincidence of the Council's events? or perhaps it all started in the home of the Italian politician and intellectual Marco Minghetti who was a friend of the both. This friendship contnued to flourish after the turbulent occurrences at Vatican I where he shared his « joy and sorrow » with Lord Acton as he wrote to Lord Gladstone[26]. They used to meet during summer months in Tegernsee near Munich in Acton's home[27]. On one occasions the British Scholar paid a visit to the Bishop in Djakovo[28].

---

[24] *Ibid., p.* 130.
[25] *Ibid.,* pp. 130-131.
[26] CBSG, p. 424.
[27] KRS, I, 112. There are only three letteres of Lord Acton to Strossmayer preserved in the Archives of the Yugoslav Academy of Zagreb. All of them dealt with family matters of Lord Acton and with the possibilities where they might meet. Cf. AJA XI A/Act. 1, 2, and 3. Acton's several telegrams to the Bishop are still kept in the same Archives. None of them has any general significance.
[28] TS, p. 20. (Some of the Bishop's letters to Lord Gladstone were translated into English by Lord Acton. See CBSG, p. 417).

Eventhough the course of their lives was not so much alike, their views, however, on the various contemporary issues were similar. First of all, both Acton and Strossmayer were deeply involved in politics and diplomacy. Their reflections on politics brought them into agreement as strong opponents of the temporal power of the pope[29]. They were against it for the variety of reasons: the Church, by becoming involved in the secular affairs, loses the sight of spiritual matters, and she is likely to neglect her mission in the world. Besides, both of them agreed that every nation is entitled to choose its rulers – Italian included[30]; secondly, they were against governmental absolutism and excessive centralism. This idea is well developed by Acton in article « Nationality » in which he even touched upon the problem of conglomeration of nationalities in the Austrian Empire with these words: « The several nationalities are at very unequal degrees of advancement, and there is no single nation which is so predominant as to overwhelm or absorb the others ».[31] The outcome of his brilliant analysis was that each and every nation should be autonomous and have self-government[32]. These ideas of Acton's most certainly remind us of those of the Bishop.

There are some more remarkable similarities between these two personalities. This particularly comes to the fore in their relationship to the papacy and to the other Christians of various churches. Acton says that « communion with Rome is dearer to him than life »[33]. As we have already seen, the Bishop had studied Protestant theology so did Acton; and this is remarkably well formulated by H. Paul: « To Protestant theology he (Acton) paid as much attention as to Catholic. Those who feared God and followed Christ in every nation belonged his household of faith »[34].

To bring to completion the striking resemblances on some other

---

[29] *Letters of Lord Acton to Mary, op. cit.* (H. Paul in his « Introductory Memoir », p. XXV.

[30] *Ibid.*

[31] *History of Freedom, op. cit.,* 296.

[32] *Ibid.,* p. 297.

[33] Quoted by H. Paul, *Letters of Lord Acton to Mary, op. cit.,* p. LII.

[34] *Ibid.,* p. XX.

subjects between Acton and Strossmayer we must speak of Acton's ideas on the two most valuable human prerogatives: conscience and individual freedom on which he had so beautifully elaborated in his two lectures: « Freedom in Antiquity »[35] and « Freedom in Christianity »[36]. The most notable resemblance is in Acton's description of human conscience with that of Bishop which we quote in its entirety: « The Christian notion of conscience imperatively demands a corresponding measure of personal liberty. The feeling of duty and responsibility to God is the only arbiter of Christian's actions. With this no human authority can be permitted to interfere. We are bound to extend to the utmost, and to guard from every encroachment, the sphere in which we can act in obedience to the sole voice of conscience, regardless of any other consideration »[37]

Furthermore, Lord Acton's approach to various problems was all the time motivated by and undertaken under historical aspect which is similar to that of Döllinger, John H. Newman and Strossmayer. Hugh MacDougall is unjustly critical of this Acton's erudite practice when he says that « Acton's case, however, was more complicated (than that of Cardinal Newman). In the first place he was not a theologian and had no deep appreciation of the science of theology apart from history. He tended to assign to history too exclusive a role in the determination of religious truth »[38]. This statement is only partially true. It seems to us that Acton was very much cognizant of the development of a dogma. Why did he accept then the dogma of papal infallibility if he were so strongly attached to history; and we all know how valiantly he fought against the defining of papal infallible teaching. In addition, his awareness of the historical process within the church – from her birth to Acton's own day – was very much alive when he stated

---

[35] *History of Freedom, op. cit.*, 1-29. This lecture was delivered by Acton on Febraury 26, 1877.

[36] *Ibid.*, pp. 30-60. This conference was given by Acton at the Bridgnorth Institution on May 28, 1877.

[37] *Ibid.*, p. 203 (His article « Political Thoughts on the Church »).

[38] H. MacDougall, *The Acton – Newman Relations. The Dilemma of Christian Liberalism* (New York, Fordham University Press, 1963), 127.

that « Christian antiquity had given way to universality, universality made way for authority »[39]. It looks to us as if Acton with his activities in Rome during Vatican I wished to forestall this « authority » turning into total absolutism. Perhaps, this was one of the reasons for his staunch opposition to defining the dogma of papal infallible teaching.

At any rate, Acton indeed shared the preceding opinion with the Bishop of Djakovo. What is more, Acton undoubtedly viewed the definition of papal infallibility with a great alarm, and he foresaw in it and so did Strossmayer an obstacle to the reunion of the Christian churches, by remarking, that « the chances of union with the Greeks, the means of discussion with the Protestantes, would vanish utterly, and Catholicism would forefeit its expending power... »[40].

3. - Acton's and Tkalac's Appraisals of the Vatican Council

Acton's views, expressed in his study « The Vatican Council » and Tkalac's Reports and their respective reflection on the issues, proceedings and happenings in the Vatican Council are in many respects similar. Of course, one has to keep in mind that Tkalac's Reports were written on the spur of the moment, while Acton's study is a result of somewhat long and deep reflections; and what is more, Acton in his encyclopedic mind is superior to Tkalac in the field of theology.

Let us make one more observation in regard to Acton's article. It is beyond our comprehension why his presentation of the Vatican Council is viewed with scorn by the Church historians and churchmen[41]. In our judgment Acton is unbiased in depecting the

---

[39] *History of Freedom, op. cit.,* p. 514 (His article « The Vatican Council »).
[40] Quote by H. MacDougall, *op. cit.,* 112. The quotation is taken out of Acton's article « The Next General Council » published in *The Chronicle* of July 13 (1867), p. 370.
[41] « In this essay (Acton's article "The Vatican Council") his (Acton's) preoccupation with the political aspects of the Council tended to blind him

events in the Council and in giving their background. This especially becomes evident if one becomes sufficiently acquainted with
Strossmayer's plans and with the Reports of I. Tkalac. It is equally
true that to follow Acton's writing is occasionally difficult since he
presupposes the knowledge of certain matters and incidents which
are actually out of reader's reach. There are several paragraphs
which are impossible to comprehend if one is not familiar with
the plans of Strossmayer; nor can one avoid thinking that he wanted to protect the reputation of his friend, Strossmayer. There is
another peculiarity about his essay on the Vatican Council: after
having presented what had preceded the Council, he concentraded
just on several principal actors, and he spun all the happenings
around them. Perhaps, this is more accurate way in presenting the
developments in the Council. (Most certainly, it is much easier to
present the ideas and activities of an individual than of o group of
persons involved in the same occurrences).

Acton's and Tkalac's appraisals of the members of the minority
and majority in the Council will offer us a better insight into the
issues that were to be deliberated. This will also help us to understand why a schism was never realized in spite of bitter disagreements in the Council. It appears here and there in the Reports of
Tkalac that he was hopefully waiting for such a thing to take place, while on the other hand Acton sometimes explicitly sometimes
implicitly placed the blame on the bishops of the minority for not
acting more energetically; they were « in the stage of inertness », he
stated[42]. Acton equally blamed them for the lack of action since the
determination in actions, in his opinion, would forestall the definition
of papal infallibility, or as he wrote « they (minority) signed protests that were of no effect. They petitioned; they did not resist »[43];
a few pages later he expressed himself more succinctly that « the
bishops (of the minority) stood on the negative. They showed no
sense of their mission to renovate Catholicism... They were content

---

to the far more important considerations ». H. MacDougall, op. cit., 117.
MacDougall's assertion cannot be acceptable to anybody who happened to
read the Essay attentively.
    [42] History of Freedom, op. cit., 526 (His article « The Vatican Council »).
    [43] Ibid., p. 527.

to leave things as they were, to gain nothing if they lost nothing, to renounce all premature strivings for reform (of the Church) if they could succeed in avoiding a doctrine which they were as unwilling to discuss as to define »[44]. Acton in this cited paragraph is referring to the speeches of some members of the opposition which were delivered in the early stages of the Council, and which the prelates like Schwarzenberg, Rauscher, Darboy, Dupanloup, Verot, Kenrick, Strossmayer and some more had cried for the reformation of the Church, and Acton is reproaching them for abandoning their earlier wholesome plan and for allowing themselves to be involved in debates of papal infallible teaching.

According to the Reports of Tkalac the weakness of the bishops of the opposition began to show in the month of April. This particularly took place prior to the voting on the Constitution « Dei Filius » in the solemn congregation of April 24, 1870. He ascribes the achievements of the majority and the defeat of the minority to the skill of the « infallibilists » whose « knowledge of matters and persons was superior to any oratory; and thus everything went their way »[45]. The conscious or subconscious awareness of the opposition of being outsmarted by their opponents' intrigues and well schemed manipulations made the minority feel « uneasy, embarrassed, hesitant and humiliated »[46]. The conclusion of the Constitution « Dei Filius » was in question; and the conclusion runs: « But since it is not sufficient to avoid heretical perversity, unless those errors are also avoided which more or less approximate it, we admonish all of their duty to observe also the constitutions and decrees by which this Holy See has proscribed and condemned similar evil opinions which are not here enumerated in detail »[47]. Mgrs La Place

---

[44] *Ibid.*, p. 526. While the opposition, in the judgment of Acton, was willing to take any kind of concessions in order to avoid the dogmatization of papal infallibility, Strossmayer on the other hand did not think like the rest of the opposition, but « he demanded (in his speech of January 24, 1870) the reformation of the Court of Rome, decentralization of the government of the Church, and decennial councils. That earnest spirit did not animate the bulk of the party » (*ibid.*).

[45] RSCV, p. 268 (Tkalac's report of April 23, 1870).

[46] *Ibid.*, p. 267.

[47] MANSI 51, 38.

and Strossmayer in their respective groups (French and German) insisted that the « conclusion should be thrown out, and the customs of ecumenical councils should be observed ». This proposal at their respective national meetings was rejected[48]; and on April 24 the opposition voted with a « placet » while Strossmayer absented himself from the solemn congregation[49].

The cited conclusion was a decisive factor in the Council since in the mind of both Pius IX[50] and of the leader of the majority, Archbishop Manning,[51] the very acceptance of it meant implicit recognition of papal infalliblity. On April 23 Tkalac had already indicated in his report to Visconti Venosta that the oppostion ceased to exist[52].

While Tkalac described the members of the minority as in a state of confusion[53] and that the Roman Curia was aware of the « limitis of courage of the opposition, and that they (Roman Curia) are not much disturbed by their demonstrations »[54], Pope Pius IX[55] and Acton indicate that they (minority) were divided among themselves by fear. The latter finds the source of their fear in the fact that a very small number of them, if they were separately questioned on the question of papal infallibility, would reject it on theo-

---

[48] RSCV, p. 268.

[49] *Ibid.;* cf. also D. BUTLER, *op. cit.,* 247 and *History of Freedom, op. cit.,* 543.

[50] Tkalac in his dispatch to Venosta of April 28 quotes Pope Pius IX: « As far as the opposition is concerned, they are divided by their own fears: that so-called opposition does not exist any more. 'Afflavit Deus et dissipati sunt' the Pope added and broke into roaring laughter » (RSCV, p. 271).

[51] Acton writes: « Archbishop Manning afterwards reminded them (the opposition) that by this vote (of April 24) they had implicitly accepted infallibility » (*History of Freedom, op. cit.,* 543). Three days later Strossmayer at the meeting of the German bishops reproached his colleagues with these words « Whoever wishes to save cabbage and goat, he is fooled by seeming concessions » (RSCV, p. 271).

[52] RSCV, p. 268. « The opposition is buried for good », Tkalac wrote to Venosta. *Ibid,* p. 270. Acton also shares Tkalac's opinion. See *History of Freedom, op. cit.,* 542-543.

[53] RSCV, p. 268. The opposing bishop are already of short temper. At their international meeting « Mgr. Hefele hollered at Strossmayer 'you caused us to lose the Council' while Mgr. Dupanloup cried at Mgr. de La Place 'you destroyed the opposition' » (*ibid.*).

[54] *Ibid.,* p. 277 (Dispatch of May 8).

[55] See the note no. 50.

logical grounds[56]. In addition, Acton also reproaches the opposition for their constant living in hope that either some incidents like « Deus ex machina » or the intervention of their respective governments would change the course of the Council in their favor[57]. The implication is very obvious: they were afraid to take the reins in their own hands. Cardinal Schwarzenberg, one of the leading forces of the opposition, shared Pope Pio IX, Acton's and Tkalac's opinions.[58] In his letters from Rome to F. Rački Strossmayer had also strongly expressed his doubts about the courage of the opposition[59].

All these actors: Acton[60], Strossmayer[61] and Tkalac agreed that the Opposition has many men of great talent. Tkalac somewhat exaggerated when he stated in his report of June 29, 1870: « When I am in the company of the opposition, I often regret that the Infall-ibilists do not have a one single great talent, a one single famous scholar nor a one great orator. The infallibilists in the assemblies appear below the most common mediocrity; their successes evidently come from the people who do not participate in the venerable sessions and who in secrecy manipulate, but their advices, sugge-stions and instructions are usually very clumsily executed »[62]. Fur-thermore, the Britsh Historian in his article « The Vatican Council »

---

[56] *History of Freedom, op. cit.*, 528.
[57] *Ibid.*, p. 525.
[58] I. Tkalac describes his encounter with Cartdinal Schwarzenberg: « One day I told Cardinal Schwarzenberg: 'Emminence, you know what the Fathers had done in Constance. Depose Pope Pius IX, proclaim an anti-pope, convoke a new council under his presidency in Constance and reform the Church *in ca-pite et in membris!* And mankind will bless your name'. 'You are right', Car-dinal answered, 'that is what should be done. But, what can you do, I am not a man of action, and my friends are not better either. It is not the papacy that frightens us (to act), it is we who are more or less old, and we do not feel the energies within ourselves to act as we should. The tendency of the education of a Catholic priest is geared to crush our natural energies and thus to makes eunuchs out of us. You see that very litle is achieved'. I said to him: What is the use to talk when you are unable to act'! The Cardinal shrugged his shoulders and said· 'To appease the conscience' ». (Dispach of Juy 21, 1870. Cf. RSCV, pp. 335-336).
[59] KRS, I, 102.
[60] « The best talents (with) the most discordant views » (*History of Freedom, op. cit.*, 532.
[61] KRS, I, 101. Cf. also R. AUBERT, *op. cit.*, 332.
[62] RSCV, p. 318. Tkalac also describes the opposition as being « proud ». *Ibid.*, p. 267.

added one more remark for the sake of clarification in regard to the bishops of the opposition. The stigma of Gallicanism was constantly attached to them so as to discredit them altogether in the eyes of the rest of the Catholic world. Therefore, he under-lined the fact that these prelates, outside of France, did not have anything to do with Gallicanism « which was essentially odious » to them[63]. Since Acton knew the « hearts and souls » of the bishops of opposition, his opinion cannot be disputed.

4 - Fr. Augustine Theiner (1804-1874)

Undoubtedly Fr. Augustine Theiner, a member of the Oratory of St. Philip Neri, belonged to the circle of Strossmayer's intima-te friends. Although Theiner was one of the most prominent scho-larly figures in the Catholic Church in the nineteenth century, at this point we are not so much concerned either with Theiner's erudition as a historian or with his numerous publications that he wrote or edited. Because of his erudition in history he also became a very close friend of Francis Rački, Lord Acton and Imbro I. Tka-lac. Theiner visited Rački in Zagreb and Strossmayer in Djakovo; the latter helped him financially in publishing some of his works. He reciprocated by providing Rački and Strossmayer with docu-ments for the history of the South Slavs. Rački and Strossmayer planned to make him an honorary member of the Yugoslav Acade-my of Science and Art in Zagreb[64]. No wonder, therefore, that as soon as Strossmayer arrived at Rome to attend the Council, he was in the company of Theiner[65].

What we are primarily concerned here with is the case of A.

---

[63] « The only bishops », Acton writes, « whose position made them ca-pable of resisting were the Germans and French; and all that Rome would have to contend with was the modern liberalism and decrepit Gallicanism of France, and the science of Germany. The Gallican school was nearly extinct; it had no footing in other countries and it was essentially odius to the libe-rals. The most serious minds of the liberal party were conscious that Rome was generous to ecclesiastical liberty as Paris ». *History of Freedom, op. cit.,* 524.

[64] KRS, I, 314.

[65] *Ibid.,* p. 100.

Theiner and his being a controversial figure in the Catholic Church: why he was deposed during the session of Vatican I by Pope Pius IX, and why the position of the Prefect of the Vatican Archives was taken away from him. Was this a result of illegally supplying the minority in the Council with secret documents, or perhaps was he a victim of Pius' IX wrath or of the revenge of the Jesuits on account of his book « The Life of Clement the Fourteenth » in which he vindicated that pope against the Jesuits. In our judgment the testimonies of Strossmayer, Tkalac, Acton and Canon Voršak can shed a lot of light on this controversial figure and his removal from his position during the time of Vatican I.

Lord Acton spoke very highly about the moral qualities and spiritual life of A. Theiner. According to him, Theiner led sometimes a very rigid life.[66] The foci of the controversary over A. Theiner were the Acts of the Council of Trent and his communicating their contents to the Fathers (minority) of the Council[67]. Lord Acton indicated that Theiner was in possession of the transcripts of the Acts of the said Council, and that Pius IX explicitly forbade their publication[68]. Acton went a little further by stating that Theiner « deemed the Concealment (of the Acts of the Council of Trent) prudent »[69].

I. Tkalac in his dispach of June 22, 1870, to Visconti Venosta was more emphatic than Acton in stressing the virtues, the erudition and the merits of Theiner whom he called the « purest and the most integer character among the Catholic clergy of our time ». What is more, Tkalac considered him as his own personal friend and the « best source of getting information whose just one word would put him in contact with the most reserved and most exclusive bishops as for instance Cardinals Rauscher and Schwarzenberg, Mgrs. Darboy, Landriot, Verot etc ». Theiner was on ami-

---

[66] *History of Freedom, op. cit.,* 411-412 and 429.
[67] F. Šišić maintains that A. Theiner had supplied Strossmayer and the rest of the opposition with the material from the Vatican Archives. Cf. KRS, I, 106, note 5.
[68] *History of Freedom, op. cit.,* 431.
[69] *Ibid.*

cable terms with the both parties of the Council: the minority and the majority. Even though he was against the dogma of papal infallibility, he never became engaged in any disputes, according to Tkalac.

Some time after Easter Sunday (1870) Theiner went to Naples to rest, and fifteen days thereafer he was notified to return to Rome instantly. As soon as he arrived at Rome, he was sent immediately to Pope Pius IX who upon seeing Theiner became « enraged like a lion ». The Pontiff asked Theiner to turn the Archives keys over to Cardoni. Pius' behavior so saddened Theiner that he began to cry like an infant. After Theiner regained his composure and the Pontiff somewhat calmed down, he asked the Pope for the reason of his dismissal. This is what the Pope answered:

« I do not feel obligated to give you the motives for my actions, but I will tell them to you anyhow. First, you have supplied these ignorants (exactly in Italian *somari* = donkeys) of the opposition with the secret books and documents, who do not know either theology or the Church history, in order to combat my dogma; secondly, you have given an advice and information to Rauscher, Schwarzenberg, Youssouf and to that '*capo-setta* Croatino' (that Croatian ring-leader) Strossmayer; thirdly, you have transmitted the documents of the Archives to that miserable Acton (in Italian *bric-cone* = rascal) who licks my feet and at the same time works with the opposition; and what is still worse, your have let him enter and have an access to the Archives »[70].

Theiner himself told all these things to Tkalac. The following is the summary of the answer that Theiner gave to the Pontiff. First of all, Theiner told Pius IX that he did not feel obliged to declare himself on this dogma (papal infallibility) – which the Pope calls « my dogma » – since he was not a bishop. Thereafter he admitted to the Pope, that after he was given the position of the Prefect of the Vatican Archives, he was in correspondence with the more learned German, French, Slav and American bishops, but he denied – by giving his sacerdotal word of honor to the Pope – that he had ever communicated any secret documents to any of them.

---

[70] RSCV, pp. 302-303.

As far as Lord Acton was concerned, he declared that he never confided any documents to Acton except those which Pius IX had ordered him to give. Cardinal Antonelli was an intermediary in this matter. He reminded the Pontiff that at that time he did not know Acton, nor did he ever allow him to pass the threshold to the Archives. The Pontiff, after having listened to Theiner's defense, calmly said to him « You are not one of ours, and you cannot be in charge of the Archives »[71].

Prior to the dismissal of Theiner a strange coincidence took place, namely, Lord Acton was in process of purchasing some rare documents and books which deal with the last three centuries of the history of the Church. Since the Jesuits, as Tkalac reports, were after Theiner, they seized this opportunity to strongly imply that Acton was procuring these historical documents from Theiner with the cash. According to Tkalac Acton knew that Theiner was in extreme danger, and he instead of coming out with the truth and of denying that he ever purchased anything from Theiner, left the scene and escaped to Florence. In the judgment of Tkalac Lord Acton had a wonderful chance to discredit the Pontiff, the Roman Curia and the Jesuits with the public statement[72].

Tkalac is in agreement with Lord Acton that Theiner was in possession of the transcripts of the documents of the Council of Trent[73]. He is more precise on this point than Acton. In his dispatch to Venosta of June 20, 1870, he stated that Theiner was granted a permission by Pius IX to publish the Acts of the said Council, but later on this plan was suspended by the explicit order of the Pontiff[74]. This most certainly indicates that during the Vatican Council Theiner had the transcripts of the documents of the Trent's Council which, of course, were the products of his personal labor. In all probability at that time the abridged documents of the Council of Trent were prepared by Theiner for publication. Sure enough, the *Acts* of the said Council were published in Zagreb under the title: A. Theiner, *Acta genuina concilii Tridentini*, Zagra-

---

[71] *Ibid.*, p. 303.
[72] *Ibid.*, pp. 303-304.
[73] *Ibid.*, p. 304.
[74] *Ibid.*, p. 313.

biae, 1874[75]; and the publictaion was financed by Strossmayer[76]. The Bishop wanted to pay « Dionička Tiskara » (The Joint Printing Shop) of Zagreb so that Theiner could collect all the rayalties of the book for himself. Most probably this was done on the part of Strossmayer in gratitude to Theiner after the latter promised that not only the *Acts* but also *Codex epistolaris,* to be published in Zagreb would contain the letters of the European kings, princes, bishops and cardinals and would serve as the interpretation to the Acts of the Trent's Council[77].

Before we bring out Strossmayer's assessment of Theiner's character we deem necessary to mention some other facts which led to the publication of the *Acts* of the Council of Trent. When Theiner was dismissed from his post, some European bishops including Strossmayer offered an asylum to him and the king of Bavaria volunteered to defray the expenses of printing of the *Acts.* Theiner refused both[73]. It is evident from the abundant correspondence between Rački and Strossmayer that neither of them gave a word of encouragement to Theiner to publish the documents. Both of them respected the private opinion of Theiner. It is true that Theiner paid a visit to Rački and Strossmayer in 1872[79] and again in June and July of 1874[30]. The first time Rački and Strossmayer learned about Theiner's intention to publish the *Acts* was when N. Voršak came to Zagreb to make arrangements on behalf of Theiner with « The Joint Printing Shop » of Zagreb. This took place in August, 1873[31], Strosmayer, after having learned this, was delighted that this great work of Theiner would be printed in Zagreb[82]. Toward the end of June, 1874, Theiner arrived at Zagreb to supervise the setting and printing of the *Acts*[83]. Besides, both Rački and Strossmayer wanted by all means to get from Theiner the transcripts of

---

75 KRS, I. 236.
76 *Ibid.,* p. 314.
77 *Ibid.*
78 RSCV, p. 313.
79 KRS, I, 186.
80 *Ibid.,* pp. 313-314.
81 *Ibid.,* p. 236.
82 *Ibid.,* p. 246.
83 *Ibid.,* pp. 313-314.

the letters of the two popes Sixtus the Fifth and Pius the Sixth which they needed so badly for the completion of another work of Theiner, the second volume of *Monumenta Slavorum meridionalium*[84] which was eventually published in Zagreb under the editorship of Rački.

While the Acts of Trent were in the process of being printed, Theiner returned to Rome and shortly thereafter died on August 10, 1874. Theiner was accompanied on this journey to Zagreb by N. Voršak, who did not return to Rome with him. The very same day, when Rački and Voršak learned of the sudden death of Theiner, Voršak returned to Rome to save the papers, correspondence and other written material which Theiner had left to him[85]. Strossmayer wholeheartedly approved the instant departure of Voršak for Rome, and the very same day he sent him a letter in German to Rome. Most probably the letter carried the instructions what to do with the material, left to Voršak by Theiner; and in another letter the Bishop manifested his feelings to Rački in regard to Theiner's bequest: « I believe that this material, confided to Voršak (by Theiner), ipso facto has become his property. Whatever is in our hands, it is ours, and we won't give it to anybody »[86]. Back to the Acts of the Council of Trent.

The pubblications of the Acts was completed by Rački, and by the end of 1874 it reached the bookstores in Rome and in some German cities[87]. The appearance of the Acts had greatly disturbed the Pontiff and the Roman Curia, so Voršak informed Rački from Rome. According to the same letter of Voršak, the Pope and the Roman Curia were attacking him because they could not do anything to the dead Theiner. The Pontiff threatened to take Voršak's name off the list of the prelates, while on the other hand Voršak was about to write a letter to Pius IX to remind him that if he and the Roman Curia did not stop marring his name and character, he would come out with the truth in the public[88] The implication of

---

[84] *Ibid.*, pp. 146 and 199.
[85] *Ibid.*, p. 315.
[86] *Ibid.*, p. 316.
[87] *Ibid.*, p. 328.
[88] *Ibid.*

Voršak's threat was that he was in possession of quite a few personal letters of Pius IX to A. Theiner which would discredit the Pontiff in the eyes of the public; this would also vindicate the innocence of A. Theiner. Unfortunately, we are not in possession of Pius' IX letters, and consequently we do not know their contents. Strossmayer, as we shall see later on, makes reference to these letters of Pius IX, and most certainly he knew their contents.

The storm over the publication of the Acts by Theiner and Rački subsided in the public, but the Roman Curia kept exercising pressure on Voršak until the beginning of 1878 when Voršak finally surrendered all the remaining documents, left to him by Theiner, to the Holy See. The case of the Acts was revived on the occasion of the death of Canon Voršak when his obituary appeared in the Vatican newspaper *L'Aurora* on February 6, 1880, with the remark that it was « his great merit that he returned Theiner's papers to Vatican »[89]. This news did not surprise Strossmayer since he had been already told by the Nuncio of Vienna about this incident[90].

There is no indication when this news was communicated to the Bishop, but we know that he wrote to Voršak and asked him for the explanation which he never received[91]. It is evident that Voršak had also turned over to the Vatican authorities *Codex epistolaris* which had to be printed in « Joint Printing Shop » of Zagreb with which Theiner had made a contract[92], plus the documents of Juraj (George) Cardinal Drašković who distinguished himself at the Council of Trent[93]. Shortly after Voršak's death, Imbro Tkalac wrote to Strossmayer from Rome that according to his information Voršak had surrendered Theiner's papers to the Vatican authorities either for cash or for some promised rewards or for both, and that none had been realized[94]. Strossmayer was not quite certain what had prompted Voršak to undertake these

---

[89] KRS, II, 256.
[90] *Ibid.*
[91] *Ibid.*
[92] *Ibid.,* p. 259.
[93] *Ibid.,* pp. 261-262.
[94] *Ibid.,* pp. 262-263.

steps, since Theiner had left his papers to Voršak with the stipulation that they be forwarded to Rački and to be eventually published in Zagreb by Rački under the auspices of the Yugoslav Academy. In the judgment of the Bishop, Voršak was an honest and learned man, but his judgment was poor, besides which he was extremely ambitious; and Voršak as such became a « victim of machiavellism of the Roman prelates »[95].

Strossmayer in his letter of February 17, 1880, to Rački made the following remarks on Theiner's character and activities:

« It remains to me to remark that the late Theiner was not only a learned man but also a saintly man – a hundred times saintlier than those who unjustly persecuted him; and on top of it he was totally innocent. That man (Theiner) was not able to perpetrate an act which might mar his conscience. The papers, which Theiner confided to Nicholas Voršak, most certainly were obtained in the honest manner and according to the regulations; but on the other hand the obituary of N. Voršak implies what the worst enemies of Theiner are still trumpeting, that he came into possession of these papers in a dishonest way. As far as I know, those papers are the transcripts which the late Theiner had procured for his scientific research legally and with the permission of higher authority, as for instance, the transcripts of the documents which pertain to the Council of Trent. Among his other papers *The Life of Benedict The Fourteenth* is found. This biography is divided into four volumes: two first volumes are already finished, the third one is in its first draft and the fourth one is only: *pieces justificatives*. Furthermore, the late (Theiner) had many letters of the late Pius IX – written in his own hand – which concern Theiner's book *The Life of Clement The Fourteenth*. At the beginning Pope Pius IX coaxed Theiner to publish *The Life of Clement The Fourteenth* against which the Jesuits raged. Thereafter Pius IX reversed himself and began to maltreat Theiner for writing that book. Permission was also granted to him by Pius IX to publish under his auspices

---

[95] *Ibid.*, p. 257. Cardinal Hergenröther was not only well acquainted with the case of Canon Voršak, but he also had his fingers in obtaining Theiner's papers from him. Cf. KRS, II, 262.

the Acts of the Council of Trent, but when the Jesuits learned it, they persuaded the Pontiff to stop its publication. On many occasions poor Theiner used to cry bitterly in front of me. God was good to him by calling him to Himself at the right moment before the Acts of the Council of Trent were published in Zagreb; otherwise they (the Roman Curia) would crush him and put him through tortures »[96].

Undoubtedly, nobody was better acquainted with the possessions and dealings of Theiner than Canon N. Voršak who was constantly in his company, and who also occasionally served as Theiner's intermediary, as for instance, in the case of pubblishing the Acts of the Council of Trent in Zagreb. Several facts from the correspondence between Voršak on one side and Strossmayer and Rački on the other are certain. First of all, Theiner himself decided on his own to have the Acts printed in Zagreb, even though some Protestants wanted to publish them at their own expense in Germany. Secondly, Theiner in 1855 had been given permission by Pius IX to publish the said Acts. As a matter of fact. about 80 pages of them were set up and rolled off the presses when all of a sudden the Pontiff, under the influence of Jesuits, ordered him to halt the publication. According to Voršak, Jesuits were prompted to act that way out of fear that the work of their confrere Pallavicini on the same Council would lose its significance in the scientific world. In addition, the publication of the Trent's Acts might eventually become an obstacle to the forthcoming ecumenical council which had been already secretly planned, and which, of course, would not have been run according to the procedures of Trent. Thirdly, Theiner had revised and abridged the original Acts of 1855 and had wanted to publish them in two volumes with the additional volume on the correspondence between the Presidents of the Council of Trent and the popes so as to illustrate how the said Council had been conducted and what sort of freedom had prevailed in it. Fourthly, the two volumes had to be printed as fast as possible and also under the utmost secrecy. I. Döllinger and Lord Acton were to write a review as soon as it came off the presses. Fifthly, Theiner had un-

---

[96] *Ibid.,* pp. 256-257.

dertaken this step under the insistence and urgency of many bishops who wanted to see these documents in the hands of the scholars[97].

As soon as « The Joint Printing Shop » of Zagreb had embarked on setting the type of the Acts, Pius IX and the Roman Curia were alarmed either by the Jesuits of Zagreb or by those in Vienna, Austria. According to the statement of Voršak the Pontiff himself had inaugurated a harangue against Theiner and the *Acts*. Scarcely a few days elapsed after Theiner's death when State Secretary Cardinal Antonelli asked for the keys to the trunks of Theiner. One trunk was half-full of documents; the other half of the trunk-load of documents was sold to Lord Acton in 1868. These documents purchased by Acton dealt solely with Scottish and English history. Theiner also made a promise to Acton to let him copy the rest of documents[98]. It is no clear from Voršak's letter if these documents were simply transcripts or original ones.

Even though Strossmayer in no document admitted that he had had access to the documents of the Council of Trent, it seems clear that he and the other bishops of the opposition had availed themselves of their contents during Vatican I sessions. It becomes equally clear, as Lord Acton states, that Pius IX « was not quite consistent » in dealing with A. Theiner: once encouraging him to publish the *Acts* of the Council of Trent and later on forbidding

---

[97] See correspondence Voršak-Rački AJA XII A 810/33 and XII A 810/34. The first letter of N. Voršak to Rački is dated Rome August 3, 1873 and the second one November 28, 1873. – Strossmayer himself became distressed after learning that the documents (transcripts) – especially the correspondence between the presidents of the Council of Trent and the Roman Curia – once in A. Tteiner's possession – were turned over to the Vatican officials by N. Voršak, and thus the scholars were deprived of an opportunity to study the Council of Trent thoroughly. Cf. KRS, II, 256. (Nicholas Voršak was officially appointed by the court of Vienna, Austria, to act as an executor of the last will of A. Theiner. He (Voršak) disposed of all belongings (except the transcripts of documents) of the late Theiner by giving them to the children of his sister. Cf. AJA XII A 810/50 – Voršak's letter to Rački, dated Rome May 29, 1879.

[98] Cf. AJA XII A 810/50. See also Voršak's letter to Strossmayer (dated Rome August 26, 1874). AJA XI A/Vor. Ni. 67. Fr. A. Theiner did not leave any kind of testament. Cf. Voršak's letter to Strossmayer (dated Rome August 13, 1874). AJA XI A/Vor. Ni. 65.

him. Sad to say, the Pontiff kept using Theiner as tool, completely disregarding his person. Besides, the rumor that Acton was indeed engaged in purchasing documents from Theiner was not unfounded, even though it did not occur during the Council but prior to it.

This sad and complex story can serve as an example what happens within the Church when basic human rights are not respected and the supreme authority uses its prerogatives whimsically and arbitrarily, if not tyrannically: It is a fact that during Vatican I the bishops were forbidden access to some documents, found in the Vatican Archives, so that they could not use them to defend and expound their proposals. This absolutist policy of Pius IX and of the Roman Curia offers us an insight into the lives and actions of honest individuals, how they behave once they are within the framework of absolutism and to what means they resort under unreasonably imposed regulations.

5. - The Opening of the Vatican Council: Freedom of Speech

From what has been said at the outset of this chapter it appears that dogmatizing papal infallible teaching was not intended to be placed on the agenda of the forthcoming Council. Pius IX himself constantly kept asserting that since this papal charisma was practically uncontested, the said dogma was no motive for him to convoke the Council, and in reality he acted as though it had been already conferred upon him[99]. All of Europe prior to the Council – especially Catholic circles – was humming with the apprehension of the definition of papal infallibility. To describe all the pertinent incidents revelant to this issue and to give a detailed picture of the Council's developments would take a lot of space and time. Our aim here is to offer the essential views of the Bishop on the major issues of the Council, this will illustrate his belligerence to papal infallibility.

From the very opening of the Council until its closing he per-

---

[99] *History of Freedom, op. cit.,* 496.

sistently accused it of depriving the bishops of the freedom which should be accorded to them on account of their divine rights and because of the practices established in the former ecumenical councils[100]. It almost looks as if he sensed immediately that they were « entrapped » after the Bull *Multiplices inter* was distributed at the beginning of December, 1869, and which contained the fixed procedures for the work of the Council.

Emil Ollivier, a French historian, took great pains in comparing the procedures at the Council of Trent with those set-up in *Multiplices inter*. The results of his research are as follows: At Trent the council Fathers had the initiative in introducing proposals for debate, while at Vatican I only the Pontiff was entitled to propose topics for discussion. A small qualification must be added: the council Fathers at Vatican I were allowed to introduce subjects for deliberation, but these had to be approved by a special commitee, appointed by the Pontiff. At Trent neither the Council's agenda nor regulations were laid down ahead of time, while Vatican I was just the opposite; various deputations at Trent to formulate decrees were named or elected by council Fathers; at Vatican I preparatory commissions had their meetings before the Council convened, and they were chosen by the Holy See. At Trent theologians submitted subjects to those with a voting right – and these topics were previously and publicly debated; – at Vatican I council Fathers were handed already formulated schemas[101]. The differences are obvious. The main divergence was that the initiative was shifted from bishops to the Pope.

The first note of protest against the set procedures in *Multiplices inter* was drafted by Strossmayer and signed by twentysix bishops (Cardinal Schwarzenberg, Haynald, Dinkel, Kenrick, Ketteler, Smičiklas, Legat, Dobrila etc.)[102] This memorandum, dated January 2, 1870, was addressed to the Pontiff. The Bishop in the

---

[100] « Strossmayer's criticism (of the suppressed freedom of speech) was not without justification » (H. Jedin, *op. cit.*, 206).

[101] É. Ollivier, *op. cit.*, I, 466-501. Cf. also J. Hennesey, *op. cit.*, 33-35.

[102] CP, pp. 285-286. Most probaly this was communicated to Cepelić and Pavić by Strossmayer himself. The style and the ideas are obviously Strossmayer's.

polite but resolute manner stated that the « members of the Council, if they deem in their conscience that something has to be brought out or proposed for the common good of the Church, have also the right to do so by their offices... and besides we follow in this matter the footsteps of the Council of Trent ». He also underlined in the same note that this is not a privilege, as some prelates wish to interpret it, but a right. Thereafter he offered the proposal that some bishops of the Council should be placed on the committee[103] which granted a permission to a certain bishop to introduce a proposal for debate. Then he concluded: « Let those bishops, who wish to bring subjects for discussion before the Council, be allowed to have a free access to that committee, and thus have an opportunity to participate in debates »[104]. The Pontiff did not find it opportune to answer this memorandum in writing, but he simply sent a message through the Secretary of the Council Mgr. Fessler; and the latter communicated orally to Cardinal Schwarzenberg that the Pontiff opined that his Bull did not abrogate unchangeable bishops' rights, and thus *Multiplices inter* « must remain unchangeable as it is »[105]. Evidently the Pontiff interpreted Strossmayer's memorandum in the sense which had been attributed to it by its originator, namely, the lack of freedom.

A short digression will clarify the background. In all probability the note of protest was written before January 2, 1870; it was in some respects a brief summary of some ideas Strossmayer had expounded in this speech of Dec. 30, 1869. From the report od Canon Voršak to Rački (dated in Rome Dec. 31, 1869) it appears that Pius IX knew that the Bishop of Djakovo had drafted the letter. There is no other way to explain the intervention of Cardinal de Luca, one of the Council's Presidents, who was sent by the Pontiff to ask Strossmayer not to speak in the general assembly.

---

[103] The Pontiff has appointed a special committee whose duty was to examine all the proposals introduced by the bishops, then this committee can refute them or accept them in consultation with the Pope.
[104] Mansi 50, 217.
[105] *Ibid.*

(Strossmayer was the first who had already submitted his name in the general assembly of Dec. 10, 1869, to be the speaker. This he had done after being approached by some French and German bishops to speak up in the Council on their behalf). When he refused to comply with the wish of the Pope, he was told by Cardinal de Luca that « he will never get a red hat, and that he is denying it to him on behalf of the Pontiff »; what is more, he also instructed Strossamayer that the « procedure laid down by the holy Father is unalterable »[106]. This mild threat and the confrontation with the « impossible » did not deter him from speaking on Dec. 30, 1869. This also accounts for the strong statement in his first speech that « he follows the dictates of his conscience and convictions ». This incident most certainly had triggered off the battle between Strossmayer and the Infallibilists (the Pontiff included) which continued relentlessly for quite some time.

In the second memorandum also of January 2, 1870, addressed to the Pontiff and signed by 41 bishops from Germany and Austria (among them Cardinal Schwarzenberg. Cardinal Rauscher and Bishop Strossmayer) they petitioned the Pope that all the speeches of the Fathers should be printed and distributed to the rest of the bishops, and also that all schemas should be given out to the bishops in order that they may have a better insight into what had to be discussed and so that they may adjust their speeches, according to the schemas[107]. It seems that this petition, too, was justified especially in view of the fact that some of the Fathers were of weak voice, and that the assembly hall in which the sessions were held was of extremely poor accoustics. Had the schemas been given, most probably many repetitions would have been avoided, and there would have been less manipulation and intrigue behind the scenes.

The Pontiff again did not acknowledge this letter in writing, but he used once again « oral communication » through Mgr. Fessler to Cardinals Rauscher and Schwarzenberg. None of the suggestions

---

[106] AJA XII A 810/22 (Correspondence Voršak-Rački).
[107] A. SPILETAK, Biskup J. J. Strossmayer, op. ct., 129-130.

was accepted by Pius IX[108]. On January 7, 1870, fifty bishops (among them Strossmayer) petitioned the Presidents of the Council that the aula should be remodeled so that the speakers can be easily heard. On the back of it one of the Presidents wrote that they would try to do something about it[109].

To the fourth memorandum of the opposition (dated March 4, 1870) ninety signatures of bishops, belonging to various national groups, were attached; this letter was an energetic protest against the Bull of the Pontiff *Apostolicis litteris* of February 22, 1870, in which still further and more precise restrictions were introduced. The new ruling of *Apostolicis litteris,* that the Council's decrees and definitions would be voted upon by numerical majority, greatly disturbed and provoked the opposition. This meant that the last weapon was taken out of the opposition hands, and the wedge between the belligerent parties of the minority and the majority was still further driven. The prelates of the opposition in their memorandum tried in vain to change the situation. Their appeal to the procedure of the Council of Trent in which Pius IV had instructed his legates at Trent that all decrees should be agreed upon by moral unanimity of the Fathers; their threat that « their conscience would be weighed down with intolerable burden, and that they would fear that the character of the Council might be called into question and its authority undermined, as lacking freedom »[110], their energetic insistence that, in defining a certain doctrine, a consent of the entire Church representation should be obtained – quoting in their favor R. Bellarmine and Vincent of Lerins[111] – all this remained like « vox clamantis in deserto ». The Cardinal Presidents replied to this memorandum by simply stating that the Bull *Apostolicis litteris* did not violate in any way the rights of bishops, and

---

[108] *Ibid.,* p. 130.
[109] *Ibid,* p. 131. Voršak in his dispatch of January 9, 1870 informs Rački that the aula in St. Peter's Basilica – where the Council sessions are held – was somewhat readjusted by heavy drapery, and the speakers can be heard easily. AJA XII A 810/23 (Correspondence Voršak-Rački).
[110] Quoted by D. Butler, *op. cit.,* 219. Cf. also R. Aubert, *op. cit.,* 334-335.
[111] A. Spiletak, *op. cit., Biskup J. J. Strossmayer, op. cit.,* 134.

that they could not change anything « what has been ordered and promulgated by the Pontiff ». Their duty was to safeguard and execute the Pope's decree[112].

Strossmayer was one of signatories of the note of protest. None of the prelates of the opposition reacted so vehemently against the newly introduced regulation as did he. His letter from Rome to F. Rački of March 8 is mixed with indignation. The letter runs:

« Here I am in a hurry with a few words. During these days they have issued 'decretum' (he is referring to *Apostolicis litteris* of Febraury 22) which totally deprives us (bishops) of freedom and which, instead of the old practice of moral unanimity, introduces numerical majority; which is drafted according to their own whims and desires. Besides, today they issued a decree " De infallibitate papae " which is so inconsiderate and absurd that nobody expected anything like that. The question is now: what? I thought that we – us bishops between hundred and hundred thirty – should be steadfast like a cliff, ascertaining, that this Council is not a true council since it is deprived of freedom and since it has replaced the eternal and immutable rule of faith and of the Catholic Tradition by the majority of votes. (The last sentence he put in Latin: 'aeternae et immutabilis Fidei and catholicae traditionis regula funditus eversa per maioritatem numericam'). It is sad that our (Croatian) bishops[113] are not willing to join this decisive act. Hence it follows that personal infallibility of the pope will be defined in the strictest form. I must remain by my convictions in order to save my conscience and honesty before God and mankind. Afterwards, may God and the luck of a hero allot me whatever it may be. I shall do what I must do, then I shal return home...

« The Roman emperors were made gods by the subservient senate; today someone (he is referring to Pius IX) is making himself a God, and we have to attach our signatures to it. I cannot bear that disgrace, and I cannot subscribe to the detriment toward

---

[112] *Ibid.*, p. 135.
[113] The Croatian bishops were members of the opposition: Djuro Smičiklas of Križevci, Juraj Dobrila of Poreč-Pula and Bartol Legat of Trieste. KRS, I, 102, note 2.

which the Church is heading. May God be with me and the rest of us »[114].

On the very same day he had already written to Rački, a letter which is relatively calm. In this letter he complained that the order in the Council was once again so arranged and restricted that there was no freedom and « they can shut up our mouths any time ». Finally, he stated that Infallibilists with their excessive demands were capable of destroying the Church. The only good thing that could come out of the Council is to prevent the evil (He meant the definition of papal infallible teaching) and prepare the way for the better and freer council whose first duty should be to reform the Roman Curia[115].

From those two letters it is evident that the bishops became infuriated when on March 8 an appendix on the papal infallibility was added to chapter eleven of the schema *De ecclesia Dei* (on the Church of God) which had already been distrituted to the Fathers on January 21, 1870. His indignation against the procedure and practices in the Council remained relentless until its very closing. In his letter from Rome to Rački of June 6 he stated that they had given up the freedom of speech, and that the majority would devide the minority by introducing an ambiguous formula on papal infallibility. At the end of the same letter he declared « Rome will never see me again »[116].

---

[114] KRS, I, 101.
[115] *Ibid.*, pp. 100-101. More or less all Church historians say — so does Cardinal Gibbons — that there was freedom of speech in the Vatican Council. « Nothing can be more untrue than to say that the Fathers of the Council of 1870 were deprived of liberties », writes J. Gibbons, *op. cit.*, p. 20. The rest of the objections against Vatican I and its practices, for instance, that various deputations were appointed by the Pontiff, that the Deputation of Faith — which was the most important body in the Council — were all the members of the majority (except Mgr. John Simor who prior to the Council in his Pastoral letter declared himself in favor of infallibility and arriving in Rome he changed his stand and switched to the minority) and that the Deputation to reject or to accept the proposals introduced by the Fathers was appointed by Pius IX himself, Cardinal Gibbons solves all these objections by stating that the Pontiff has the right, the majority rules and that the authority and the person of the Pontiff had to be protected by all means. *Op. cit.*, pp. 180-182
[116] KRS, I, 107.

6. - Strossmayer's Plans in the Council

It is obvious from all the reports that he was against any kind of definition of papal infallibility; he did not want to make any compromises in regard to his question. Only under this perspective can his other movements within the committees outside of the Council can be understood. Besides, of course, he held his unchangeable position that the Church was in no need of new dogmas, and that he wanted to discuss current problems of that epoch which troubled the world in general and the Catholic Church in particular. Papal infallibility hardly fitted into his concept of the Church.

Undoubtedly, his opposition to defining this dogma was greatly intensified by the manipulations of the members of the majority and especially those of Archbishop Manning whose living quarters were the centre of intrigues[117]. In addition, it is hardly believable, after careful perusing the reports, that there was much of good will displayed on the side of the Pontiff or on the side of the majority toward the minority and their pleas[118]. The tension between these two parties reached its peak by the end of February and by the beginning of March when it became obvious that the schema *De summo pontifice* would be introduced and it would get priority before even the Church and her structures were debated at all.

For the sake of better understanding of the Council and of the position of the minority it is necessary to point out that the members of the minority had already petitioned the Pontiff in their letter of January 12 not to place papal infallibility on the agenda of the

---

[117] D. BUTLER, *op. cit.* 141. We do not hold that Strossmayer's feelings toward Archibishop Manning were cordial all the time. On the other hand, it is evident from the Bishop's writings, as he began to move closer and closer to the acceptance of the Vatican Decrees, that his attitude toward Manning commenced to change and assume the form of friendliness. In his Pastoral letter of March, 1877, he paid a great tribute to the endeavors and accomplishements of the Archbishop of Westminster and Lord Spencer. Cf. GBBS, V (1877), 63-66 and especially p. 65. Besides, the Bishop of Djakovo sent a telegram to the Archbishop of Westminster on the occasion of his sacerdotal golden jubilee.

[118] D. BUTLER, *op. cit.*, 221.

Council. The main points of this letter are: first, it is strange that some bishops (the majority) approve what ought to be proven; secondly, it is unnecessary to define this dogma further since the Catholics already obey and respect the decrees of the Holy See, and since erudite and holy men teach that whatever the pope teaches *ex cathedra* on matters of faith and morals is irreformable even without the consent of the Church. However, they had qualified the latter by stating that there are quite a few objections to it in the Church Fathers and in other Church documents[119]; and unless these objections were resolved the doctrine of papal infallible prerogative could not be defined as being God's revealed truth. Besides, if this doctrine were defined, it would give a chance to some governments to intensify their attacks on the Church and her rights, and it would also cause great difficulty to the Catholics. On account of this they suggested that the best solution to the question of papal infallibility and of the rights of pontifical primacy would be to remain by the definitions of the Councils of Florence and Trent, and that these formulations might serve as an open door to the Greek Orthodox. They also professed that an ecumenical council is not valid without the pope, but on the other hand they called to the

---

[119] Undoubtedly, the members of the minority had particularly in mind the case of Pope Honorius who – on account of his two letters to Sergius, Patriarch of Costantinople – was condemned as a heretic along with the other leading Monothelites by the Sixth Ecumenical Council in 681. It is unquestionable that Pope Honorius sided with the so-called heretics. Mgr. K. Hefele wrote during the Vatican Council *Causa Papae Honorii*, Naples, 1870. Cf. H. KÜNG, *Structures of the Church, op cit.*, 260-261, note 25, and RSCV, p. 262.

In my dissertation presented at St. Anthony's College (Romae, 1947) *Doctrina Praecipuorum Monotheletarum Saeculi VI et VII* I analysed the teaching of the Monothelites and arrived at the conclusion that they were not real heretics but their principal fault was, not using the proper terms. In reality they taught the orthodox doctrine but they refused to use the word « two ». Pope Honorius did the same thing. It is anoter question whether or not the two « heretical » letters of Pope Honorius were *ex cathedra* pronouncement. I maintain they were.

Cardinal Newman in his debate with Lord Gladstone over the papal infallibility opines that « Honorius words were not ex Cathedra, and therefore did not proceed from his infallibility ». *Newman and Gladstone: The Vatican Decrees* (Introduction by Alvan S. Ryan) (University of Notre Dame Press, 1962), 179. In my opinion Newman's interpretation of Honorius' case deserves special attention – especially pp. 180 and 200. It seems that there is some discrepancy in his approach to the problem.

Pontiff's attention the fact that according to R. Bellarmine, in defining a certain doctrine the apostolic tradition and the testimony of other churches is required[120]. This document manifests best the position of the majority of the opposition not solely in regard to papal infallible teaching but also in regard to the requirements for dogmatizing a certain doctrine: concurrence and testimony of the churches.

Most certainly the protest of the minority of May 8 was the most strongly worded document signed by 71 prelates and addressed to the Cardinal Presidents. This document was drafted in connection with the change of procedure of April 29 when the Presidents had interrupted the debate on catechism and Church discipline, and had proposed a discussion of the primacy and infallibility of the Roman pontiff. The Presidents motivated this unexpected change by the explicit desire of many Fathers who wanted to discuss these topics which in recent times had created grave anxieties in the souls of faithful[121].

In this memorandum the members of the minority expressed that, in spite of their ardent desire to bring to an end the existing discordance in the Council, they felt it imperative to inform the Presidents that the new order was not in accordance with the nature of matters under the discussion, nor did it serve the welfare of the Church and the repute of the Holy See. In their judgment it was impossible to discuss one part of the Church without the others. This meant that the entire structure of the Church ought to be canvassed and the rights of all her members be established. On this point they formulated their thoughts in the following manner:

« The Church of Christ and the Roman pontiff are not one and the same subject, and since the infallibility of the Church and that of the pope is defended, then it becomes clear that the infallibility of the Roman pontiff cannot be discussed before the doctrine of the supreme teaching authority of the holy mother Church is cleared up and before the relationship between the teaching of the Ro-

---

[120] Mansi 51, 678-679.
[121] *Ibid.*, 467.

man pontiff and the infallibility of the magisterium of the Church of Christ is secured. Furthermore, it is necessary that each debate begins with that what is certain and plain, and about what there cannot be disputes. The infallibility of the Church of Christ is held by all Catholics, and there is no doubt about it; this, however, cannot be ascertained about personal infallibility of the Roman pontiff. First of all, the Church and her infallible magisterium are bound to be deliberated, and then the teaching authority which pertains to the Roman pontiff within the Church of God; and this order is followed by more learned theologians. Finally according to the schema of March 6 (appendix added to chapter eleven of 'De ecclesia Dei') it should be defined that the infallibility of the Roman pontiff and that of the Church covers the same object. How can this conscientiously be examined and judged, and how can this object (of the infallibility) be defined if the Church and the object which falls within the scope of her infallibility are not debated? »

They also unhesitantly expressed the fear that if solely the prerogatives of the pontiff were defined, this would create new prejudices against the Church instead of making her more presentable to the world. They felt obligated to resist this change of procedure as strongly as possible in spite of their love and respect for the Pontiff and in spite of the repeated calumnies thrown upon them[122].

Implications are also found in the said Memorandum that the original plans for convoking the Council, outlined in the Bull of June 9, 1868, and in another papal allocutions to remedy the then existing evils, were changed, and that the Pontiff himself has contributed to it[123]. The Presidents were reminded of the awareness

---

122   Pius IX used to call the bishops of the opposition « Pontius Pilates » and occasionally referred to them as « the enemies of God ». Cf. RSCV, pp. 258 and 277. Naturally, some prelates of the opposition reciprocated by labeling the Pontiff (especially Mgr. Maret) with such epithets as « imbecile », « ignorant », « liar ». Mgr. Maret even put Pius mental sanity in question, and that he should be dethroned. Cf. RSCV, p. 262.

123   « It was not until March 1 that Pope confirmed the decision; and on March 6 the public announcement was made that the infallibility was to come before the Council », writes D. BUTLER, op. cit., p. 286. Secretary of State Cardinal Antonelli on March 25 « strongly urged » the Pontiff to withdraw the infallibility question. « The Pope answer was 'I have the holy Virgin with me: I will go on!' » (op. cit., p. 282). Cf. also H. JEDIN, op. cit., 214.

of the public of this sudden switch[124], and the signatories found it extremely difficult to defend the honor and authority of the Holy See in face of all things that have been done by a certain group of the Fathers who were using the Council as a tool in vindicating the opinions of some theological schools. In addition, they stated that if they would work out the entire doctrine of the Church, the forthcoming feast of Pentecost would be a joyous event, but as the matters stood it would be a day of sorrow. (One wonders how they could accomplish all that in such a short time).

The conclusions of their Memorandum, which touches upon the way they and their petitions were ignored in the Council, assumes a form of some resignation mixed with exasperation or better yet of total powerlessness: « We feel somewhat satisfied that we have manifested our convictions without submitting any petitions. It is incongruous with our episcopal dignity, it is inappropriate to the office that we perform in the Council and to the rights which belong to us as to the members of the Council that we submit any petitions any more since we have learned from the past experiences that our petitions do not deserve any consideration; and they are not even worthy of any reply. Nothing else is left to us but to voice our criticism in protesting against the reversal of the procedure which we maintain to be detrimental to the Church and to the Holy See; and thus we free ourselves of any responsability before men and before the judgement of God from all evil consequences which hence will arise in the near future, and they are already appearing. Let this letter of ours be an eternal testimony to it »[125]. This letter was read at the meeting of the Cardinal Presidents, and no answer was given. This annotation was scribbled on the back of it by Mgr. Fessler, the General Secretary of the Council[126].

The chief reason why we have brought the preceding letters of protest of the opposition was that one can see the plans of the mi-

---

[124] It is interesting that the very same idea was expressed by Tkalac in his dispatch of May 8; then he added: « It becomes obvious that the sole purpose for convoking the Council was to obtain the dogmatization of the infallibility » (RSCV, p 276). Quirinus also goes along the same lines. Cf. D. BUTLER, op. cit., 225.

[125] MANSI 51, 727-732.

[126] A. SPILETAK, op. cit., 145.

nority, what they intended to discuss and how they felt about the
procedures and the other matters in the Council. Undoubtedly,
there were many divergent views among them and what course
they should have undertaken in counteracting the schemes of the
majority. At this place it should be said that the French opposition
was more moderate than German. This should not surprise anybody
since there were so many forces at work in France which were unfavorable to the French bishops. It suffices to mention that the French
clergy and even personnel of the chancery offices from all over France kept bombarding the Vatican with their petitions that papal infallibility should be dogmatized[127].

Therefore, there is no wonder that Mgrs. Darboy and Dupanloup kept reminding the opposition that « they should proceed with
the utmost caution as not to arouse in the Pontiff any doubts about
their orthodoxy ».[128] Hefele and Strossmayer held the furthest flank
of the opposition, and Cardinal Rauscher at the beginning shared
their constancy and implacability. At the international meeting of
January 24, 1870, held in Rauscher's quaters, he remarked that « if
we accept this schema (De ecclesia Dei), then we (bishops) will be
simply chaplains of the pope », Strossmayer at the same gathering
advocated the use of parliamentary means in order to protract the
debates until the end of the month of June (when it gets hot in
Rome), and thus to fight point by point[129]. Evidently this was the
advocacy of filibustering.

When on March 6 the topic of papal infallibility was inserted
into the schema De ecclesia Dei, great uneasiness was created
among the bishops of the minority. On March 12 the meeting of
the Austrian and German bishops was held, and Ketteler and Strossmayer engaged in a heated discussion on the course of counteraction to
be taken. While Ketteler upheld « the use of the utmost modera-
tion », Strossmayer was extremely radical in his proposal. There-

---

127 RSCV, p. 254. Louis Veuillot did more than his share in this campaign. Strossmayer, several years after the Vatican Council, calls him *papa
laicus infaillible et intollerable* who divided the church of France and hated
Mgr. Dupanloup. Cf. KRS, III, 346.

128 RSCV, p. 251.

129 *Ibid.*, p. 233.

after Ketteler quit the meeting, and Strossmayer declared that he would do the same thing if they (the opposition) did not approve of his policy. For a moment the bishops remained silent, then Mgr. K. Hefele stated that there was only difference in form, and that they shared Strossmayer's views. Thereupon the bishops asked him to draft a proposal[130], and he immediately complied. This is the text of Strossmayer's proposal:

« 1. Mgr. Strossmayer will take charge of speaking up in each congregation and also in the solemn session and of making known in the name of the opposition, or if he is not authorized by it, then in his own name that he protests against each decree of the current Council upon which it (the Council) would vote, for this Council is deprived of the essential characteristics of an ecumenical council such as of freedom of speech and of the due respect for the apostolic rights of the episcopate; furthermore, that the decision of the majority of votes is contrary to all the former councils[137] where the decrees were voted upon by the entire church (on the basis) of the near unanimity which represents the consensus of the universal Church.

« 2. If this proposal is rejected, the opposition – in order to save its conscience – will propose the dissolution of the current Council.

« 3. If the dissolution of the Council is rejected, the opposition will protest, with the manifesto addressed to 'Urbi et Orbi', against the violation perpetrated against it (the opposition), then the opposition will quit the Council in spite of threats of anathema, and it will appeal to a council which is going to be free and canonical »[132].

Strossmayer's propositions were heard with a deep silence. Cardinals Rauscher and Schwarzenberg with K. Hefele declared themselves in favor of them, and promised to propose them to the French and American bishops for discussion[133].

---

130   *Ibid.*, p. 241.
131   This can be said to a great extent about the Council of Trent bu not about « all the other ecumenical councils ».
132   *Ibid.*, pp. 241-242.
133   *Ibid.*, p. 242.

Several more remarks must be brought out. First of all, Strossmayer wanted to quit the Council. On April 20 he expressed himself unequivocally on this matter in his letter to Rački: « This coming Sunday, April 24, a solemn session will be held in which
I must say 'non placet'[134] and this should be done by the entire oppostion, then we should walk out and free ourselves of any responsibility. However, I cherish no hopes that the opposition will have
that much courage. It is said (by the opposition): 'O, my God,
what consequences from this act (of walking out on the Council)
will follow', and we the blind men do not see that on account of
our compliance the worst consequences will befall the Church »[135].
Lord Acton also refers to this plan of Strossmayer in his study
« The Vatican Council »[136].

Even though Strossmayer's propositions were ill-fated and never carried out, the opposition apparently did not cease to search
for a more moderate formula and policy in counteracting the plans
of the majority in the Council. At the meeting of March 30 Mgr. K.
Hefele had brought out another suggestion with the following
points: 1st, that the pope does not have the right to decide on matters of faith and morals if a considerable number of bishops oppose
such a decree; 2nd, the pope must not side with one party in the
Council; 3rd, if the decisions reached are contrary to the Tradition

---

134   He did not attend that public congregation but absented himself.
135   KRS, I, 102.
136   « To wait for unanimity was to wait for ever, and to admit that a
minority could prevent or nullify the dogmatic action of the papacy was to
renounce infallibility. No alternative remained to the opposing bishops but
to break up the Council. The most eminent (Acton meant Strossmayer) among
them accepted this conclusion, and stated it in a paper declaring that the
absolute and indisputable law of the Church had been violated by the Regulation (of February 22) allowing articles of faith to be decreed on which the
episcopate was not morally unanimous; and that the Council, no longer possessing in the eyes of the bishops and of the world the indispensable condition of liberty and legality, would be inevitably rejected. To avert a public
scandal, and to save the honour of the Holy See, it was proposed that some
unopposed decrees should be proclaimed in solemn session and the Council
immediately prorogued », writes Lord Acton in History of Freedom, op. cit.,
540. The similarity between Strossmayer's proposal and Acton's description
is so striking that no one can have any doubt about « the most eminent
among them » was the Bishop of Djakovo.

of the Church, they neither obligate the Fathers who protest against them nor their faithfull[137]. Mgrs. Hefele and Ginoulhiac were nominated to give it a final form and then bring it up for a discussion. Strangely enough Hefele's recommendation was never drafted, let alone brought up either before any national or international meeting of the opposition[138]. It shared the same fate as Strossmayer's offer.

Perhaps Odo Russell's report will clarify best the attitude and the motives of Mgrs. Ketteler and Hefele who « warned them (the opposition) against the rupture with Rome which could not benefit the Catholic Church, since the history of Councils proved that the bishops who had attempted it had stood out in the cold without achieving their objective in the end »[139]. This also elucidates where Hefele and Strossmayer stood and where they parted: the former wanted at all costs to work through and remain in the Council while the latter intended to walk out on it, as actually occurred at the last stages of the Council. Both British writers Odo Russell and Lord Acton, vis à vis the opposition and their maneuvers in the Council are correct: the first finds the cause in their reluctance to leave the Council while the second one attributes it to the « inertness » and « fear » of the opposition; and both latter elements stem from the fear of walking out of the Council.

In connection with this topic there are more incidents in regard to Strossmayer's position versus the Council. First of all, he did break up the Council on March 22. This was precipitated by his speech with supposedly « offended the pious ears » of the majority, and it was considered « the one real 'scene' of the Council »[140]. We quote a portion of his oration which created that commotion and which brought to an end the session for that day that one may see better the mentality which prevailed in the Council. It runs:

---

[137] RSCV, p. 255.
[138] Cf. *Ibid.*, pp. 261, 271 and 277. K. Hefele in his conversation with Tkalac accused Mgr. Ginoulhiac for the lack of courage to write the chartered proposal. See RSCV, p. 261.
[139] N. Blakiston, *The Roman Question*, 440.
[140] Cf. D. Butler, *op. cit.*, 236; H. Jedin, *op. cit.*, 208, and R. Aubert, *op. cit.*, 336-337.

« My second remark concerns the paragraph (which begins with these words) 'Nemo siquidem ignorat proscripta a Tridentinis patribus haereses etc'. (Everybody knows that the heresies were condemned by the Fathers of the Council of Trent). This statement, Venerable Fathers, concerns Protestantism; the venerable bishops, who worked on correcting this text, maintain that the source and origin of all evils and errors, which have inundated the world from the time of the Council of Trent until now, is Protestantism; and they even call Protestantism and its subsidiaries in the following paragraph an 'impious pestilence whose venomous virus has gotten even a hold of the sons of the Church'. To put at ease these men, who are more erudite and distinguished than myself, I wish to say that the first paragraph seemes to me it is neither in conformity with the truth and let alone with charity.

« It is not in conformity with truth. It is true, however, that the Protestants carry the responsibility for refuting and despising this authority of the Catholic Church by submitting to the subjective judgment and opinion not the religious matters, as the schema states, but the matters of faith, that is, the eternal and unchangeable truths of faith. There is no doubt that through the breath of this human pride and corruption the source to many evils was open within the Church, certainly, rationalism, criticism and some other ugly errors have their origin in it. But we have to know that the seed of Protestantism and rationalism – which are connected with each other -- was in existence prior to the sixteenth century; it existed in the so called humanism and laxism which some distingui- shed men in Protestantism indeed incautiously favored and propagated. Had the seed of Protestantism and rationalism not preexisted it is hardly conceivable that such an insignificant spark could have caused such a conflagration in the centre of Europe which we were unable to extinguish until this very day.

« Secondly, nobody can deny that the scorn of the Church, religion, faith and of every authority just as well the most pernicious doctrines without the paternity and cognation of Protestantism originated in the midst of the Catholic nation – at the time of Voltaire and the Encyclopedists. These doctrines did not come to us through the intervention of Protestantism, but they were inaugurated among the Catholic people: this corruption of heart and spirit, as it is known, has caused such a massacre that, by destroying all the foundations of human society, it filled the regions in a never heard of manner with human corpses and blood. Nobody can say that this infection is somebody else's but our own which we should expiate with bloody tears, and whose poison is still spreading, and it threatens with great dangers the present society.

« Finally, we must refute – we even must condemn – that the members of the venerable deputation while writing the genealogy of naturalism, materialism, pantheism, atheism – all these without any specification attribute to Protestantism. There is no doubt that these doctrines are very dangerous; equally so there is no doubt that all means are to be employed to eradicate them from human conscience and from the entire world. As far as I remember the first venerable speaker said that materialism and other similar errors had originated at the time of the Council of Nicaea in the school of Alexandria and from there they began to spread; therefore I deem that it is not in conformity with the facts to ascribe these most pernicious errors solely to Protestantism. Besides, there are also among the Protestants some grave men – they are indeed grave – who had offered a great help and support to th Church and us in combatting these errors and monstrosities. I shall mention only one of the old ones, Leibnitz, a learned and well acquainted man with the institutions of the Catholic Church and also a courageous man in battling against the errors and eliminating evils who also employed all his abilities to establish peace among the Christian communities.

« I would like to say a little more on this matter. All of you remember how you shuddered over the terrible book of (Ernest) Renan in which he attacked the divinity of our Lord Jeus Christ. Marvelous things had been said by bishops and theologians in refuting this error – indeed marvelous and of every praise worthy. There is no doubt that we also recall that there were glorious men among the Protestants who had courageously attacked the book and defended Jesus Christ. I shall mention one or two. Who does not know Guizot who responded, and whose meditations on faith -- of course with a few exceptions – I would like to see in your hands (the Fathers murmur in protest) – if possible; he writes about such things which we would never expect to hear from him: many topics discussed in his books deserve our admiration. Therefore, I maintain that there are many men among the Protestants in Germany, England and the United States of America who follow the footsteps of men like this, and who love our Lord Jesus Christ; and they deserve the words of Great Augustine to be applied to them 'They err indeed but they err in good faith (murmurs): they are heretics, heretics; but no one holds them for heretics' ».

(At this point Strossmayer was interrupted)

The President, Cardinal de Angelis: « I pray you, Rt. Rev. Father, to refrain from words that cause scandal to some Fathers ». Strossmayer went on in the same sense with words no caught by the stenographers; but he was cut short by Cardinal Capalti, one of the Presidents, who said that it was not a question of Protestants but of Protestantism, not of the persons but of the heresy; modern errors do arise from the principle of Protestantism, private judgment; therefore it is not against charity to say that these monsters of error are derived from Protestantism.

Strossmayer: « Most cordially I thank your Eminence for this instruction; but your argument does not convince me that all these errors are to be attributed to Protestants. I believe that there exists in Protestantism not merely one or two, but a crowd of men who still love Jeus Christ » (Murmur).

Cardinal Capalti: « I beg that you stick to what the schema says. This is the expression which is applied to the Protestants. It is said that the errors – condemned by the Fathers at the Council of Trent – became divided into manyfold and diverse sects. You can see, therefore, that Protestants are not mentioned; the sects are only mentioned which are condemned by the Council of Trent. The venerable Fathers will judge about the other numerous sects which have derived from the first heresy. It seems to me, indeed it seems that there is nothing which might offend the Protestants. Therefore I beg you that you desist from such speech, which, I must frankly say, offends to ears of very many bishops ».

Strossmayer answers: « I finish. I must certainly know many men who live among Protestants and who wish from the bottom of thei heart that nothing should be put into the texts which would prevent the efficacy of the grace of God which is also at work among them. I also know that at the Council of Trent, whenever Protestantism was discussed, the problem was approached with the utmost caution, prudence and charity. The Council of Trent says that the Council was convoked at Trent – on the border of Germany – to offer an opportunity to Protestants to come to the Council. At the end the Council of Trent also says: if the Protestants would come into our midst, we would receive them with love and kindness; none the less we have discussed their matter in such a way that it seemed that we did not discuss so much our own cause as theirs. I would like that they don't... ».

(Strossmayer was interrupted again).

Cardinal Capalti: « Our most Holy Father took care of that matter, after having arranged ecumenical council, when he invited all the Protestants with the apostolic letter. If they wish to return to the light, let them do it without a delay; and they will find a motherly heart in the Roman Pontiff and also in this Ecumenical Council (Signs of approval are being heard). Let us rather affirm that the Church was always the most gentle mother; let us not make such comparisons which somehow are offensive to the zeal of the shepherds of the Church. The Church was always full of love toward all those who are in error or who are heretics; this did not prevent her, however, to condemn the errors and at the same time to ascertain the truth about the doctrine. It seems to me, I repeat, it seems to me if we wish to speak truthfully your remarks in regard to this matter are not based on the text of the Schema which might give a chance to Protestants to continue their hatred toward the Catholic Church ».

Strossmayer: « I finish; but against one observation of your Eminence I must say just one word... ». (He was interrupted again).

Capalti tried to speak, but immediately, Fathers on all sides murmuring, Strossmayer said: « I attribute this to the deplorable conditions of this Council ». (An uproar of indignation made it almost impossible to hear what he said).

Strossmayer went on: « I would like to make a third observation, which is going to be short, extremely short, and which concerns the essence of things; and it so moves my conscience that I can by no means keep silence. It was said that we would vote; in the dec-cree, which was given to us as a supplement to regulate the proce-dure of the Council, it is said that questions are to be settled by a majority of votes. Against this some bishops have put in a state-ment, asking if the ancient rule of moral unanimity... ».

The speaker's words were made inaudible by the renewed and increased murmur of general indignation.

Cardinal Capalti: « This does not belong to the present discus-sion ». Vehement applause followed. Strossmayer tried to go on. Most of the Fathers shouted him down; they almost raged; many called on him to come down.

Strossmayer: « Your Eminence certainly should pardon me. I respect the rights of the Presidents. I certainly if the old rule, which is eternal and immutable, of a moral unanimity, morally unanimous... ». The speaker's voice was drowned in the uproar of indignation. Strossmayer said: « I protest against any interruption, I... ».

Fathers rising called out: « We protest against you ».

Strossmayer: « I protest against any interruption ».

The First President rang his bell again and again.

The Fathers generally: « We wish him to come down; let him come down ».

Strossmayer: « I protest against... » (And he began to come down). The indignant Fathers left their seats, all murmuring dif-ferent thinghs. Some said: « These men are against the infallibi-lity of the Pope; is this man (Strossmayer) infallible himself! » Others: « He is Lucifer, anathema, anathema! » Others: « He is another Lucifer, let him be cast out! » And all cried out: « Come down, come down ». But he kept on saying: « I protest, I pro-test », and came down.[141]

Nobody can believe that the prelates had acted toward Stross-mayer according to their position and dignity[142]. What caused their undignified behavior is hard to say. We do not believe, however,

141 Mansi 51, 74-77.
142 R. Aubert, op. cit., 337.

that it was solely his bold defense of Protestants and his advocacy of being more charitable in dealing with the other Christians which precipitated such an uproar in the general congregation and brought that session to an abrupt end; nor are we of the opinion that he, in this particular instance, was off the topic which would have warranted the intervention of the Presidents except, of course, if we assume that they can exercise their presidential rights arbitrarily. It is possible that Strossmayer's boldness and his continuous assertion of his independence became intolerable to the Infallibilists and to the Roman Curia who wanted to see every bishop to fall « in line »[143]. It can be said, however, that Strossmayer was out of order on one point, that is, when he brought in his heated debate with Cardinal Capalti a moral unanimity – required for defining articles of faith – but again he threw this in when the tumult of the Fathers was in full swing. Therefore his mention of a moral unanimity was no cause at all, but it rather was an additional fuel to the already blazing fire.

The following day the Bishop drew up a note of protest (sent to the Presidents) in which he required satisfaction, stating that he was not certain if there was place for him any more in the Council where freedom of bishops was suppressed – as it was the case with his oration of the previous day and where articles of faith are defined « in the new and unheard of way in the Church of God »[144].

---

[143] « ... Strossmayer... was called twice to order by the Cardinal Speaker », writes Odo Russell on Dec. 30, 1869, « but the Bishop, less obedient than his predecessors (on the ambo), asserted his independence, repeated the sentences for which he had been reproved and completed his oration amidst the approbation of the Fathers of the opposition... » (N. Blakiston, op. cit., 377). One can hardly share Cardinal Gibbons' opinion: « When the Bishop would see the hand (of one of the five Presidents) in close proximity to the bell he would dexterously return to his subject, and thus avert the humiliation of an admonition ». Op. cit., p. 27.

[144] History of Freedom, op. cit., 542. The question of moral unanimity even after the month of February used to come up from time to time in the circle of bishops outside the Council. On May 12 Mgr. Riccio (who voted non placet in the fourth solemn session of July 18 but later on he switched his vote), Bishop of Cajazzo, approached Strossmayer and told him that more than 150 Italian bishops would side with the opposing bishops, if the Italian government would offer them protection against the revenge of the Holy See. The purport of Mgr. Riccio's visit to the Bishop of Djakovo was that he intervenes, on their behalf, with the Italian government. Strossmayer

In any case, Strossmayer and his speech greatly contributed to the fact that the language in the schema on the Protestants was considerably toned down[145]. It is interesting that immediately after the oration was delivered, he was complemented by his colleagues, but later on Cardinal Schwarzenberg told him that « while he approves of his ideas, he disapproves of his violence », to which Strossmayer retorted: « If there were any violence, the Janizaries of the Vatican are responsible for it »[146].

Neither O. Russell nor Lord Acton mention any attempted violence on Strossmayer's life whereas « Letters from Rome » and Imbro I. Tkalac allege that Mgr. Castaldi, the Pope's ceremoniarius, had jumped upon the tribune from where Strossmayer spoke, and cried out that « he would throw headlong this heretic »[147]. Stross-mayer, several years after this incident had taken place in the council, recounted it to his friend, French publicist Compte Begouen, and he did not say a word to him about anybody's intending to do him a physical harm. However, he had mentioned in this interview that the police had tried to secure their way by force into the hall to protect his life or that of whoever happened to be in danger. Strossmayer also communicated to Begouen that the most vociferous against him had been Spanish and Italian bishops while a great number of French – especially Mgr. Place of Marseille – and German bishops had clamored in his favor[148]. It appears that the voices of the minority were simply drowned by those of the majority. This becomes even more evident from the records of the stenographers; who simply put in writing the outcries of the majority. Three days after the incident Mgr. Castaldi publicly said that the only reason for his mounting the rostrum had been to open the

---

denied having either direct or indirect contact with the said Government and advised Riccio that one of the Italian hierarchy should contact the Italian officials. Cf. RSCV, p. 280.

[145] D. BUTLER, *op. cit.,* 238-241. Cf. also N. C. EBERHARDT, *op. cit.,* 539; RSCV, p. 251, and H. JEDIN, *op. cit.,* pp. 206-207.

[146] RSCV, p. 250.

[147] *Ibid.,* pp. 248-249.

[148] C. BEGOUEN, *loc. cit.,* pp. 69-70. See also E. OLLIVIER, *op. cit.,* II, 246-247.

grill for Strossmayer that he might come down[149]. The most remarkable observation on this scandalous uproar in the Council against Strossmayer was made by O. Russell: « The consequences of this incident may become very serious if cleverly handled by the opposition »[150]. The opposition did not press the issue, and it remained as « the memory of the past » as Strossmayer stated to Begouen.

(During the course of the Vatican Council four solemn sessions, over which the Pontiff himself presided, were held: December 8, 1869, and January 6, April 24 and July 18, 1870. Strossmayer only attended the first two, while from that of April 24 he absented himself on account of the conclusion of the schema in which implicitly papal infallibility was inserted. The last and final solemn congregation of July 18 he refused to attend with the rest of the opposing bishops. In this session papal primacy and infallibility were officially proclaimed).

Undoubltedly, the most crucial moment for him during the session of the entire Vatican Council was the solemn congregation of April 24 when he was actually left completely isolated. In spite of his being versed in parliamentary procedures this caused in him some consternation not being certain either to attend the session and vote « non placet » or to absent himself[151]. Tkalac claims that Strossmayer opted for the latter on his advice[152]. We are of the opinion if anybody had to do anything with his decision, it was Lord Acton. This again confirms that the Bishop did not abandon the idea of walking out of the Council. This plan was shared by Lord

---

[149] RSCV, p. 250.

[150] N. BLAKISTON, op. cit., 412. The above statement of the British Envoy is significant. He had a great admiration for Lord Acton's talents, energies, and virtues, whom he regarded to be the soul of the opposing bishops. Ibid., p. 385 and passim. Odo Russell expressed his mind on the controversy of infallibility with these words: « I admire his (Acton's) creation, I bow before his genius and I wish the opposition all the success they have so earnestly at heart, but I adhere to my conviction that humanity will gain more in the end by the dogmatic definition of Papal Infallibility than by the contrary » (ibid., pp. 385-386).

[151] RSCV, p. 265.

[152] Ibid., p. 270.

Acton, too[153], and according to Russel, Lord Gladstone was in favor of it[154].

Strossmayer with the other eighty bishops of the opposition on June 4, 1870, had handed a letter of protest to the Presidents. In this short letter they complained that it was contrary to the procedures of general congregations to stop the debate on the schema « De ecclesia Die » which (the cloture) was requested by one hundred-fifty signatures of the majority. They reiterated that a doctrine which is about to be defined as revealed by God cannot be brought to a close without giving a chance to all the Fathers to pass their judgment on it[155]. This indicates that they were referring once again to moral unanimity. The General Secretary of the Council, Mgr. Fessler, gave an oral reply to Cardinal Schwarzenberg. The answer that the Presidents had proceeded according to the regulations set down by the Pontiff himself, and subsequently they could not do anything about it[156].

Toward the end of the Council Strossmayer changed somewhat his attitude; his belligerency lessened considerably. We do not maintain that this change in him occurred due to the influence of F. Rački, since he shared the Bishop's opinion on papal infallibility[157]; it should not be excluded, however, as possibility that Cardinal Antonelli, with whom he kept contacts during the stormy days of the Council, gave him a hint on what was going on in the Vatican vis à vis his person[158]. In any case, the Bishop in his letter to Rački

---

153 « However, Acton who knows his men and is in favor of a protest and departure 'en masse' of the Opposition, still thinks it possible at the last moment, so I hope I may be mistaken in my estimate of the character of R. C. Bishops of the Opposition ». N. Blakiston, op. cit., 442 (Dispatch of June 9, 1870).

154 « Mr. Gladstone... thinks that if the Opposition Bishops could join in a protest against Infallibility and leave Rome 'en masse' it would be a great blow to Ecumenicity » (ibid., p. 441).

155 Mansi 52, 444.

156 Ibid.

157 « ... the greatest blessing that could befall the Church and the Holy See would be the postponement of the Council... », writes Rački to Strossmayer on July 3. KRS, I, 104. In the same letter Rački writes that « those in Rome are preoccupied with infallibility instead with the reunion with the Eastern Church ». Ibid., p. 105.

158 Ibid., p. 107.

of April 24 strongly indicated what sort of situation existed in Rome: « Here (in Rome) there is an immense corruption. These Romans employ the same weapons against me which the Germans and the Hungarians used against me in order to paralyse my political influence »[159]. When Strossmayer was notified by Rački that people would like to arrange ovations in Zagreb and Slavonski Brod on the occasion of his return from Rome[160], he replied to him on July 6 that he would rather return without any ovations. « It is my duty », he continued, « to save myself to our nation as much as possible. Today I have to be more cautious than ever before. The Roman Curia would like to see me destroy myself and our government wishes me the same thing. In these circumstances I have to be careful. First of all, however, conscience and honesty are to be saved. If the latter can be accomplished, and if at the same time one can remain considerate as not to give an opportunity to the enemy (the Roman Curia) to get rid of me, I think this is our duty... »[161]. At this point we should add that Strossmayer in his last letter from Rome of July 9 had unequivocally put the blame on the opposition for the lack of courage, and consequently « the Pontiff would win to his and to the Church detriment »[162].

By the report of Tkalac of June 6 Strossmayer still was in favor of attending the final solemn session and of refuting in it the entire schema[163]. By June 27 he suggested to the opposition to go to solemn session and to disprove all the decrees reached in the Council by voting « non placet ». This proposal was listened to with a due respect at the international meeting of the opposing bishops, but was rejected[164]. Finally, we find Tkalac on July 17 having a dinner with the Hungarian bishops who accused Strossmayer of being an « inspirateur » of the idea of absentism from the solemn session of July 18[165]. Both Tkalac and the Hungarian hierar-

[159] *Ibid.*, p. 102.
[160] *Ibid.*, pp. 105-106.
[161] *Ibid.*, pp. 106-107.
[162] *Ibid.*, p. 108.
[163] RSCV, p. 296.
[164] *Ibid*, pp. 317-318.
[165] *Ibid.*, p. 332. However, the Hungarian bishops showed « admiration for Strossmayer's talents and courage », reports Tkalac (*ibid.*, p. 333).

chy were correct as far as Strossmayer's attitude or rather his change of the attitude is concerned. The Bishop wanted the whole opposition to cast their votes by « non placet » in the solemn session, but when he perceived that there would be a small number of those who would say « non placet » then he commenced to advocate absentism so as not to become conspicuous in the eyes of the Roman Curia. This perfectly fits into his plans expressed to Rački « of saving himself to his nation ». Strossmayer's suggested plan to the opposition of walking out of the Council had finally become a reality at the very end of the session of the Council – of course, in much milder form than he had originally envisioned. Had the opposition complied with the plan of Strossmayer of the month of March when he proposed walking out on the Council, what the outcome of the Council would have been, it is difficult to say.

Undoubtedly, the best picture of the last days of the Council and of the stand of the opposition is offered in this letter, addressed to the Pontiff himself, of July 17, on the very eve of the solemn session. This letter was signed by fifty-five bishops, Strossmayer among them:

« Most Holy Father:

In the general Congregation held on the 13th of this month we gave our votes on the schema of the first Dogmatic Constitution concerning the Church of Christ.

Your Holiness is aware that 88 Fathers, urged by conscience and moved by love of Holy Church, gave their votes in the words 'non placet'; 62 others in the words 'placet iuxta modum'; finally about 76 were absent and gave no vote. Others had returned to their dioceses on account of illness or other serious reasons. Thus our votes are known to Your Holiness and manifest to the world; and it is notorious how many bishops endorse our view; in this manner we have discharged the office and duty which lies upon us.

Nothing has happened since to change our opinion, nay rather these have been many and serious events which do not allow us to depart from our position. We therefore declare that we renew and confirm the votes already given.

Confirming our votes therefore by this present document, we have decided to be absent from the Public Session on the 18th of this month. For the filial piety and reverence, which very recently brought our representatives to the feet of Your Holiness, do not allow us in a cause so closely concerning Your Holiness to say 'non placet' openly and in the face of the Father.

Moreover, the votes to be given in Solemn Session would only repeat those already given in General Congregation.

We return, therefore, without delay to our flocks, to whom, after so long an absence, the apprehensions of war and their most urgent spiritual wants render us so necessary; grieving that in the existing sad condition of things, we shall find the peace and tranquillity of consciences disturbed.

Meanwhile, with our whole heart, commending the Church of God and Your Holiness, to whom we avow our unaltered faith and obedience, to the grace and protection of our Lord Jeus Christ, we are, of Your Holiness, the most devoted and obedient sons »[166].

A brief explanation is postulated at this place in connection with the above quoted letter. The signatories of the letters, by stating that « there have been many and very serious events which do not allow us to depart from our position », most certainly had in mind the clause « and that such definitions of the Roman Pontiff are therefore irreformable because of their nature, but not because of the agreement of the Church « which had been added to the definition of papal infallible teaching on July 16, and had been approved by a large majority of votes. Whether or not the Fathers had sufficient time to deliberate this clause and to envision its implications is a question which continues to engage Church historians and theologians.

7 - His Arguments against the Dogmatization of Papal Infallibility

It has been stated several times that Strossmayer was against defining any new dogmas and that the existing dogmas – in his judgment – if applied and interpreted correctly, would suffice to remedy the present ills of the Church and of human society. However, when

---

[166] Mansi 52, 1325-1326.

he attacked the Code of Canon Low for some of its inadequate and obsolete laws and for the dubious origin of some of them, and when he insisted on forming an international commission composed of the most erudite men to bring the Code of Canon Law up to date, he ventured to state that according to Vincent of Lerins even a dogma can undergo a certain growth which has to be of the same gender and in the same sense[167]. The Bishop believed, in other words, in the development of a dogma even though, as we shall see later on, he was not so susceptible to this reality in regard to the dogma of papal infallibility.

At this point it is of particular interest to us to see what stand Strossmayer had taken on the dogma of Immaculate Conception, proclaimed by Pius IX in 1854, since in this instance papal infallibility was in its fulness exercised. As far as we know there was only one of the opposing bishops in the Vatican Council who had questioned the validity of the above dogma; and that was Archbishop Kenrick of St. Louis, Mo[168]. Strossmayer, on the other hand, had attached some explantion of his to this dogma. This was manifested in his Pastoral Letter of Febraury 21, 1855, addressed to his clergy: « My Dear Sons and Brothers! We announce to you a great joy in the Lord that the supreme Pontiff Pius IX, a common Father and Shepherd of all believers, has declared the doctrine of the Immaculate Conception of the Bl. V. Mary a dogmatic one; and thereby he proposed it to all of the Church of God to be believed with the certitude of irreformable faith by the privilege of his authority. This happiest event, which is very much in accordance with our desires and piety, please explain to the faithful – entrusted to your care – on the Feast of the Annunciation (March 25) ». Hereafter he urged his clergy to explain this dogma on the basis of the Bull *Ineffabilis Deus;* then he requested them most earnestly and emphatically to stress to their faithful the following passage of his Pastoral: « Nothing new is introduced into the Church by this dogmatic definition except only that, what prior to this (definition) has been tacitly believed in the hearts (by con-

---

167   Mansi 50, 488. Cf. *Symbolism*, II, 67 in the notes.
168   *History of Freedom, op. cit.,* 544-545.

sensus) of all the faithful, is now explicitly and by the solemn profession of faith acknowledged and believed; and that this growth of faith is of the same gender, of the same contents and of the same meaning »[169]. The last clause of the cited paragraph is quotation of Vincent of Lerins.

From the above interpretation, given by the Bishop, of the dogma of the Immaculate Conception several things become apparent. First of all, he admits the dogma, defined by Pius IX, due to his papal position within the Church; secondly, he affirms that the doctrine of the Immaculate Conception is in harmony with the wishes and piety of the faithful; thirdly, he denies that anything new is brought into the Church as far as faith is concerned, and he qualifies it by stating that the only novelty is in the mode, that is, what has been previously tacitly believed, now it is professed explicitly; fourthly, he specifies the transition from a tacit belief to the explicit one when he utters that the dogma at both stages (tacit and explicit) is of the same kind, with the same contents and with the same meaning which points out again that the Pontiff's solemn declaration only added a new mode; fifthly, it appears from the context that he does not invest the inerrancy or as he calls it the « certitude of faith » in the Pontiff but it is rather found and deposited in the « consensus of the faithful »; sixthly, it becomes evident from the way he had formulated it that the Pontiff is simply the voice or the mouth piece of the entire Church. At any rate, it appears to us that, whoever accepted the dogma of the Immaculate Conception, he *materialiter* endorsed papal infallibility; and the only thing, that was left, was its formal recognition which actually was a matter of time.

The reasoning of Strossmayer on this point we cannot detach from that of J. A. Möhier. There is a striking similarity between these two personalities on this issue. Möhler also places a great emphasis on the « general sense » of the Church; and the community is in possession of Christ's promises and gifts[170]. Further-

---

[169] CP, p. 271 (Document is registered under no. 146 in the archives of the Diocese of Djakovo).

[170] « The general sense decides against particular opinion – the judgment of the Church against that of the individual: the Church interprets

more, he discovers the inerrancy of the Church « in the episcopacy united with the general head and centre... for, it represents the universal Church, and one doctrine of faith, falsely explained by it, would render the whole a prey to error »[171]. Undoubtedly, Strossmayer was cognizant of the fact as J. H. Newman was[172] that Pius IX consulted bishops, cardinals and even a certain segment of faithful prior to the dogmatization of the Immaculate Conception; and the Bishop on numerous occasions in his writings referred to this fact.

However, the most astonishing resemblance between the Bishop and Möhler is grounded in their views on personal infallibility. Even though Strossmayer did express only implicitly on what grounds he recognized the above mentioned dogma, we feel justified in assuming on the basis, of course, of what has been said earlier that he did in the sense which Möhler so beautifully had formulated: « To no individual, considered a such, does infallibility belong; for the Catholic, as is clear from the preceding observations, regards the individual only as a member of the whole; as living and breathing in the Church. When his feelings, thoughts, and will, are conformable to her spirit, then only individual attains the inerrability. Were the Church to conceive the relation of the individual to the whole in an opposite sense, then she would destroy the very notion of community... »[173]. We, most certainly, perceive in this statement a great likeness between him and the Bishop according to whom « the feelings, thoughts and will » of Pius IX were in total accord with those of the Christian commu-

---

the Sacred Scriptures. The Church is the body of the Lord... He dwells in the comunity; all His promises, all His gifts are bequeathed to the community – but to no individual, as such, since the time of the apostles », writes Möhler in *Symbolism*, II, 34-35.

[171]   *Ibid*, p. 77.

[172]   Quoted by Jean Guitton, *The Church and the Laity* (Alba House, Staten Island, N. Y., 1965), p. 31. See also Cardinal Newman's article « On Consulting the Faithful in Matters of Doctrine », reproduced by J. Guitton from *The Rambler, op. cit.*, pp. 63-111 – especially pages 77-78. Strossmayer in his Pastoral letter of 1881 follows Newman's footsteps. Excerpts from this Pastoral are found in Mansi 53, 1000. Cf. also TS, p. 437.

[173]   *Symbolism*, II, 10. E. Hocedez maintains that Möhler was on the road of becoming an infallibilist. E. HOCEDEZ, *op. cit.*, 248.

nity. In the Bishop's dependence on Möhler we discover the reason why he had so frequently reiterated in the Vatican Council, in his struggle against dogmatization of papal infallibility, « personal and absolute infallibility ».

Furthermore, in our judgment the influence of Vincent of Lerins was more powerful on him than that of Möhler or for that matter of anybody else except, perhaps, of St. Cyprian. His attachment and devotion to Vincent of Lerins never left him, but stayed with him until the moment he expired. It seems as though he was obsessed by Vincent's classical work « Commonitorium ». This especially goes for Vincent's statement: « In ipsa item ecclesia catholica magnopere currandum est ut id tenemus quod ubique quod semper, quod ab omnibus creditum est » (PL, L, 640) — (In the [same] Catholic Church a special care must be taken that we maintain what has always been believed, at all times, in all places by all the faithful »). It is practically impossible to find any of his Pastoral letters in which he would not have made a reference to Vincent of Lerins. Sometimes this reference would be like a thunderbolt out of the blue sky as it is the case in his correspondence with Lord Gladstone[174].

Some more remarks ought to be made before we bring out his arguments against the dogmatization of papal infallibility. Now and then the Bishop might look at first glance to be inconsistent in his views especially vis à vis papal infallibility, but on the other hand we must keep in mind that he was not precise all the time in expressing his thoughts, and that he was occasionally carried away by his sentiments. His Pastoral Letter of June 4, 1859, in which he praises papacy to the sky, is the epitome. In describing why bishops have to go « ad limina » he alleges among other reasons that the Bishop activities in their respective dioceses « can be either approved or corrected by the judgment of the infallibile authority... by the one who is the heir of the power, love and mercy of the Lord... »[175]. It would be presumptuous to think that

---

[174] CBSG, p. 438 (Strossmayer's letter of April 11, 1878 to Gladstone). Cf. also KRS, IV, 230; GBBS, XXI (1893), 38, and *ibid.*, XXVI (1898), 45 and passim.
[175] JJS-DK, p. 427.

he had in mind papal infallibility. One more thing ought to be added in order to understand better his position on the dogma of papal infallibilty; and this concerns his notion of the growth of a dogma.

He undoubtedly admits the development of a doctrine, but it looks though that he was so forcefully attached to his own interpretation of the theological ideas of St. Cyprian, Vincent Lerins and of the other Church Fathers that it was hard and painful for him to make a further step. This stagnation, so evidently displayed by him in the Vatican Council, must be ascribed to his inner theological formation and partly to his fervent dislike for the dogma of infallibility which would bring eventually great difficulties upon the Church.

In addition, we believe that Lord Acton had in mind Strossmayer when he stated that there would be an extremely small number of the opposing bishops who would absolutely reject the doctrine of papal prerogative[176]; and the Bishop was one of this small number. Nobody can deny that during Vatican I it was excessively difficult for him to embrace Möhler's conception that the faithful during the course of history « obtain a clearer and more intuitive knowledge » of a certain doctrine contained in the Scripture[177]; nor was he susceptibible to the allegory of his intimate friend, Vladimir Soloviev, of an accorn and a potential oak tree which grows out of it. (Naturally, Soloviev developed this idea quite a few years after Vatican I). In the mind of Soloviev primacy and papal infallibility were acorned in the holy Scripture and in the early Christian Tradition, and later on they have reached their full growth in all their dimensions[178]. He simply – almost obstinately – stuck to the principle of Vincent of Lerins « quod ubique, quod semper, quod ab omnibus creditum est » of which Möhler wrote: « How desirable it were, that we could find everywhere such clear notions of the progressive development of Christian

---

176 *History of Freedom, op. cit.,* 528. Cf. also J. Oʙᴇʀšᴋɪ, *Hrvati..,* *op. cit ,* 24-25.

177 *Symbolism, op. cit.,* II, 54.

178 V. Sᴏʟᴏᴠɪᴇᴠ, *op. cit.,* 116-117.

dogmas, as are here advanced by Vincentius! »[179]. In spite of his intransigency on this issue in Vatican I, later he would align himself with the conceptions of J. A. Möhler.

We sincerely profess that we do not know to what extent his stand on this charism of the pope was influenced by the schemes and manipulations perpetrated in the Council by the Pontiff himself, the Infallibilists and the Roman Curia by changing and rearranging the procedures in the Council to fit their plans. We are not certain either if he had been irritated by some statements of Pius IX, which can be hardly theologically correct and justifiable, as for example, when he stated « I am the Tradition », or when he told Cardinal Schwarzenberg: « I, as John Mastai, (Pius' family name) believed in the infallibility; as Pope, I do not ask the Council for anything, the Holy Spirit will enlighten »[180]. However, it is evident that he resented greatly the set-up in the Council which saw placed on the key deputations solely those who were in favor of papal infallibility except Mgr. John Simor[181]. Nobody wishes to deny ecumenical character of Vatican I, but it was a great anomaly that 40% of the entire European episcopate were Italians; the five Presidents of the assemblies were Italians after Cardinal Reisach died; two-thirds of the consultants and all the secretaries, except Mgr. Fessler, were also Italians[182]. Naturally, all this was in a direct conflict with his fundamental notion of the universality of the Church.

It has been repeatedly pointed out that papal infallibility did not fit in his ecclesiological conceptions but on the other side we should not neglect to bring up his further objections against it, of which some can be classified as of theological nature, while the others belong to the sphere of forewarning and practictability. Practically at the very beginning of the Council, in his speech

---

[179] *Symbolism, op. cit.*, II, 67 in the note.
[180] E. OLLIVIER, *op. cit.*, I, 535. Fr. C. Schrader admitted to Tkalac that it was not fair on the part of Pope Pius IX to throw the responsibility for dogmatizing infallibility on the Roman Curia and the Jesuites. Then Fr. Schrader made the following observation on the Pontiff's stand in regard to his dogma: « What one wants, he gets » (RSCV, p. 337).
[181] D. BUTLER, *op. cit.*, 147.
[182] R. AUBERT, *op. cit.*, 324-325.

of January 24, 1870, he warned the council Fathers not to drag « this power (papacy) – given to us by God to protect the spiritual welfare of all – into something which is not opportune... and which would mean to comprise this divine institution in the eyes of nations if we, in our ardent affection, keep on exaggerating the rights of papacy »[183].

Regardless of what someone might opine of Vatican I and its positive effects and achievements in establishing the prerogatives of the Roman pontiff, we affirm that Strossmayer's forboding and premonition were correct, viewed in the light of the subsequent incidents which had taken place in the later months of the Council and what had been written and said against papacy by some opposing bishops[184]. We do not intend to go into this, but on the other hand we feel tempted and urged to cite some observations or rather reflections of I. Tkalac, expressed so succinctly in his last report from Rome to Visconti Venosta of July 21, 1870 – just a few days after the Constitution had been solemnly promulgated. Tkalac – as it has been stated previously – was a liberal but well versed in the topics debated in the Council and also well acquainted with the incidents – most probably not less than Lord Acton and Odo Russell. His reflections sound somewhat exaggerated, but nobody can deny that they contain a grain of truth. Besides, we deem them interesting especially in view of the present upheaval within the Church. Here are some of his reflective thoughts:

« The triumph of the (papal) infallibility and that of the society of Jesus is accomplished, but it was purchased by the price of blood. Papal infallibility has destroyed the infallibility of the Church and that of the episcopate united in an ecumenical council; it erased with the stroke of a sponge the apostolic institution of episcopate and of holding general councils, and it has crowned the edifice of papal absolutism which had been on the march sin-

---

[183] MANSI 50, 484. This also offered a chance to the Bishop to publicly defend Mgr. Dupanloup against the attacks – launched by some Catholic newspapers. It is obvious that he had in mind Louis Veuillot and his newspaper L'Univers. Ibid.

[184] Mgrs. Dupanloup, Kenrick, Rausher, Hefele. Cf. RSCV, p. 263.

ce the nineth century... it will take several generations of struggle until this dogma establishes itself and finds its place in the new organisation of Catholicism. The intoxication with papal omnipotence will redouble the outcry of the Hussite Cardinal Schwarzenberg 'reformatio in capite et membris'.

« This papal superhuman authority has paid very dearly for its apotheosis. It was anatomized, cut and dissected like a cadaver, and this is the greatest merit of Minority; neither a fiber nor a artery (of it) was left untouched and unscathed. Since the time of the Council of Costance the papacy did not suffer such an affront and humiliation. It was reproached with all infamies, lies, frauds and faults through which it was formed and maintained. The authors of 'Janus' were not so cruel as Schwarzenberg, Hefele, Dinkel and Americans Purcel and Verot and Greek Youssouff. Mgr. Purcel has condemned (papal) temporal power as a pestilence which the Roman Curia attempts to save by way of one dogma in order to exploit the patient (papal temporal power) which is in the process of putrefaction and decomposition. Mgr. Verot said that an ounce of genuine faith is worthier than million books of Roman teachings...

« The Jesuits have debased the episcopate and have canonically destroyed it; the episcopate, in return, will revenge and debase papacy; and the authority will be corroded. So much evil is mutually (on both sides) done that it goes without saying that they fought against themselves and inflicted almost incurable wounds upon themselves. Hatreds are awakened which neither time nor the change of circumstances will appease and assuave. The abyss, created between the papacy and the episcopate by this Council, will devour the authority of the both, and especially in the countries where Catholics live in communion with Protestants and Schismatics and where scientific theology will not be able to resist the influence of heterodox doctrines »[185].

---

[185] *Ibid.,* pp. 335-336. Tkalac's dislike for the Jesuits was not an isolated case, it was shared by Lord Acton who, however, made a distinction between those Jesuits who worked directly for Pope Pius IX whose « instrument » he became, and those with their Father General, Roothan, who did not want to identify the Order with the writings of the *Civiltà Cattolica.*

Let us return to some other arguments of Strossmayer against papal infallibility. When finally it became evident during the heat of debates that papal prerogative would be made into a dogma, he in his last speech, full of arguments against it, threw in some more suggestions as to divert the Council from defining it. First of all, he highly praised the Council of Trent for refraining from dogmatizing it; and when Archbishop Manning and some other prelates of the majority stated that the said Council had not a chance to define it, he retorted: « If this chance (vis à vis Protestants who had made questionable the supreme authority of the Church) had not been offered to the Council of Trent, then there would never be a chance to define it ». To his former statement that the Catholics listen to the Holy See he added that « it is dangerous to contradict the pronouncements of pope even in the instances when it seems that we are justified by our conscience to do so... »[186]. What is more, the Church of God in her existence of eighteen centuries rather preferred to exercise the charism of infallibility than to make it into a dogma[187].

These recommendations he deduced from analyzing the Church Fathers. Naturally, he elaborated first on his favorite theologian St. Cyprian, according to whom there is « one episcopate and one flock which is fed by the consensus of all the apostles ». Needless to say, that he was driving at the unity of the epscopate with the head and also at the moral unanimity in the Council. In relation to this he took into consideration the biblical texts Matthew ch. 16

See *History of Freedom, op. cit.,* 497-498. Cardinal Newman wrote to Mgr. Ullathorne on January 28, 1870 — after having stated in the same letter that no doctrine *de fide* can be a « luxury » — then he continued to say that « others doubting about the capacity possessed by bishops, drawn from all corners of the earth, to judge what is fitting for European society, and then again angry with the Holy See for listening to the flattery of a clique of Jesuits, Redemptorists and converts ». D. Butler, *op. cit.,* 183. (Newman later on was greatly distressed over the fact that this letter had become public. He said that this letter « was one of the most confidential that I never wrote in my life ».The question of this letter became an issue when Newman entered into a public debate with Lord Gladstone. See *Newman and Gladstone: The Vatican Decrees, op. cit.,* 168).

186 Mansi 52, 394.
187 *Ibid.,* 403.

and John ch. 21 « from which », as he uttered, « some prelates deduce with such certainly personal and absolute inerrancy of pope to what I cannot subscribe »[188]. In his mind all bishops are the shepherds and the pontiff is « the heir of the whole plenitude of power which pertained to Peter ». His dialectics found its great support in the dispute over the re-baptizing of heretics between St. Cyprian and Pope Stephen, and Firmilian and the said Pontiff; and it was unconceivable to him how a Saint of Cyprian's caliber could have resisted the Roman Pontiff, had papal inerrancy been so evident. « At least in third century », he went on to argue, « nothing had been known about personal and absolute infallibility of the Roman pontiff ». The African Saint, however, had been cognizant of the inerrancy of the Church and of that of pope « when the latter is initmately and undividedly united with the rest of the Church »[189]. His interpretation of the famous text of Irenaeus « all Churches in all places are in agreement with the Church of Rome concerning the 'potentior principalitas' is to be understood in the sense that the testimonies of the other Churches must be added to the principal holder of the Tradition which is the Church of Rome. St. Augustine's declaration that the consensus of people in matters of faith « keeps him in the Catholic Church » received the same explication and was aligned with those of Irenaeus and Cyprian[190].

In the Bishop's mind it was not sufficient to define a certain doctrine on the basis of the universal consensus of the Church at the fixed period of her history; one also ought to look into the antiquity of the Church to see what she believed in the preceding centuries. To corroborate his stand he quoted once again Vincent of Lerins' assertion *quod semper, quod ubique, quod ab omnibus creditum*. On the grounds of it he deduced that every doctrine *de fide* required these three elements: « antiquity, universality and consensus », these factors form one undivided entity, and that they cannot be separated from one another by sophism and subtle words[191].

---

[188]   *Ibid.*, 393.
[189]   *Ibid.*, 393-395.
[190]   *Ibid*, 400.
[191]   *Ibid.*

He obstinately insisted that every doctrine must have been manifested in each century and persistent through the centuries if it were to be defined. Though this might look ideal, in practicality it is unacceptable, and on the part of the Bishop it was grossly exaggerated. Most likely this was the crux of his difficulty in accepting the pope's infallibility. There is no other reasonable explanation for the fact that even in the subsequent years after he had professed and embraced the pope's prerogative, this problem kept popping up in his mind and he was constantly citing Vincent of Lerins. He expounded the teaching of Vincent of Lerins to the effect that the custodians of the deposit of faith are the entire Church and the universal body of the episcopate, and subsequently he came to the conclusion that « Vincent of Lerins did not know anything about personal and absolute infallibility of pope... It is my belief », he said, « if we wish to follow his doctrine and footsteps, let us not define anything without the censensus of all... »[192].

No matter how much we may disapprove of his interpretation of Vincent of Lerins, he still was logical, in terms of his notion of the Church. In his personal note of protest – addressed to the Cardinal Presidents – against making papal prerogative into a dogma he referred as « the most dangerous and perilous thing to the repute of the Church and of the Holy See », and begged the Pontiff to exercise humility and self-denial rather than to press for the definition of his personal prerogative. His two principal reasons were as follows: first, « when the prerogative od infallibility is discussed, neither the head has to be separated from the body nor the body from the head. We ascribe the infallibility to the whole body of the Church; it is superfluous to question in what of the same body is the seat of infallibility. We know that a human body has a soul, but the question remains unresolved in what part of the body the soul has its seat »; secondly, « there are quite a few objections against papal infallibility which is impossible to solve »[193].

---

[192] *Ibid.,* 400-401.
[193] Mansi 51, 1030. Strossmayer held that the inerrancy of the Church is voiced through the episcopate united with the pope. This by no means places him in the same category of I. Döllinger who did no believe in

In the latter part he most certainly alluded to the historical incidents which are difficult to reconcile with papal charism of infalliblity, for instance, the case of Pope Honorius who was condemned as a heretic quite a few times.

Another letter of protest runs somewhat parallel to the above cited one in the sense that everything in the Council is geared to assume the form of a strict legalism. In this note he blasted the Deputation on Faith for having so poorly drafted chapters ten and eleven on the Church of God that « nothing more shallow and more meager can be imagined than these two chapters) », and for not saying a word about the rights of bishops, but above all else he attacked the said chapters for making the primacy of the pope so « legalistic and contentious » instead of presenting it in so beautiful a fashion that pope's primacy by itself « would enhance everybody to love, obedience and admiration toward it »[194].

He proffered some more arguments which are of religio-social nature. In the first place, he contended that this papal prerogative is not in conformity with the mentality of modern educated men who detest to see such a power deposited into one mortal human being subject to all human weaknesses and vicissitudes. Furthermore, he warned the Council Fathers that the enemies of the Church were exactly waiting for something like it to defined in the Council so that they might expose the Church herself and her authority to all sorts of ridicule and also to discredit her in the eyes of the faithful and nations. As a matter of fact, he showed them a book by the title *The Necessities of our Epoch* with such contents, namely, that a certain segment of people were eagerly expecting such definition. According to his own testimony that book made him « so agitated that it brought tears to his eyes » (He did not mention

---

the infallibility of the united episcopate with the Roman pontiff, but he rather perceived it in the approval and ratification rendered by the entire Church. Cf. *History of Freedom, op. cit.,* 545.

[194] Mansi 51, 730-731. In the same letter he stressed his great surprise in seeing in the Schema on the Church that nobody can appeal from the pope to the ecumenical council since this is a *passe;* and it should not be revived. *Ibid.* On this point he was not quite consistent especially in view of his advocacy of walking out on the Council and appealing to another as we have seen earlier.

the name of the author of this book). At last he resorted to the time of St. Augustine and his struggle against the Manicheans who, for the very same reasons, ridiculed the Catholic Church for basing everything on the authority in her function[195]. (This parallel, drawn by him, between the old and modern Manicheans was not unfounded). This preservation of his was accompanied by murmurs of some of the Fathers, but he was not interrupted.

Finally, a few words on his favorite topic, ecumenism and the prospective reunion of the Eastern and Western Church. It appears that during Vatican I some of the Prelates directly or indirectly had touched upon pan-Slavism, and most certainly they had in mind Strossmayer. It is true, however, that he in his irenic advocacy of the reunification of Christians had included not only the Eastern and South-Slav Schismatics but he also pleaded in the Council not to write anything into decrees which might be offensive to the Protestants and to their religious feelings.

It almost seems from many insinuations that a certain compaign was waged against him on account of his ecumenical ideas and of his strong support for the reunion of the Greek Orthodox and Catholic Church. This had inundated not solely the circles in Rome, but it had spread to the other capital cities of the world, for instance, London and its leading newspaper, *The London Times*. This paper in its writings had gone so far as to state in its issue of May 1, 1870, that Strossmayer wanted to fuse the Catholic minority in South-East Europe with the Greek Orthodox Slavs for the sake of obtaining political unity of the South-Slav nations. Since similar and tendentious statements kept appearing in the British press, he was approached and asked by the British bishops to clear up the matter by issuing a communique; eventually he did comply with their wishes[196]. His communique under his name was published in *The Tablet*[197].

---

[195] Mansi 52, 402-403. It is noteworthy that Cardinal Newman in his confidential letter to his Bishop Ullathorne counted also on the mentality of the « European society ». See D. Butler, *op. cit.*, p. 182.

[196] KRS, I, 107-108.

[197] *Ibid.*, pp. 105-106. Unfortunately, Strossamayer — due to his preoccupations with the matters of the Council — did not have the time to write

In spite of all these unfavorable rumors concerning his Slavism and pan-Slavism he did not become frightened enough not to point out that the new dogma would be in the way to reunion of the Churches. Several times during the session of Vatican I he stressed that the various Eastern Churches cherish extremely their autonomy and their particular rights; and « if this planned definition becomes a reality, I am afraid that all the endeavors of bringing the Slav nations into the union with the chair of Peter wil become fruitless »[198].

After having exhausted all his arguments against papal infallibility and while pleading in his last speech with the Pontiff and the Fathers of the Council to refrain from defining this dogma, he injected the hope that « the Pontiff will save us from our anxieties »[199]. It almost sounds from the context that he was referring to his own personal and inner difficulties in accepting the dogma about to be defined.

In conclusion, it is apparent that the Bishop was fearful of the extreme Church theocracy. It almost appears from his writings and speeches that any either pre-Christian or Christian theocracy was tyrannical; it confounded Heavenly and earthly orders, spirit and matter, the affairs of the Church with those of State. Furthermore, under this perspective he was unable to find a sufficient room for Christian freedom to properly function in so huge a structure of theocracy since the Christian freedom in the final analysis is a renunciation of all claims to earthly powers and those supposedly

---

the aforementioned communique, but he rather asked N. Voršak to compose it, on his behalf. He told Voršak what to write, but unfortunetely the Canon did not formulate the Bishop's thoughts correctly: the whole communique sounded as though Strossmayer all along wanted to set up a trap for the Slavs of the Greek Orthodox Church by founding the Yugoslav Academy and the University of Zagreb. Since this communique was also published in the newspaper in Austria, Hungary and Croatia he felt a need to tell Rački to insert, at least in the Croatian newspapers, the following notice: « We know from very reliable sources that the Communique published in the British press did not come directly from the Bishop. Whatever in the said dispach can be wrongly misinterpreted is by no means the conviction of the Bishop » (*ibid.*, p. 107).

[198] Mansi 52, 403.
[199] *Ibid.*, 404.

spiritual ones which operate in the earthly fashion; and they are tinted by secular spirit.

There is another undercurrent of thought in all Strossmayer's ecclesiological ideas which is akin to the previous one. We have no documentation as to whether or not he was acquainted with the writings and ideas of Feodor Dostoievsky, but it is a most remarkable coincidence that Dostoievsky, Vladimir Soloviev and the Bishop shared the same outlook on power and human freedom as they should be practiced and understood in the genuine Christian sense. Dostoevsky in his master piece « The Grand Inquisitor » gave the interpretation to the three temptations to which Christ was subjected in the desert: to change stone into bread, to become a master of earthly kingdoms, and to perform a miracle. Christ refused most emphatically all the three suggestions, for He did not want to win human spirit either by bread or by might or by miracles but simply by His love and by man's free exercise of freedom in responding to God. The same explanations was given by Soloviev in his work *The Story about the Anti-Christ*[200]. Strossmayer on numerous occasions interpreted another incident from Christ's life, in the same sense: Christ fled into mountains when the multitude of people, after having being fed miraculously by Christ in the desert, intended to make Him a king. In the Bishop's interpretation Christ was not after any earthly power, nor did He want to win human souls and minds by miracles but by love. Since the Church is « the being of the being of Christ », then there is no wonder that Strossmayer time and again insisted that the only means that the Church can use in her divine mission is the love. Too much emphasis on power within the Church can only blur her focal point, the love, and thus drive people away. This also must be kept in mind in order to interpret correctly his strife against and his stand on papal infallibility and primacy.

---

200 NICHOLAS BERDYAEV, *Dostoevsky* translated by Donald Attwater) (Cleveland and New York, Meridian Books, The World Publishing Co., 1968), 188-212.

VI

AFTER THE FIRST VATICAN COUNCIL

After the Bull « Pastor Aeternus » – which contains the dogmas of papal primacy and infallibility – had been solemnly proclaimed in the solemn session of July 18, 1870, and after the opposing bishops, having handed a letter to the Pontiff, had left for their homes and dioceses without attending the solemn session, the period that followed can be characterized as a period of hesitation, struggle and pressure from Rome on the bishops of the minority to declare themselves in favor of the dogma of papal infallibility.

The French opposing bishops were the first to submit one by one their acceptance, and they were followed by the Germans. Finally, the most solid block of them all, the Hungarian bishops accepted the dogma. A special pressure from Rome was exercised upon Cardinal Schwarzenberg, Archbishop Kenrick of St. Louis, Mo. and Mgr. Haynald, who hesitated for a while then at last gave in[1]. It is ironical that the opposing bishops, who insisted so much in the Council on moral unanimity in defining a certain doctrine, would be the first ones to give their signatures and approval to what they so bitterly fought against; in other words, to become the means in accomplishing moral unanimity instead of numerical majority as it had been enacted by the regulations of Vatican I which (numerical majority) was the target of their attacks. At any rate, moral unanimity, if not in Council itself, then afterwards, was achieved on the doctrine af papal primacy and infallibility.

---

[1] Cf. D. BUTLER, op. cit., 417-438. It is interesting to note at this point that as late as 1875 Mgr. Haynald, Archbispop of Kalocsa, Hungary still kept denying ecumenicity to Vatican I. Canon N. Voršak in his letter from Rome (written on Easter Sunday, 1875) notifies Strossmayer that he had read the copy of the letter of Haynald, addressed to Cardinal Antonelli, in which the Archbishop of Kalocsa recognizes papal infallibility but negates ecumenicity to Vatican I. AJA XI A/Vor. Ni. 80 (Correspondence Voršak-Strossmayer).

After reading their declarations on the acceptance of papal charism one gets the most certain impression that they had at their hearts the welfare of the Church, and that none of them wanted to separate himself from Rome. Had not good will and loyalty prevailed on the part of the minority, the Church might have had the second edition of Protestantism in Europe. They deserve everybody's admiration, especially in view how they as bishops were treated by the Pontiff and the Chairmen of the Council who constantly ignored their petitions, protests, and paid no attention to their many wholesome ideas for the betterment of the Church.

We maintain, however, that there was something particular about Strossmayer in the post-Council years. While the Council was in session and while he knew what slanderous remarks Pius IX had made about him, he never reciprocated, nor did he go personally to the Pontiff to beg or to plead for anything; he thought that the Council was the place where all disagreements and grievances should be resolved. Time and again he asserted that he had never said anything disparaging or slighting against the Pontiff. It is a fact that he was extremely critical of the Roman Curia and of its personnel but he placed a line of demarcation all the time between the papacy and the Roman prelates. He referred to the dogma of papal infallibility to be a « disgrace » and a « shame » to the Church of God; he even stated that the Pontiff wanted them to act like a « Roman subservient senate as to make him a god ». It appears from the documents containing these remarks that they were uttered in the fit of anger and because of great disappointments for the lack of understanding on the part of those who wanted by *fas et nefas* to define this dogma of papal prerogative, and, of course, because he all along was convinced that this defined doctrine would be a detriment to the Church and to her future welfare.

After the closing of Vatican I Strossmayer still continued to be the centre of attention, especially in the central Europe in the years of 1870 and 1871. During this period the Prelate exchanged a few letters with I. Döllinger, Lord Acton and Professor Reinkens; all these letters were published by Prof. Schulte, chief organizer of Old Catholic movement. Both Teodor Granderath, S. J., in his famous work *Geschichte des vatikanischen Conzils* and Janko Oberški, founding his total research on Granderath's scientific results, in his booklet *Hrvati prema nepogrješivosti papinoj prigodom Vatikanskog Sabora 1869-1870* (Croats vs. Papal Infallibility at Vatican I) had eleborated on this correspondence of Strossmayer. Neither Granderath nor Oberški, in discussing Strossmayer and his posittion toward the Vatican definitions and the Prelate's correspondence with the German dissenters, did not have any other documents but the said letters; hence both scholars were occasionally doubtful. We cannot understand why Oberški did not make use of Strossmayer's Pastorals, which were easily available to him. Neither Granderath's nor Oberški's presentation of Strossmayer and of his case is complete and satisfactory.

At any rate, it becomes evident from the analysis of Bishop's letters that the Bishop of Djakovo did not comply with the wishes of either Reinkens or Shulte of Friedrich which had been expressed in their respective letters (By the way, none of these letters are preserved in the Archives of the Yugoslav Academy of Zagreb) to Strossmayer. From this correspondence, as it is presented by Granderath and Oberški, several facts become evident. First of all, they (German dissenters) wanted him to join their ranks; and Prof. Friedrich had gone in his letter as far as to beg Strossmayer to consecrate one of them to bishopric. (Strossmayer did not answer Friedrich's letter). It is true that the Prelate had denied in his letter to Reinkens the legality to Vatican I and the validity to its definitions, but on the other hand he had explicitly stated several times that he was a « thorn in the eyes of the governments of Vienna and Budapest and that he wanted by all means to preserve himself to his poor nation; and he would rather see the Austro-Hungarian episcopate to continue the struggle against Rome ». (Isn't this in accord with Strossmayer letter to Rački from Rome)? Besides, he had indicated unequivocally in his letters that he would never separate himself from Rome. Both Granderath and Oberški allege that the Vatican kept pressure on the disobedient bishops by denying the answer to their petitions (which the Bishop in his letter to Reinkens calls « tyranny »). Strossmayer in his sizeable correspondence never mentioned that such a pressure was practiced by Rome against him.

Strossmayer's letters flow with kindness and politeness; and it seems that he wanted to keep these individuals in union with the chair of St. Peter[2]. Therefore, we are justified in asserting that he never cherished for a single moment the idea of joining the Old Catholic movement of Germany. Even though he did keep contact with his close friend Döllinger for several years, this does not indicate that he accepted Döllinger's ideas[3] which were quite divergent from his especially in ecclesiology: The German theologian and historian taught that the definitions of a council are valid if approved by the entire Church and not solely by the bishops. It is too sad that F. Rački censored the passage in the Bishop's *Travelog* which dealt with his meeting with Döllinger, for this might supply us with a better insight into the person of the German Historian and Theologian. We must not omit the Bishop's last letter from Rome (to Rački) of July 9, 1870 in which he stated: « if our nation were mature, it would free itself from the foreign tutelage in politics and from the Romanism (spirituality of Rome) in the religious field »[4]. This by no means points out that he wanted to break off the ties with Rome. This has to be understood in the context of his bitter criticism of the Roman Curia which should be reformed by the « freer council »[5], and accused the same for its « blindness and haughtiness » [6]; in other words, he did not want to see the Roman mentality to get hold of his nation. Had he planned to sever the bonds with Rome, most certainly he would have accepted wholeheartedly the invitation of the German dissenters and of that of F. Rački to have arranged ovations for him in Zagreb and Slavonski Brod on his return from Rome. At first, he refused Rački's suggestion for fear of compromising himself in the eyes of Rome;

---

[2] J. OBERŠKI, *Hrvati...*, op. cit., 53-59.

[3] « Strossmayer's hesitations lasted longer. He seems at first to have been disposed to dally with the Old Catholic movement, writing to Döllinger and other leaders that he did not recognize the ecumenicity of the Council or the validity of its decrees, on account of the lack of proper liberty; but he made it clear he would join in no revolt, no schismatical movement » (D. BUTLER, op. cit., 423). Cf. also N. C. EBERHARDT, op. cit., II, 541.

[4] KRS, I, 108.

[5] *Ibid.*, p. 101.

[6] *Ibid.*, p. 107.

thereafter he left the whole matter to the discretion of the Croatian Historian[7].

In any case, the historians claim that Strossmayer had accepted « Pastor Aeternus » either in December, 1872, or in January, 1873, when the said Constitution was published in the newly founded organ of the Diocese of Djakovo GBBS (Glanisk biskupija Bosanske i Sriemske) in nos. 1 and 2 of January 15 and 31, 1873[8]. In Mansi « Acta Conciliorum » it is found under no. 83 that « Strossmayer, Bishop of Bosnia, in the general congregation of the 13th of July (1870), had voted « non placet » on the Constitution; he did not attend the Solemn Congregation (of July 18th) »[9]. Further down, the authors of Mansi report: « ... the diocesan organ Glasnik has published in nos. 1 and 2 of 1873, by the order of the same Bishop (Strossmayer), the Constitution « Pastor Aeternus » which (a copy of GBBS) later on the same Bishop Strossmayer, while dwelling in Rome because of his health, gave personally the above publication to the supreme Pontiff, Pope Pius IX, and the latter handed it over to the Council's Undersecretary, Ludovico Jacobini, to have it placed with the other documents of the Vatican Council »[10]. According to the quoted document it becomes apparent that Strossmayer in January, 1873, really recognized the Constitution Pastor Aeternus, but there are some other incidents and documents, as for instance Strossmeyer's letter to Rački from Rome of February, 1873, which makes Mansi's contention very doubtful. On account of these discrepancies we would like to present the entire course of subsequent events after Vatican I in regard to Strossmayer's recognition of papal infallibility.

---

[7] Ibid., pp. 106-107. On two other different occasions he wrote to Rački from Rome that « he would tell him certain incidents when they meet ». Many a time the Bishop in his correspondence with Rački was fearful of putting in writing the names of his informants or to communicate his plans.

[8] « Finally he (Strossmayer) published the decrees in December, 1872 » (D. Butler, op. cit., 423). They were published in January, 1873. The Croatian historian, F. Šišić, also maintains that the Prelate was reconciled with the Holy See when the Constitution « Pastor Aeternus » was printed in the said diocesan Organ. See KRS, I, 208 note 1. It is also the contention of J. Oberški that Strossmayer embraced the decrees of the Vatican Council in January, 1873. Cf J. Oberški, Hrvati..., op. cit., 59.

[9] Mansi 53, 997.

[10] Ibid., 997-998.

In the months of November and December of 1871 and also in the month of January, 1872, Strossmayer was in Rome. In his letter from Rome (dated December 4, 1871) he notified F. Rački: « I was (in audience) with the Pope; I could not have complied with his (Pius IX) wish. The rest of it I'll tell you when we meet »[11]. We cannot think of any other desire of the Pontiff but that he wanted Strossmayer to admit *Pastor Aeternus*. The Prelate in his « pro memoria », sent to the Italian government from Vienna, Austria, in March 1871, praised its present policy toward the Catholic Church in allowing her to exercise unhampered her divine mission; then he added that he did not approve of its policy in trying to win by all means the Pontiff to its side so that the liberty of the Catholic Church might become subject to the Pontiff's arbitrariness « which is nothing else but to pave the road to the slavery of the Church and that the Pope can practically exercise personal infallibility. It is easy to foresee », he continued to say, « how the supreme Pontiff can abuse this greatest privilege (infallibility) and make it detrimental to the Church and to Italy as well »[12]. In the years of 1871 and 1872 Strossmayer was still strongly opposing papal infallibility.

Within the scope of this topic falls the spurious speech of Strossmayer. The authors of Mansi also contend that the Prelate, by refuting the forged speech imputed to him, had recognized *Pastor Aeternus*. Since this bogus speech had created such a commotion in the Christian world, it deserves our attention in three aspects: first, how it came into existence, secondly how he reacted to it, and thirdly how the authors of Mansi looked upon it. During the Vatican Council a forged speech of the fifth oration of Strossmayer under the title « Papa e Vangelo, (discorso) di un vescovo al Concilio Vaticano » first appeared in Florence, Italy and later on in Germany, England, South America and even in his native land[13].

---

11 KRS, IV, 419.
12 Carte Minghetti, Cartone 84, fasc. III.
13 A. SPILETAK, *op. cit.*, 156. Cf. also the letter of Canon Voršak in GBBS, I (1873), no. 3. The Prelate wrote in his Pastoral letter « Sts. Cyril and Methodius » of 1881: « Several years ago an abominable speech, under my name, circulated almost over the whole world which (speech), by its form and contents is so strange to me, as is that place (Buenos Aires) where a fallen away priest penitently admitted that he had forged that speech, offering me

This spurious speech under the name of Strossmayer circulated here in the United States of America in 1877[14]. The same speech reappeared once again in circulation in USA in the year 1889. This time, however, Bishop C. Maes of Covington, Ky. had notified him about it and asked him to refute it; Strossmayer had complied with the wish of Mgr. Maes[15]. The bogus speech was also published in *The Manchester Guardian* in the issue of June 28, 1871; a copy of it is found in the British Museum, printed at the Nile Mission, Cairo, as late as of 1928 without indicating that it is a forgery[16]. As far as we know this counterfeit speech was published in 1967 in Belgrade, Yugoslavia, in the collection « Besede » (The Selection of Famous Speeches)[17]. Dr. Berislav Gavranović, O.F.M. in his article *Dr. Josip Juraj Strossmayer* in the Franciscan Review *Dobri Pastir* has brought the original oration of Strossmayer (as it was delivered in the Vatican Council on June 2, 1870) and its forgery

---

satisfaction through his confessor... the speech caused not a small anguish to quite a few Catholics » (MANSI 53, 999). See also TS, pp. 430-431.

[14] Canon N. Voršak's letter to Strossmayer (dated Rome March 13, 1877) AJA XI A/Vor. Ni. 103. In the same letter the Canon notifies his friend Strossmayer that « Pope Pius IX and some Cardinals of the Roman Curia were jubilant over the incident ». The implication was that they had been glad in Rome to see Strossmayer compromised more and more in the eyes of the Catholic world – even in the United States of America. We were unable to procure an English copy of the forged speech.

[15] A copy (written in Latin) of Mgr. C. Maes' letter to Strossamayer is found in the Archives of the Diocese of Covington, Ky. under the number 277. The date is illegible, but it is evident that it was written between May 27 and May 29, 1889 since it is placed in Maes' correspondence between the mentioned dates. In the last paragraph the Bishop of Covington asks Strossmayer « if he would be so kind as to refute (the forgery), and he would publish it (Strossmayer's reply) in English ». Since the news of the Diocese of Covington prior to 1894 was carried in the leading newspapers of Cincinnati, Ohio as for instance: The Catholic Telegraph, Der Wahrheitsfreund, the late Mgr. Paul E. Ryan checked these papers for me and found nothing. He also checked some other secular newspapers in Cincinnati (The Cincinnati Commercial Gazette, The Cincinnati Enquirer, The Time-Star, Cincinnati Freie Presse, The Cincinnati Methodist Weekly and The Western Christian Advocate) and no trace of Strossmayer's refutation was found, and this can only mean that it was published somewhere else. Cf. A. SPITELAK, *Strossmayer i pape*, 182-183 and p. 254 on Strossmayer's answer to Bishop Maes.

[16] D. BUTLER, *op. cit.*, 423 note 9.

[17] This forgery is found in the mentioned edition, pp. 309-313. Cf. Dr. B. GAVRANOVIĆ, O.F.M., « Dr. Josip Juraj Strossmayer », in *Dobri Pastir*, XVII-XVIII (Sarajevo, 1968), 189.

so that the readers of Yugoslavia might see what a striking difference exists between these two speeches.

It is unnecessary to quote the forged speech in its entirety since
its author had summarized his main ideas in five points:

« First, Jesus Christ had given equal jurisdiction and power
to Peter and to the rest of the Apostles.

« Second, the Apostles did not recognize St. Peter as a vicar
of Christ, nor did they consider him as to be infallible teacher
of the Church.

« Third, Peter never thought of himself to be a pope, nor
did he act like one.

« Fourth, the councils, held during the first four centuries, had
given an honor to the pope on account of his residing in the most
important city of Rome – only honor was given to the pope – and
by no means the supreme power.

« Fifth, the Church Fathers had never understood the famous
(biblical) text 'you are Peter and on this rock I will build my
church' to mean that the Church is built on Peter but on the rock
(non super Petrum sed super petram), that is, on the sincere faith
of that apostle (Peter) »[18].

The appearance of the spurious speech in the weekly *Kremser
Wochenblatt* under the title *The Speech of Bishop Strossmayer in
the Vatican Council 1870* provoked Strossmayer and Bishop Fessler.
A copy of that newspaper was sent to the Bishop of Djakovo. At
the same time Mgr. J. Fessler of St. Polten, the former Secretary
of the Vatican Council, asked him to make a statement in regard
to the forged speech, what Strossmayer did on March 18, 1872.
This is his answer to Bishop Fessler:

« You know just as well as all those who had participaded in
the (Vatican) Council that I had never delivered such a speech
which is attributed to me. My principles are basilically different
from those found in the spurious speech. I am aware that I had
never asserted anything which might undermine the authority of
the Holy See, nor had I said anything which might harm the unity

---

[18]　B. Gavranović, *loc. cit.*, p. 187.

of the Church. I authorize you, Most Rev. Bishop, that you may use this statement of mine »[19].

The author of the unauthentic speech was a fallen-away Catholic priest, Dr. Jose Augustin de Escudero, a Mexican by birth and former monk of the Order of St. Augustin. He declared himself to be the forgerer in the review *America del Sud* whose contributor for a few years he had been and later on he became its editor. In the mentioned review Escudero wrote an article *The Truth in Vatican* in which he publicly admitted that he had falsified the speech. A copy of this magazine, accompanied with the letter of Father Pedro Stollenwerk of Buenos Aires, Argentina (dated 18, 1876) was sent to the Bishop of Bosnia and Sriem[20].

The principal reason why we have mentioned this forged speech whose authenticity was so often denied by Strossmayer himself and by Canon N. Voršak in the Roman ond other European newspapers[21] and which caused much annoyance to the Bishop during his life, was that the Church authorities in Rome considered his repudiation of the forgery as the acceptance of papal infallibility[22].

This confirms that the authors of Mansi did not have any other documents to corroborate their contention that Strossmayer had accepted the dogma of papal infallibility except his refutation of the falsified speech, and that he had supposedly ordered the Constitution *Pastor Aeternus* to be published in GBBS. Let us return once again to GBBS.

First of all, there is no word in GBBS that the Bishop issued the order to publish the said Constitution. As a matter of fact, it appears from the note, that the Editors of GBBS had done it on their own, which is inserted in GBBS and it runs: « A lot is being

---

[19] Mansi 53, 997. Cf. A. Spiletak, *J. J. Strossmayer, op. cit.,* 148. Strossmayer's letter was published on April 6, 1872 in *Neue Tiroler Stimmen. Ibid.*

[20] Mansi 53, 998. Cf. A. Spiletak, *J. J. Strossmayer.., op. cit.,* 149. Dr. J. A. de Escudéro accepted Protestantism and got married. Later on, his marriage was validated by Rome. He traveled extensively all over Europe and South America. *Ibid.*

[21] A. Spiletak, *J. J. Strossmayer..., op. cit.,* 154-156.

[22] « He (Strossmayer) accepted the Constitution (Pastor Aeternus) by protesting against the pamphlet 'Papa e Vangelo, discorso di un vescovo al Concilio' » (Mansi 53, 997)

written and said all over about the Vatican Council and especially
about the Constitution on *The Church of Christ*. The text of it as
it is published in various political newspapers is neither correct nor
reliable. On account of this it is necessary to inform our reader-
ship about the fourth solemn Congregation, held July 18, 1870 »[23].
There are no other annotations; the text was published in Latin instead of Croatian. At any rate, the practice of the Editors of GBBS
is at least strange, and especially in view that they wanted to « inform » the public by means of using Latin language. (Did the Croatian public posses sufficient knowledge of Latin to form its opinion
on the dogma of papal infallibility?) Furthermore, everybody would
expect that the Bishop would write an introduction to the newly
founded diocesan organ, but it was done by the editorial staff. For
the year of 1873 Strossmayer did not even write the Lenten Pastoral; it was composed by Vicar General, Joseph Matić and was
published in GBBS. (However, he did write a Pastoral for the
year of 1874 – see GBBS, v. II, no. 3, pp. 17-23). It is strange,
but at the same time it looks to us as if the Prelate did not want
to associate himself with the first issues of his diocesan official review. Whatever the motives of the editorial staff might have been
in publishing the Vatican decrees in GBBS, the fact remains that
the Bishop did not protest against their decision. This is perfectly
in accord with his respect for everybody's freedom, conscience and
convictions. It was said by him so many times « It is a sin against
the Holy Spirit to go against someone's religion and convictions ».
If the conscience and convictions of the Editors dictated them to have
the decrees published, most certainly he did not wish to be in the
way. In such a delicate matter as the dogma of infallibility he refrained from imposing upon anybody his personal persuasions.

Strossmayer's letter to Rački from Rome (dated Febraury 5,
1873) makes his acceptance of papal prerogative of infallibility more
doubtful. « During these days I was with the Pope », he notified
Rački. « He received me very nicely. What the newspapers are

---

[23]   GBBS, I (1873), of January 15, no. 1, pp. 5-6 and no. 2 of January 31,
pp. 11-12. (By the way, GBBS was published for quite a few years in the
city of Osijek and not in Djakovo).

trumpeting about my submission, it is a fable. I will recount the entire incident to you when I return »[24]. Not only did the authors of Mansi interpret this audience of the Prelate with Pius IX and his handing a copy of GBBS over to him, in which the Constitution *Pastor Aeternus* is found, as the official acceptance of papal infallibility, but somehow various newspapers were tipped off on this incident; and they offered the same comment on their pages. In any case, Strossmayer denied any « submission » to the Vatican decrees, but on the other side we have no written documents saying how the incident had occurred. We cannot envision that the Bishop had two faces in this respect: to accept papal infallibility on one hand and refute it on the other, as he did in the letter to Rački. What is more, it appears from one letter of Canon Voršak (dated Rome March 13, 1874) to Strossmayer that the Bishop of Djakovo had also a difficulty in accepting the following sentence of the Canon on papal primacy « or if anyone says that his power (of the Pontiff) is not ordinary and immediate either over each and every Church or over each and every shepherd and faithful member: let him be anathema » which he had strongly attacked in Vatican I; and in 1874 there was a strong rumor in the circles of Vatican: if he (Strossmayer) denied « ordinary and immediate power of the Pontiff », he would be considered a heretic[25]. No other documents on this issue are available to us which might tell us unequivocally what his stand was in this respect, or if he had any theological objections to the above statement. At any rate, these persistent rumors indicate that the problem of Strossmayer was not settled yet.

In spite of Strossmayer's two private audiences with Pius IX (in 1871 and 1873) we do not believe that cordial relations were reestablished between the Pontiff and himself as they had been prior to Vatican I[26]. The reasons are obvious: his refusal to accept the dogma of infallibility and his financial subsidising the work of Fr. A. Theiner *Acta genuina concilii Tridentini*. We should not

---

[24] KRS, I, 208.
[25] AJA XI A/Vor. Ni. 51 (Correspondence Voršak-Strossmayer).
[26] Voršak in his letter to Strossmayer (dated Rome February 28, 1865) reports that Pius IX had highly praised Strossmayer in the presence of Fr. Theiner. AJA XI A/Vor. Ni. 1 (Correspondence Voršak-Strossmayer).

omit to mention either that he used to stay in Rome for a month or two without presenting himself to the Pontiff; he simply ignored the Vatican protocol[27]. Naturally, all these factors kept aggravating and straining the relationship between these two personalities.

On the other hand, having in mind the Prelate's sincerity and openness we can hardly imagine that he did not communicate his theological difficulties to the Pontiff and that the latter was somewhat understanding toward him; otherwise we are unable to explain why they (in the Vatican) did not put any pressure on him and force him to sign the Vatican decrees as they did on the other bishops of the opposition, as for instance on Mgr. Haynald. No doubt Cardinal Franchi, intimate friend of both Pius IX and Strossmayer, served as intermediary between these two individuals so as to smooth out the grievances and also to explain the position of the Prelate in more detail to the Pontiff. This is apparent from the letter of Canon Voršak (dated Rome, May 18, 1873)[28]. As the time went on, the intermediary role of Cardinal Franchi became obvious, especially in January, 1875[29]. On January 16, 1875, Strossmayer wrote to Rački from Rome: « I shall reconcile with the Pope out of love for my friend (Canon Voršak)... Cardinal Franchi was by me yesterday... »[30]. In December 6, 1875 we find the Prelate once again in Rome. On December 6, 1875 he wrote to Rački: « One of these days I'll go to see the Pope even though I don't like to do it and to listen to his drudgery; but since it has to be, it has to »[31]. On both occasions he did have an audience with Pius IX, and there-

---

[27] « Had the Bishop followed my advice, he would have reconciled himself with the Roman Curia a long time ago. It is too late now... The Bishop does not want to follow protocol «, writes Voršak to Rački. Cf. KRS, I, 389-390.

[28] AJA XI A/Vor. Ni. 44 (Correspondence Voršak-Strossmayer).

[29] « Thank God », writes Canon Voršak to Rački, « I succeeded in convincing the Bishop that he should see the Pope. During these days Cardinal Franchi acted as an intermediary between the Pope and the Bishop » (KRS, I, 334 – letter dated January 16, 1875).

[30] KRS, I, 333. Rački in his letter to Strossmayer encouraged him to « approach » the Pope. Cf. KRS, I, 337.

[31] KRS, I, 386.

after with Cardinal Antonelli. According to his letter of December 25, 1875, he was received friendly by both[32].

With the year of 1877 it seems to us a great change in both Piu IX and Strossmayer had taken place. On the occasion of the fiftieth anniversary of Pius' episcopacy the Prelate of Djakovo wrote a lenghthy Pastoral (dated April 28, 1877). This letter is the manifestation of his childlike fidelity and love not only toward the office of the Roman pontiff but equally so to his person. At this point we are not concerned with his personal sentiments toward the Pontiff, which pop up here and there, as we are with its contents; nor are we preoccupied with his plans how the Pontiff's anniversary should be celebrated in each parish of his diocese and how he would lead Croatian pilgrims to the Eternal City. Perhaps no other Pastoral or speech of his is so rich with his reflections on numerous quotations, taken from the Church Fathers, as it is this one. The title of the said Pastoral can be *The Position and the Prerogatives of St. Peter's Successors in the Church of God.*

As in so many other places and instances so in this Pastoral, too, he does not omit to state that the Church is the being of the being of Christ, she is a living organism in which Christ resides, she exists and lives by the power of the One who is the source of every being and life. The following statements are of particular interest. First and foremost, the Roman pontiff is not only in possession of the supreme power as to preserve the unity in the Church, but this power is also « ordinary and immediate » over the other shepherds, churches and faithful[33]. The prerogatives of St. Peter are transmitted to his successors in their completeness, or as he says « Peter, you will resurrect in your successors in the place where they had crucified you »[34]. Furthermore, the Church of Rome is the only one which is entitled to solve any dissesions, and her judgment has to be accepted by everybody[35]. In his Pastoral he directly discusses the inerrancy of the Church but implicitly and indirectly he touches

---

[32]   *Ibid.,* p. 389. The Bishop kept constant contact with Cardinal Antonelli – even during the stormy Council. Cf. KRS, I, 107.

[33]   GBBS, V (1877), 80.

[34]   *Ibid.,* p. 79.

[35]   *Ibid.,* p. 88.

upon the inerrancy of the Roman pontiff when he says: « When the supreme ecclesiastical authority acts on behalf of the entire Church, it acts in such a manner that it becomes evident that the complete Church body acts through it and in it », or when, a few lines further down, he states: « When the supreme Church power speaks in the name of the entire Church, and when it defines (or as he says « when it makes something into a law ») something for the entire world, it is doing it with such carefulness, caution and provision that it becomes evident to everybody that through it the Church speaks and defines ». According to him, the supreme ecclesiastical authority « draws its all decisions out of the holy and eternal bequest which Christ and the Apostles had deposited into the bosom of the Church... and also out of consciousness of the entire Christian world »[36]. In order to confirm his reasoning he alleges the way how the dogma of the Immaculate Conception was defined; and this has been done when « the supreme Church authority had asked all the bishops (not all of them) and their churches for the opinion on this matter before making it into an irreformable decision »[37].

As we see, he did not come out unequivocally with the dogma of papal infallibility; nor did he mention it by name. Most probably the reason is to be sought in the fact that it was very difficult for him to embrace the last sentence of the definition of papal infallibility « ... and that such definitions of the Roman Pontiff are therefore irreformable because of their nature, but not because of the agreement of the Church », as we shall see later on. To what extent – if at all – the person of Pius IX had contributed to the Prelate's wavering in giving his assent to the dogma, we do not know; nor are we in possession of any documents which might point out in the direction that his personal pride was in the way. We cannot separate, however, the Prelate from the historical incidents which he mentions in the said Pastoral, let alone from his stand on the inerrancy of the Church. Time and again he reiterated that man's greatness is found in his humility, and that this was

---

[36] *Ibid.*, p. 83.
[37] *Ibid.*

particularly manifested in the case of Fenelon who had submitted his opinion to the judgment of the Church. St. Cyprian, in spite of his disagreement with Pope Stephen over rebaptizing heretics, never separated himself from the chair of St. Peter[38]. He also contends that the Church cannot err in the matters of a certain doctrine, but she can err in choosing less correct terms to express it. Due to the presence of Christ in the Church this can never become detrimental to her[39]. Let everybody judge wheter these factors have anything to do with his case.

Prior to Strossmayer's visit to Rome with the Croatian pilgrimage in 1877 Pius IX expressed his desire of « eagerly waiting to see the Bishop of Djakovo »[40]. During his sojourn in Rome he delivered a sermon on May 31, 1877, which actually was a panegyric to the papacy. Even though he uttered in this speech: « In this our epoch the conscience and the soul of the entire mankind has responded to the word and decision of Pius IX when he, following the footsteps of the holy fathers and of the Church councils, has proclaimed the Immaculate Conception an article of faith »[41], he did not utter a word on papal infallibility. Every reader and listener would expect from the context of the said sermon that he would mention papal charism, especially when he asserted that « papacy is the source and basis of truth, life and victory »[42], but again, no trace of papal infallibility. In his Pastoral « The Unity of the Church » of 1877, in which among other things he interprets the famous text « You are Peter and on this rock I will build my Church », he does not say a word on the infallible teaching of the Roman pontiff. He, however, states that these biblical words « do not solely betoken a mere honor, but they denote the most genuine supreme authority in the Church of God which (the supreme ecclesiastical authority) is the guarantee to her eternity and invincibility, and it is also the source and centre of the ecclesial unity... »[43].

---

[38] *Ibid.*, p. 82.
[39] *Ibid.*, p. 83.
[40] KRS, II, 108.
[41] GBBS, V (1877), 149-158. We quote by CP, p. 141.
[42] CP, p. 144.
[43] TS, pp. 401-402.

Furthermore, Cepelić and Pavić in the compiled list of the documents which the Bishop of Djakovo ordered to be published in GBBS, the constitution *Pastor Aeternus* is not listed. However, they mention the order of the Prelate of 1877 under no. 333 to have « The Creed of the Council of Trent » published which contains the following words in parentheses « I unhesitatingly accept and profess all the doctrine (especially those concerning the primacy of the Roman Pontiff and his infallible teaching)... »[44].

Strossmayer, during the reign of Pius IX, did not accept explicitly and unequivocally the dogma of papal infallibility, or at least he did not accord recognition to it in the sense and in so many words as those in the Vatican expected him to do. Since he had never written a word about it, it is difficult to penetrate into the dephts of the soul of the Bishop to see his inner struggle and obstacles in accepting this dogma. His frequent reference to the works of the Jesuit theologian, Giovanni Perrone, indicate that he kept studying and reflecting on the papal charism of infallibility in the post-Council years. What is more, we are not presumptuous in believing that neither Pius IX nor any of the Vatican leading men had considered any Pastoral or any other document of Strossmayer to be a genuine document of his recognition of papal infallibility. This becomes manifest in view of the fact that a great portion of his Pastoral of 1881 on *Sts. Cyril and Methodius* was translated and added to the other documents of Mansi which deal with Strossmayer and in which (portion) he accepted and elaborated on papal infallible teaching. (This is a document of his recognition of the dogma).

Before we discuss the above mentioned Pastoral, we would like to mention some other documents of the Prelate which preceded and which have a bearing on this topic. Surprisingly enough, by the election of Leo XIII for the pope on February 20, 1878, the Bishop made one more stride toward the recognition of papal prerogative and Vatican I. This is especially evident in his Pastoral (written on February 22, 1878) on the occasion of the election of

---

[44] CP, p. 147. Cf. *The Church Teaches, op. cit.*, 8, and also GBBS, V (1877), 51-53.

Leo XIII to the office of the Roman pontiff. If this document is perused carefully, one can easily perceive that it can serve as a preface to his prolific Pastoral of 1881, and that his difficulties were resolved and he was ready to embrace the decrees of the First Vatican Council wholeheartedly. What is more, in this writing of his he began to reverse himself on many points against which he had fought previously.

For the first time in his post-Council years, as far as we know, he embarked on praising Vatican I which he called the « most illustrious and most significant event of the nineteenth century and which should be repeated; it was said that through this Council the word of God was exposed to arbitrariness (sic!) ». Thereafter, he asserted that the word of God cannot be jeopardized by anybody's arbitrariness since it lives in the soul and the consciousness of the entire Church of God; and the soul and the consciousness of the Church are the dwelling place and the shelter of the word of God into which, as St. Irenaeus says, 'Dominus et Apostoli in eam, videlicet Ecclesiam, ceu in dive quoddam depositorium, quidquid veritatis est, contulerunt'[45]. Secondly, in his mind Christ Himself and His divine will act through the teaching Church, and this also excludes any kind of arbitrariness[46]. In addition, in this document he unequivocally recognizes that there is a progress in faith, but again he qualifies it by quoting Vincent of Lerins, namely that the growth must be « in eodem dogmate, in eodem sensu, in eadem sententia ». Subsequently, he offers the following comment: « Divine truth by its very nature is unchangeable, but at the same time it is inexhaustible. It in its divine kernel carries everything which can serve to all epochs and to the needs of all nations of all ages ». It is a sacred duty of the Church to keep constantly drawing out of this « divine inheritance » a right spiritual food at the precise moment in order to quench the spiritual hunger of the nations[47]. Time and again he urges that we should listen to the teaching of the Roman Church, which has kept the word of God pure and intact

---

[45]   GBBS, VI (1878), 7.
[46]   *Ibid.*, p. 8.
[47]   *Ibid.*, p. 7.

all the time while the other churches in the course of their history have faltered[48]. Consequently, the principal custodians of the divine inheritance are St. Peter's successors; and « The One, who had revealed once upon a time the mystery of Christ's being to Peter, will protect Peter's successors that neither the blood nor the flesh should lead them into an error »[49].

There is another text which is more revelant to the topic. This text is found in his study *The Paintings in the Cathedral of Djakovo*. This lengthy article is serialized in the issue of GBBS of 1873, 1874 and 1878. The pertinent text, found in the first number of GBBS of 1878, deals with the painting of the Austrian famous artist Overbeck. The Artist – most probably under the suggestion of the Bishop himself – had painted on the walls of the Cathedral the throne of St. Peter (Cathedra S. Petri) with the dove hovering over it. He gives the following interpretation to the painting: « The throne is a visible sign of the supreme authority which St. Peter and his successors as the teachers (doctors) of the universal Church possess; for this reason the dove is hovering over the throne to denote supernatural assistance of the Holy Spirit which enlightens and protects the supreme teacher of the universal Church as not to fall into an error when he interprets to the world the mysteries of the holy faith of Jesus. By the side of this symbol two angels stand – attired like deacons – and incence the throne of Peter; and this represents the obedience and devotion which the world owes to the supreme anthority in the Church of God »[50].

When Leo XIII had published his encyclical *Grande Munus* on the Slav Apostles, Sts. Cyril and Methodius, Strossmayer, hereafter, also wrote a lengthy Pastoral on the same Apostles, describing their loyalty and reverence to the Holy See and at the same time expressing on behalf of all the Slavs a gratitude to his personal friend, Leo XIII, for showing his great love toward the Slav nations. The authors of Mansi had translated and incorporated into the documents the passage of Strossmayer's Pastoral which treat the prima-

---

[48] *Ibid.,* pp. 6 and 9.
[49] *Ibid.,* p. 7.
[50] *Ibid.,* p. 2. See also TS, p. 273.

cy and infallibility of the Roman pontiff. We shall bring on these pages excerpts from his Pastoral for the variety of reasons: First of all, that a reader can see what a change occurred in the mind of the Bishop on these issues and how he reversed himself in offering a new interpretation to some biblical texts; secondly, that a reader can become acquainted with his ideas in interpreting papal infallible teaching which were accepted by the Church authorities; thirdly, these passages will also indicate his concern over the spiritual welfare of the Slav Schismatics and over their reunion with the Church of Rome. It is probable that he wanted to utilize this opportunity, when Leo XIII pubicly showed his love and concern for the Slavs with his encyclical *Grande Munus,* to come out so strongly in favor of papal infallibility, hoping that Leo's generosity and benignity might paralyse unfavorable reactions on the side of the Slav Greek Orthodox to his acceptance of papal defined prerogative; or perhaps it was coincidental when all his inner difficulties and struggles came to an end; and this happened to be the most suitable time to pronounce his convictions on the issue of papal infallible teaching.

The passages of the mentioned Pastoral letter run:

« When I take all this into consideration and when I compare it with the present situation which prevails among the Slavs, then I would like to exclaim from the bottom of my heart: Slavs, Slavs, my brothers in Christ! If only my weak voice might reach all of you, I would tell you; you (Slavs) accept the holy Scriptures as the word cf God and you venerate it as the eternal truth; is it possible that you cannot perceive the significance, dignity, clarity and decisiveness in the words of Christ, reported by Matthew in ch. 16 'you are Peter and on this rock I will build my church. And the gates of the underworld can never hold out against it. I will give you the keys of the kingdom of heaven: whatever you bind on earth shall be considered bound in heaven; whatever you loose on earth shall be loosed in heaven'. – I maintain that undoubtedly in these cited words it is not the question of some frivolous title or of some external honor, but they concern indeed the essential structure of the Church of God; the very key-stone, which is the foundation and ultimate source of her power and authority upon which (Peter) her certainty and eternity rest. Every word of the quoted sentence, the precision of the allegory and comparison indicate this. – Is it possible, Slavs, that the importance of the words of Christ, brought by John in ch. 21, can escape your keen mind and ardent heart when Christ asks Peter three times if he loves Him; this was done to remind Peter of his uncertainty, of his three-time denial and also of the value of love through which in Christianity one can only obtain honor and grace; but above all else this was said and confirmed three times by God Himself 'feed my sheep, feed my lambs' to emphasize the primacy of Peter which should never been forgotten in the world and which should be repeated hundreds and hundreds of times until the end of the world..

« I would bring this doctrine to an end, taken out of the lives of our Apostles (Cyril and Methodius), had I not heard frequently with my own ears unorthodox and sometimes even ridiculous accusations against the Holy See, and on account of this matter I feel forced to retrospect. It is namely said: after the promulgation of the dogma of papal infallibility everything in the Church is subject to arbitrariness against which neither any particular right nor custom can be defended; it is sometimes alleged that the Holy See is after the international power while it is known that Christ had said 'my kingdom is not of this world', and that He had fled into mountains when over-enthusiastic mob wanted to make Him a king. Neither of these accusations has any basis in reality.

« As far as the first (accusation) is concerned, first of all, it has to be mentioned that the Slav word 'nepogrešivost' (infallibility) as it is used by us around here, through which we profess the doctrine of the mother Church, is not correct. This expression can easily mislead an unlearned man as though the Church would teach that the pontiff cannot sin while the Christian doctrine says: a pope cannot err when he, as the supreme shepherd and teacher of the Church, in the solemn manner promulgates and explains doctrine of the holy faith. Perhaps, the expression 'nezabludivost' (inerrancy) would be more in conformity with the Christian teaching. Regardless what term would be more suitable (to express it), it is undoubtful that – by this definition of papal infallibility – nothing new was introduced into the Church. The Church of God, just as well as her eternal Groom (Jesus Christ), is unchangeable;

she is the same today, tomorrow and will remain the same all the time. Her marvelous inner structure is indistructable since she is the genuine mystical body of Christ. Infallibility of the Church and that of pontiff is the very same thing: nobody can separate in the Church of God the body from the head or the head (pope) from the body. When the holy Church promulgates and explains holy doctrine, she is doing it through the mouth of the head; when the head is performing this act, he draws the eternal truth from the same holy and unchangeable sources, imbued with the same spirit as the Church herself. When the Fathers at the Council of Chalcedon, while listening to the Epistle (Epistola ad Flavianum) of St. Leo the Great, elatedly exclaimed: 'All of us believe this, this is the true faith of the Church of God, through the mouth of Leo St. Peter had spoken'; in this fashion through the mouth of pontiff the Church guards and protects the Christian people against any error and deceit. When Pius IX in our own time proclaimed the doctrine of the Immaculate Conception of the B. V. Mary as a dogma of the holy faith, he did it by following the holy Tradition which had commenced in the stable of Bethlehem and kept growing more and more in its volume and becoming clearer and clearer up to the time of St. Augustine, and afer St. Augustine it (the doctrine of the Immaculate Conception) has reached its maturity and completeness in our own epoch; and due to this process it has reached the stage when – so to speak – every Christian child had this doctrine on his lips; Pius IX did proclaim this dogma, after having consulted and asked for the testimony all his brethren and co-teachers, surrounded by the group of bishops. Therefore, it is entirely wrong to state that the Church has become intollerable and arbitrary since yesterday...

« When the holy father – in rare cases alone as the head of the Church and as the supreme techer of Christian nations – proclaims some Christian doctrine as a dogma of faith, we the Catholics maintain and believe that the dogma is undoubtedly revealed by God. What is more, we are convinced that through the mouth of pontiff Peter himself speaks to whom Christ had addressed these words – after having professed that He is the Son of the living God – 'it was not flesh and blood that revealed this to you but my Father in heaven'; this was done — so to speak — by St. Peter himself whom Christ had made the eternal and indestructible foundation of His Church and to whom He had confided in the special manner the keys of heaven and also the spiritual care of sheep and lambs. However, whoever is well acquainted with the structures of the Church, he will recognize that the source of the holy truth in the Church are so clear and distinct since the work of the Holy Spirit is manifested so livingly and forcefully in the communal consciousness of the Church. Therefore, it is even impossible under any human aspect that the supreme teacher can err since he draws, explains and develops the Christian truth, taken from these sources and from the communal consciousness of the Church. It is wrong and totally unjustifiable to ascertain that the dogma of papal infallibility has brought into the Church some sort of arbitrariness of which the world should be apprehensive: where Christ lives and the Holy Spirit reigns there cannot be any talk about arbitrariness...

« I am convinced that the entire world in today's confusion and uncertainty — which has crept into the souls and lives of the nation — should be especially grateful to God for elevating one human being (pope) in this world above the human dust and confusion and for entrusting to him the holy mission and the right to announce fearlessly a pure and intact truth to mankind, and thus to defend and save freedom of conscience and that of nations. This is the immortal mission of the Roman pontiffs which they knew to perform not only while sitting on their shining chairs but also while in prisons, catacombs and even on the cross. If the voice of pope could be drowned, then the world would feel that something totally essential is gone out of its moral life. That would be the eclipse which would herald the ever-lasting darkness »[51].

After a careful perusing of these several paragraphs one can readily observe that on quite a few points the Bishop had reversed his opinions, especially if they are viewed in the light of his speeches delivered in the First Vatican Council. This factor is also evi-

---

[51] Mansi 53, 999-1001.

dent in the interpretation of the biblical texts which he had put in question at Vatican I; there is also an astonishing difference in his view of the growth of a dogma which he had finally interpreted in the sense of J. A. Möhler: a dogma becomes « clearer and clearer » in the mind of the Christian community as the time marches on. It is also a fact that, while accepting the dogma of papal charism, he still had preserved some of his original ideas, expressed at Vatican I. This is particularly obvious in his statement « nobody can separate in the Church of God the body from the head (pope) or the head from the body », or « the pontiff is the mouth of the Church ».

These statements are found word for word in his own note of protest which he had handed to the Presidents of the Council. It is true that he had paraphrased quite a few times after the year of 1881 the definition of papal infallible teaching: « We, with the approval of the sacred council, teach and define that it is a divinely revealed dogma: that the Roman Pontiff, when he speaks ex cathedra, that is, when, acting in the office of shepherd and teacher of all Christians, he defines, by virtue of his supreme apostolic authority, doctrine concerning faith or morals to be held by the universal Church, possesses through the divine assistance promised to him in the person of St. Peter, the infallibility with which the divine Redeemer willed his Church to be endowed in defining doctrine concerning faith and morals; and that such definitions of the Roman Pontiff are herefore irreformable because of their nature, but not because of the agreement of the Church »[52], but – as far as we know – he had never quoted or paraphrased the last sentence of the definition « such definitions of the Roman Pontiff are therefore irreformable because of their nature, but not because of the agreement of the Church ». What we wish to inculcate is that he considered papal definitions to be irreformable but he never mentioned « but not because of the agreement of the Church ».

He did not bother to make a distinction between a « consent » and a *consensus*. He was more or less preoccupied with consensus of

---

[52] *The Church Teaches, op. cit.*, 102.

the Church. It is not excluded that he did not take seriously enough the words *ex sese, non autem ex consensu ecclesiae* in the formula of definition since they had been inserted at the last moment of Vatican I out of spite for those who had opposed the dogma. Let it be as it may, Strossmayer's friend, Vladimir Soloviev, who had written his famous book *Russia and the Universal Church* under the Prelate's influence, had gone a bit further, by explaining papal infallibility and *ex sese, non autem ex consensu ecclesiae* in the strictest sense[53]. Strossmayer on the other hand, being a practical man and by his very nature anti-legalistic, placed the whole emphasis on the « consciousnes of the Church », or as Pope Pius XII in Bull *Munificentissimus Deus* on the Assumption of the Bl. V. Mary of November 1, 1950 says « Haec singularis catholicorum Antistitum et fidelium conspiratio... »[54], or as Vatican II states that « The entire body of the faithful, anointed as they are by the Holy One, cannot err in matters of belief... they show universal agreement in matters of faith and morals. That discernment in matters of faith is aroused and sustained by the Spirit of truth »[55]. Regardless what interpretation can be attributed to the words *ex sese, non autem ex consensu ecclesiae,* the fact remains that the pontiffs prior to their dogmatical pronouncements had searched the mind of the Church, or as Strossmayer said so many times they look into « consciousness of the Church ».

Our presentation of Strossmayer's views on papal prerogative would not be complete without bringing in some other ideas of his on this problem. This especially deserves our attention, since he had written quite a few times, on this topic after the year of 1881. First of all, his notion of the mission of the Church is the search

---

[53] V. Soloviev says: « It was not by means of a general consultation but (as Jesus Christ bore witness) with the direct assistance of the Heavenly Father that Peter formulated the fundamental dogma of our religion; and his word defined the faith of Christians by its own inherent power, not by the consent of others – *ex sese, non autem ex consensu ecclesiae* ». *Op cit.,* p. 89 and passim.

[54] *Acta Apostolicae Sedis,* 40 (1950), 755.

[55] *The Sixteen Documents of Vatican II* (Boston, Mass., Daughters of St. Paul), 122. Cf. also J. A. Möhler, *Symbolism,* II, 38-39.

for and preservation of truth. This is one of the essential missions of the Church. On account of this he maintained that the Church had come into existence with the creation of man. Man is of dual nature: one is corporal which is sustained by natural laws and the other one is a spiritual one which constantly, due to its inherent spirit given to it by God Himself, searches for eternal truth. Therefore, men of all epochs, and especially great Greek and Roman philosophers, who sought the truth and lived up to it, were some kind of a Church. This again had assumed a more concrete form of a church in the Jewish patriarchs and prophets until it was finally realized in her total fulness by Jesus Christ and on the day of the first Pentecost[56]. Mankind never ceased to use its efforts in preserving the spark of God's truth; and the Church at present is exercising this duty in its fulness.

His second argument in favor of papal infallibility was that the Church is the « being of the very being of Christ », and she as such must be infallible, too, as is her own Groom (Jesus Christ); otherwise the teaching of Christ were liable to turn into sheer human opinions. For this very reason he placed the mission of the Church and her infallibility side by side. They are her inner qualities, given to her for the benefit and salvation of mankind. This inerrancy is bestowed upon the entire Church, which is the bearer and manifestation of the holy Tradition, but it is foremost conferred upon the visible and official teaching authority through which Christ himself speaks. He argues in quite a few places this way: Christ has founded a visible church and has instituted a visible and official magisterium, to whom He (Christ) transferred His own authority. Therefore, this magisterium is in possession of the same authoritative credentials which Christ enjoyed, and subsequently the judgments and pronouncements of this magisterium can claim the authority of Christ Himself. Of course, this is only in force while they are united with the head of the Church, since in the special manner Christ speaks through the Roman pontiff when he instructs the entire Christian world on the matters of faith and morals and

---

[56] TS, pp. 437-438.

when he settles disagreements and dissensions within the Church, by discerning the truth and separating it from error[57].

In another place he becomes more specific by presenting in what sense the teaching authority is the property of the Christian community: « This holy magisterium is the sacred inheritance of the entire Church of God; it does not only belong to the official teaching Church whose property is the apostolic magisterium, but it is also the possession of the learning Church which accepts the holy doctrine from the priests and bishops and implements it in their lives »[58]. This confirms once again that he by all means, even after having accepted the doctrine of papal infallibility, wanted to preserve the unity in the Church under every aspect, and could not have looked upon the pontiff either lording over the Christian community or being severed from it. In addition, this has also served him to eliminate in his own eyes and in those of the world any possibility of papal or of the magisterium arbitrariness. Pope and the magisterium have not only to look into « consciousness of the Church », but it seems to us that the charism of their infallibility attains the fulness of their function in « the response and implementation of the faithful » of what they have heard from the legitimate apostleship.

In many places Strossmayer, in order to justify the existence of the inerrancy and that of the supreme ecclesiastical power, makes a reference to the structure of every well organized society which must have a head. He even goes as far as to quote Cicero, in his debate with the Greek Orthodox bishops, that according to Cicero the Roman consuls under certain circumstances had had an

---

[57] KRS, IV, 221-222. Cf. *ibid.*, pp. 229-230, and also GBBS, XXVI (1898), 28-31. According to the Bishop « Christ is the genuine and invisible foundation of the Church, and St. Peter is the authentic but visible basis of the Church of God » GBBS, V (1877), 78.

[58] GBBS, XXI (1893), 35. See also *ibid.*, pp. 34 and 37. Karl Adam shares Strossmayer's opinion: « The living community of the faithful, hearing and obeying the revelation which the teaching authority proclaims, itself shares in the infallibility of the Church as it accepts this revelation, cherishes it and bears fruit. Such is the nature of the influence which the community exercised in the development of dogma ». KARL ADAM, *The Spirit of Catholicism* (New York, Macmillan, 1930), 135.

absolute power; and this power had been regulated by some extraordinary laws[59]. The implication is obvious: the monarchical power of pope, or if you wish to call it an absolute power, is subject to and regulated by the existing inner forces and laws within the Church as for instance the holy Scripture, Tradition and her very structure.

We earnestly hope that nobody will be tempted as to state, on account of the presented facts, that Strossmayer was a heretic. This period of almost eleven years was a time of inner struggle and of earnest study of this controversial subject. His frequent reference to the works of Perrone (especially to his « Praelectiones Theologicae » – « de Romano Pontifice ») undoubtedly indicate that he was not only preoccupied with papal infallible teaching as such, but he was equally concerned with the historical facts in which the Roman Pontiffs have erred, as in the case of Pope Honorius.

It looks as if he solved this problem by believing that Pope Honorius had not strayed in matters of faith but the whole difficulty had been caused by not choosing the most appropriate expressions. Be that as it may, in his Pastoral letters of 1877 and 1878 he time and again reiterated that the Church is patient, loving and undestanding – or at least it should be – with those who falter or waver for the variety of reasons in accepting decisions of the Church.

It is a strange coincidence that he had mentioned in his Pastoral letter of 1877 the case of the Church of Sirmium – and he happened to be the Bishop of that Church – that that Church in the fourth century happened to be reluctant to embrace the decrees of Nicaea, but « the Church more with patience and love than with severity and harshness had won (the Church of Sirmium) to her side to accept the Nicene's decisions »[60].

Surely he identified his own case with that of the Church of Sirmium. His loyalty and firm adhesion to the chair of St. Peter most certainly earned him the love, patience and understanding of Rome by allowing him enough time to think the matters over and by refraining from making any pressure on him. We do believe that

---

[59] KRS, IV, 510.
[60] GBBS, V (1877), 82.

this attitude toward him was to some extent exercised by Rome, of course, besides the facts that those in Rome were cognizant that the Bishop of Djakovo was an extremely hard « nut to crack » and that his fame in the world and his services rendered to the Church might cause her considerable unpleasantness.

VII

ROLE IN EUROPE

> « Only sword and blood will regenerate
> Europe ». This was Strossmayer's most
> favorite expression when he happened
> to discuss European political problems[1].

1. - Strossmayer's Pan-Slavism and Yugoslavism

Perhaps there was no individual of fame in the recent times, as of whom so many untrue and contradictory statements had been made as of the Bishop of Djakovo; and this specifically goes for his pan-Slavism and Yugoslavism. This is evident in his native land where it is still generally accepted that he was the father of the political unity of the South Slav nations, and, naturally, under the influence of this misunderstanding the foreign writers followed the same thread of thoughts. It seems that nobody has bothered either in his native land or outside to find his basic political and other conceptions without which it is impossible to appraise him.

Undoubtely, all those, who tend to present him either as a pan-Slavist or a Yugoslav, give the impression that he was exclusivist, and nothing is further from the truth than to ascertain this since any sort of exclusivism was not only alien but odious to him. One can justifiably affirm that he regarded himself not only a Slav but a European as well. He loved his native soil and all the Slav nations, but he never emancipated himself nor the Slav nations from the European family. It is, however, an undeniable fact that he has cherished a tremendous affection (on this topic in many instances he was too sentimental) toward the Slav race, motivated by the situation in which the Slavs were neglected and exploited.

---

[1] CHARLES LOISEAU, *loc. cit.,* p. 32.

His love for his nation and for the other Slavic groups went to the extreme as any reaction does, but no exclusivism can be detected. He strongly believed in messianism of the Russians and of the South Slav nations, but again this had to be exercised within the framework of the European nations and political affairs. In other words, he was in search of finding a proper place for the Slav na tions of the European continent without ever making their presen ce either antagonistic or dangerous to the other European national groups. As a matter of fact, the way he envisioned the presence of the Russians and of the other Slavic groups in Europe should be of benefit to Europe. At any rate, he was a Slavophil, but a Slavophil of a special kind.

Strossmayer was not akin to the Russian Slavophils. While the Russian Slavophils strongly believed in the power and orthodoxy of their common people (muzhiks), Strossmayer opined that the people should move ahead and become ennobled by enlightenment, Christianity and modern achievements. In the mind of the Russian Slavophils there was a lot of room for stagnation, which was their chief trait, while in Strossmayer's mind everything is fire, every-thing is in motion. While the Russian Slavophils were inimical to anything Western, he was a strong advocate of westernizing the Slavs and still preserving their Slav identity. All these characteristics of the Bishop are amply evidenced in his undertakings which have been treated already.

Undoubtely, in his early years he had occasionally mentioned the word pan-Slavism »[2], but his pan-Slavism should not be con-founded by any means with that of Father George Križanić, another Croatian clergyman of the seventeenth century, who had stron-gly advocated not only the reunion of the Eastern and Western Churches and the worship in the vernacular but also dreamed of the Russian protectorate over the Slav nations without having them lose their national independence[3].

---

[2] « Our future is in pan-Slavism », Strossmayer wrote to his friend Andrija T. Brlić on June 23, 1849. JJS-DK, 45.
[3] Cf. Hans Kohn, *Pan-Slavism — its History and Ideology* (Notre Dame, University of Notre Dame Press, 1953). Kohn writes: « The best known fo-rerunner of modern Pan-Slavism, the 17th century Croatian priest Krizanic,

It is true that the Russian Pan-Slavists of the nineteenth century had considered Križanić as their progenitor[4], but as will be shown here, Strossmayer did not have anything to do with their ideology. In 1849 he used the expression *pan-Slavism* in connection with the Russian intervention in the inner affairs of the Austrian Monarchy, and said that the other Slav nations within the Monarchy should use it for their national advantage in securing their national independence within the Monarchy. In other words, the Russian presence would serve as a vehicle to obtaining liberty and by no means of becoming tutor to the other Slav nations. On the same occasion and in the same document he commenced to elaborate on the reunion of the Churches (Eastern and Western). The realization of this goal, namely, the unity of the Greek Orthodox and of the Roman Catholic Slavs in the Church of Rome, meant some kind of pan-Slavism to him[5]. This should not induce anybody to conclude that Strossmayer worked on dissolving the Austrian Monarchy by advocating national independence for the Slavic nations[6].

The observation of the British historian R. Seton-Watson on this topic deserves to be cited: « In the true political significance of the word, he (Strossmayer) was anything but Pan-Slav. Like Palacky (Czech historian and the Prelate's friend) and many other distinguished Slavs in the Habsburg Monarchy, he believed in the mission of Austria, and desired to see her great and prosperous »[7].

In 1861 Strossmayer in his letter to Baron Janković complained how he had been spied upon (during Bach's despotism) and had been under « gruesome police survelliance » on account of his supposed *pan-Slavism* which (pan-Slavism) was nothing else in reality but his

---

during his long sojourn in Russia, was the first to subordinate religious missionary zeal to the emphasis on the need for political emancipation and progress of the Slavs. In the second half of the 19th century this Catholic Pan-Slavism, aiming at reunion of the Churches under Rome and of the Slavs under Russia, will be represented by another Croat priest, Bishop Strossmayer » (p. 51). In another place he calls the Bishop a « Pan-Slav » *ibid.*, p. 151).

[4] MICHAEL BORO PETROVICH, *The Emergence of Russian Panslavism 1856-1870* (New York, Columbia University Press, 1956), 6.

[5] JJS-DK, p. 45.

[6] CHARLES and BARBARA JELAVICH, *op. cit.*, 166.

[7] R. SETON-WATSON, *The Southern Slav Question..*, *op. cit.*, 128-129.

financial support of various Slav writers to enable them to publish
their works[8].

In all fairnes to the Bishop we must underscore at this place that
he was often unrestrained in expressing his Slavic sentiments and
constantly reiterating in his documents « the mission of the Slav race », most probably this has occasioned many unfounded accusations
against him[9]. There is no document written by him which would
indicate that he wanted to see the Slav nations united under Russian protection; what he actually desired and worked for was to
bring the Eastern Church into the union with that of Rome and
to establish more brotherly and more workable relations among
the Slavs. Only in this respect he can be thought of as a pan-Slav.
Perhaps his Yugoslavism might shed some more light on this topic.

Strossmayer's Yugoslavism is complex and hard to comprehend
at the first glance. In approaching this subject one ought to keep
constantly in mind that we are dealing here with the man full of idealism and honesty; one also has to put aside the crude realities of
politics, human passions, selfishness, all sorts of antagonism and
various idealogies and also one must never forget in what envi-
ronments he grew up and lived. This particularly pertains to this
topic. As earlier stated, it is generally accepted that he was the father of Yugoslavia in the political sense. Undoubtedly, some politicians of later times have projected their own ideas into Strossmayer's mind and have worked accordingly. We acknowledge that
he did give an occasion to this political adventure. At least it can
be stated that he gave something to the architects of political Yugoslavism to build upon or at least a name to lean on. On account
of this subject's complexity several facts ought to be brought out.

First of all, the movements during the years of his schooling
and thereafter and his varied contacts with some leading individuals
contributed to his political formation in regard to the Slav nations.

---

    [8] TS, p. 29.
    [9] « If we are intelligent enough, Austria (the Monarchy) will be pre-
dominently Slav », Strossmayer wrote to Andrija T. Brlić on August 31, 1849.
JJS-DK, p. 70. As late as October 8, 1888 he wrote to Princess L. Trubeckoi
that he understood by his people and homeland « the entire Slav family »
(AJA XI A4/III 6).

Those years in Europe can be characterized as a time when different nations were in search of their national reunification and of identity.

While young Strossmayer dwelled in Budapest, he came in contact with the Slovak poet Jan Kollar, who was one of the greatest forces among the Slavs. His influence was felt everywhere, especially among the leading Croats, as for istance, Ljudevit, Gaj, Strossmayer and so on. Kollar advocated that only four literary languages among the Slav nations should be developed and cherished and all dialects should be eliminated. These languages are to be: Russian, Czech, Polish and Illyrian or Yugoslav[10]. It appears that the Bishop wholeheartedly accepted Kollar's proposal and remained faithful to it, even in founding the Yugoslav Academy of Zagreb.

In his speech of April 29, 1861, delivered in the Diet in Zagreb, Strossmayer expounded the need for establishing the Yugoslav Academy of Science and Art (for which he pledged 50,000 florins) and why the name « Yugoslav » instead of « Croatian » ought to be given. His constant conviction was that no nation or the race can progress and grow culturally or scientifically as long as that nation or a race is divided linguistically. The first prerequisite, in his judgment, was to do away with the dialects and to establish one literary language. In this oration he drew a parallel between the German and the Roman nations on one side and South Slavs on the other. Then he contended that neither Italy nor France nor Germany was able to make much progress until each of them had created one literary language. For the very same reason he advocated that among the Southern Slavs (Serbs, Croats, Slovenians and Bulgarians) one single literary language must be formed, and thus all the scholars from these regions would be enabled to collaborate with one another and to become more creative[11]. At the very beginning two leading scholars were elected to the most important positions in the Yugoslav Academy: Canon Dr. Francis Rački (Croat) became its President and the Serbian scholar, Djuro Daničić, its Secretary with the assigned duty to produce a Dictionary[12].

---

[10] TS, pp. 4 and 80.
[11] TS, pp. 131-132.
[12] TS, p. 164. (Strossmayer's speech on the solemn opening of the Yugoslav Academy of Science and Art). The Prelate asked his friend the

At this place it has to be remarked that Strossmayer, Rački, Daničić had considered that Serbs, Croats, Bulgarians and Slovenians are one and the same nation; they are simply the tribes and their respective languages are dialects. The national sameness of the Serbs and Croats was particulary stressed[13]. It is evident that the platform for the close cooperation among the Southern Slavs must be the creation of the common language.

This idea of fraternal cooperation among the related Slavs is also expressed in a painting – inspired by the Bishop and executed by the great artist Seitz – in the Cathedral of Djakovo. The painting depicts the birth of Christ with Slavs from the mentioned countries in their national costumes coming to adore the infant Jesus[14].

It must be stressed here that Strossmayer's notion of a nation has undergone some development. It is evident in all documents that prior to his public political life, which began in 1860, he used to stress more forcefully his being a Slav or a Yugoslav than being a Croat. Besides, there are also indications that during this period of time, and especially while he was in Vienna, that he even dreamed of annexing Vojvodina to the Triune Kingdom of Croatia[15].

At any rate, he was extremely aware that the Southern Slavs were culturally and otherwise unproductive except for the republic of Dubrovnik and some Dalmatian cities where culture has flourished until the beginning of the nineteenth century when Dubrovnik has lost its freedom and independence. This also was hightened by the fact that the Southern Slavs had spent so much time in the Turkish slavery and in continual warfares against the

---

Serbian Prince Milan Obrenović to allow Djuro Daničić to come to Zagreb and to become a secretary and a member of the Yugoslav Academy. Cf. KRS, I, pp. 33, 51 and passim.

[13] See TADE SMIČIKLAS, « Misli i djela biskupa Strossmayera » (The Ideas and the Works of Bishop Strossmayer), in Rad Yuguslavenske Akademije Znanosti i Umjetnosti, v. LXXXIX (Zagreb, 1888), pp. 210-224, especially see pp. 215-216 and 223.

[14] GBBS, XI (1883), 21.

[15] JJS-DK, p. 51 and passim. This Strossamayer's article was originally published in the newspapers Narodne Novine in Zagreb in the issue of August 14, 1849. See ibid, p. 50, note 1. In his oration, delivered in the Croatian Diet in Zagreb on July 5, 1861, he emphasizes that he is a « Croat and a Slav ». Cf. TS, p. 144.

Turks, and that this had left them neither time nor opportunity to grow[16]. Since under Napoleon I the republic of Dubrovnik ceased to exist, in Strossmaye's mind Zagreb – another Croatian city – had to take over not only the political but also the cultural leadership among the Croats and all other Southern Slavs. This was also postulated by the fact that the city of Zagreb has been regarded the holder of the Croatian King Zvonimir's Crown, which has served as a symbol of the Croatian independence vis à vis the Austrians and Hungarians[17]. For these reasons he attributed the adjective « Yugoslav » instead of « Croatian » to the newly founded Academy so as to indicate that this scientific and cultural institution ought to be of service to all Southern Slavs, and that it was expected to house all the Yugoslav scholars and offer them the means to publish their works. This was the primary objective of his Yugoslavism, namely, to unite the Southern Slavs in the sense of culture and to coordinate their creativity. Italian historian A. Tamborra perceived it best when he stated that Strossmayer intended to achive religious and cultural unity among the Serbs, Croats, Slovenians and Bulgarians[18].

How feasible Strossmayer's Yugoslavism was in practice is difficult to say, especially in view of the fact that he wanted each Slav group of people to preserve its historical name and to remain politically indipendent within its own historial territorial boundaries. How this brotherly cooperation among the Slavs – as it was envisioned by the Prelate – would function in religion and culture presented many difficulties to superficial interpreters of Strossmayer's Yugoslavism. Therefore nobody should wonder that almost as a rule it was and still is accepted that this cultural and religious Yugoslavism of Strossmayer meant the first step toward the national political reunion of all Southern Slavs in one state; this was realized in 1918, with the exception of the Bulgarians[19].

---

[16] See TS, pp. 183-184 (Strossmayer's speech delivered on November 9, 1884 on the occasion of the solemn opening of the Art Gallery in Zagreb).

[17] Cf. TS, pp. 132, 134, 141, 183 and passim.

[18] A. TAMBORRA, op. cit., 128.

[19] See Dr. B. GAVRANOVIĆ, loc. cit., pp. 181-182. Gavranović's formulation of Strossmayer's ideas is extremely confused: once he claims that

The British historian R. Seton-Watson, who was well acquainted with Strossmayer's ideas, opined since the realization of national and political union with the other Southern Slavs outside of the Austrian Monarchy could be achieved only by war[20] this political reunion simply meant the union of the Croats and the Serbs who happened to live in the Croatian historical provinces within the Austrian Monarch: Croatia Proper, Slavonia, Istra, Dalmatia, Bosnia and Herzegovina, with Zagreb as their capital city.

We maintain that the best interpreters of certain ideas are their originators, in this case Canon F. Rački and Strossmayer himself. Rački in his lengthy article, published in Obzor under the title *The Toughts on the Encyclical of Pope Leo XIII of September 30, 1880*[21], discussed the Slav question in all its ramifications. He has defined it in the following manner: « The Slav Question is not the matter either of national or political unity, since in every and single Slav tribe the national characteristics and particularities are so conditioned by their historical growth that every one of them (Slav tribes) wishes to live its own life. The Slav question is con-

---

Strossmayer's yugoslavism was of a religious and cultural nature and a few lines farther he quotes a text which he ascribes to the Prelate supposedly written in 1874 without indicating its source. IVAN MUŽIĆ in his book *Hrvatska politika i jugoslavenska ideja* (Croatian Politics and Yugoslav Idea), (Split, 1969), follows the pattern of Gavranović, pp. 21-29. Mužić commits the same error by basing his opinion upon one doubful text of Strossmayer which is completely in contradiction with the political notions of the Prelate.

Hans Kohn falls into the same error. He writes: « I am a Catholic, and the Servians are Orthodox, but it is a difference of unimportant details, and I shall be well content to be under political administration of Servia ». H. KOHN, *op. cit.,* 55. This was supposedly said by the Bishop in 1876 to Rev. Malcolm MacCall which the latter communicated to Lord Gladstone. See H. Kohn, *op. cit.,* 269. On another page (*op. cit.,* p. 151) Kohn unequivocally affirms that the founding of the Yugoslav Academy seemed to be the first step toward the political union of the four Slav nations: Croats, Serbs, Slovenians and Bulgarians. We do not doubt either Kohn's or M. MacCall's sincerity, but the former especially is deducing too much from the British clergyman's statement as to indicate that Strossmayer wanted the political union of the Southern Slavs.

[20] Cf. R. SETON-WATSON, *The Southern Slav Question...*, *op. cit.,* 335-344. Seton-Watson's prediction, pronounced in the year 1911, was correct.

[21] Pope Leo XIII Encyclical is known by the name « Grande Munus », and it concerns the Slav missionaries, St. Cyril and Methodius. In all probability the said Pope wrote this Encyclical under the influence of Strossmayer so as to indicate the unity of the Slavs in religious field, too.

cerned with the liberaton of each Slav tribe from the yoke and hegemony which in the past kept them captives. At this stage the Slav question rests at present ». A few lines further he speaks of forming « Slavic States » in South East Europe after the Slavs are liberated from the Turks. He finally concludes that « the countries of Bohemia, Poland, and Croatia will sooner or later obtain the same position (in the Austrian Monarchy) which Hungary enjoys »[22].

The Yugoslav idea was never popular among the general populace of Croatia, and the naming of the Academy « Yugoslav » in the capital city (Zagreb) of Croatia met with great criticism on the part of the Croats; and what is more, the resistance to the Yugoslav idea actually grew more intensive as time went on. On the twenty-fifth anniversary of the Academy, Rački in his extensive report on the achievements of the Academy preoccupied himself with this criticism and attempted to offer the reasons why it was called « Yugoslav » instead of Croatian. Undoubtedly, Rački shared the opinion of the Bishop that the common platform, which is one common language, should be created. Then he concluded his reasoning with these words: « For this very reason it was intended that in its (Academy) very name (Yugoslav) its aim is clearly expressed which is to unite in the scientific field all the akin tribes of the Southern Slavs. This name (Yugoslav) neither deprives any tribe of its national characteristics nor does it intend to violate the sentiments of any tribe. Therefore, let them have the common banner under which they should gather as a one national entity for the cultural purposes »[23]. Strossmayer, after having read Rački's Report, had expressed his total agreement with him and had thanked him most cordially[24].

It is actually inconceivable that the Bishop of Djakovo meant by « Yugoslavism » national and political unity of the Southern Slavs. First of all, this would be in a direct conflict with his notion of national independence in which there are two predominant fac-

---

[22] KRS, II, 317-318. See also *ibid.*, p. 322 where he advocates the tolerance and cooperation between the Croatian Catholic and the Serbian Orthodox priests.

[23] KRS, IV, 336 and passim.

[24] *Ibid.*, p. 334.

tors: one is historic, and the other, equally important, consists of and the tribal desire to live separately and independently. This moment has been already treated. Besides, we should never forget that he wanted, as has been stressed so many times in these pages, to establish among the Southern Slavs the most cordial cooperation and brotherly love which would eventually result in the religious reunion. There are also indications here and there in his documents that he expected Montenegro and Serbia to be of help to Croatia in obtaining its freedom and independence within the Monarchy since these Slav provinces had « free hands »[25]. In addition, had he planned national and political union of the Southern Slavs then his intensive work on establishing concordats between Serbia and Montenegro with the Holy See would not have much meaning.

His position on the statehood of Croatia can also shed light on his « Yugoslavism ». His struggle in the Emperor's Council in Vienna and his debates with Count Borelli amply testify that he wanted by all means to incorporate into Croatia another province, Dalmatia, which he often refers to as « the sister and the crown of the entire Croatia ». Strossmayer's position on the union of Bosnia and Herzegovina with the rest of the Croatian provinces was somewhat different. More will be said on this topic later on. As early as 1859, just before Strossmayer had entered into the political arena, in the document (dated May 1, 1859) it becomes discernible that he regarded Bosnia a part of Croatia. In this document, by which he had donated 20,000 florins for the support of St. Jerome's Chapter in Rome, he inserted certain provisions censoring who could be aggregated to the said Chapter. The document says: « Only those (priests) are to be accepted who are wholeheartedly devoted to the Church and to the Holy See; ... they ought to be born of the Slav parents from Croatia, Slavonia, Dalmatia and Bosnia; and they are also expected to know the Croatian language... »[26]. In his letter to Fr. Ivan Vujičić, O.F.M. (dated February 7, 1892) he unequivocally affirmed: « When Bosnia once becomes totally free, or which is the same, when she is annexed

---

[25] Ibid., II, p. 205 and passim.
[26] Quoted by CP, pp. 319-320.

to us (to the rest of Croatia) in one statehood and national body... »[27].

Strossmayer never ceased to dream that Croatia would one day become free and take the reins of its future into its own hands by freeing itself from the Hungarians. On this topic he elaborated extensively in his lengthy letter of December 2, 1885, to Mgr. Nuncio Vannutelli in Vienna[28].

It should be noted that his notion of the organization of the Catholic Church in Croatia runs parallel to his conception of the Croatian political independence. When the hierarchical structure of the Church in Bosnia was in process of being organized, he came out wholeheartedly against creating either an archbishopric or a metropolitan in Sarajevo (capital city of Bosnia) since « there should be only one metropolitan for the entire South » in Zagreb, except for Split where a metropolitan must be reestablished on account of the past[29]. All these factors manifestly indicate that the Prelate whished to see Croatia organized as one entity in every respect.

We conclude this subject with the words of Revs. Milko Cepelić (Strossmayer's secretary for many years) and of Matija Pavić (Bishop's intimate friend) who were thoroughly acquainted with the Prelate's ideas: « Here we would like to state this: the Bishop, since the very beginning of his public life – since 1860 until now – had always in his mind only one goal, one aim – which was: the reunion of all the Croatian provinces into one single Croatia and into the independent statehood of Croatia within the realm of the Habsburg Monarchy. This was his alpha and omega... He had never changed his position on this basic program... His gaze was neither fixed on or turned to Vienna nor Budapest nor Belgrade – as some would like to ascertain – but he has solely looked toward Zagreb »[30].

---

[27] KRS, IV, 306. The Croatian historian Dr. F. Šišić in his study *Herceg-Bosna prigodom aneksije* (Zagreb, Tiskara hrvatske stranke prava D. D., 1908) argues that Bosnia and Hercegovina are to be annexed to the kingdom of Croatia on the basis of geographical, ethnographical, historical and political reasons. See especially *ibid.*, p. 41.

[28] Quoted by A. SPILETAK, « Bishop J. Strossmayer and the Eastern Church », in BS, XXIII (1935), 303-304.

[29] KRS, II, 252. (This letter to F. Rački is of January 27, 1880).

[30] CP, p. 428. See also IVO BODGAN, « Strossmayer », in *Hrvatska Revija*

2 - Strossmayer vs. the Austrian Monarchy and Germany

The former topic is not complete without bringing in Strossmayer's views on the Austrian Monarchy and its role in the European political theatre. It is not our aim at this place to go into details in displaying his relationship to the already existing set-up in
the Monarchy and his most earnest desire to reform it so that it
might serve the interests of all the nations; rather, we limit ourselves to stressing what role he assigned to it so that it might meet
equally and justly the needs of a multiplicity of nations.

First of all, he, like so many other politicians of his time as
for instance his friend Francis Palacky, Dr. L. Rieger and so many
others, was of the opinion that if Austria did not exist, a wise politician should create one. This was, of course, motivated by the desire to preserve political balance of power and peace on the European continent. The Monarchy, by its geographical position in the
heart of Europe and by its conglomeration of nations, was able to
fulfill this mission. In spite of the blatant realities in the Monarchy,
which were in direct conflict with his views, he remained scrupu-
lously faithful to the Austrian Dynasty and the destiny and mission
of the Monarchy in Europe. His thoughts on this topic were formulated best in his « pro memoria » to the Russian government
and in his correspondence with Lord W. Gladstone. It is interesting
to note that the British statesman manifested his ardent desire to
discuss privately with Strossmayer the existing situation in the Austrian Monarchy and also its role in Europe[31], but unfortunately the
plan was never realized.

The Bishop in his uncurbed enthusiasm for the Monarchy and
its mission wrote to Gladstone that his love for the Monarchy was
so great that he would give his life to save that « great » country[32],

---

(Argentina, Buenos Aires), III 1955), pp. 227-264. Unfortuntely Ivo Bog-
dan did not use any kind of documentation in his study, and for some unknown reasons he became engaged in polemics, therefore his presentation
of the Bishop is quite confused.

[31]   CBSG, p. 441. It is sad that some of Gladstone's letters to Strossmayer are not preserved.

[32]   *Ibid.*, p. 439 (Strossmayer's letter to Gladstone of March 13, 1879).

while in his « pro memoria » he wrote more soberly, stating that
« the sincere friends of the (Austrian) Dynasty and of the entire
Monarchy are desiring more than they are justified to expect »[33].
Regardless of his attachment to the Austrian Dynasty he did not
neglect to communicate to his friend Gladstone and to the Russian
government that neither the Austrian Dynasty nor the Monarchy
as such was capable of fulfilling its mission. According to his opinion, if the Monarchy wished to meet the expectations of the world,
then she must relinquish her unjust and insatiable desires – and
this especially goes for the Hungarians and must accord a total
freedom to each individual national group in her territory[34]. These
prerequisites in the Prelate's mind were *conditio sine qua non* to
bring up the Monarchy to the task that it was to perform in Europe.

The role of the Austrian Monarchy in Europe the Bishop has
formulated with these words: « (Austria) has... a providential destiny. It must become, amid the events which have already come to
pass and which will still occur towards the end of our century,
a great neutral state, strictly based upon truth and justice, to prevent in Europe the clash between the German element and the Slav
element: to form the guarantee of a durable peace; to assist sincerely and efficaciously the peoples of the Balkans in their just and
meritorious aims... Let us hope that the force of its pressing needs
and the course of nature will prove stronger than the blindness
of the men who have guided it hitherto »[35]. According to him the
Austrian Monarchy, due to the diversity of nationalities (German,
Hungarians and Slavs) was expected to serve as an intermediary
between the Germans and the Slavs in the arisen disputes[36] while
Great Britain, due to its insular position, must play « the part of
arbiter »[37]. In addition, he kept urging the Russian government

---

[33]   KRS, II, 57.
[34]   CBSG, p. 439 and also see KRS, II, 57.
[35]   CBSG, p. 441. See also his « pro memoria » in KRS, II, 56.
[36]   « But I hope », he writes to Gladstone, « with my whole heart that
it will be for advantage of the state to which I belong, and which seems
to have the exalted mission of interponing between great nations, to prevent
conflict and to bring about a solution of the most intricate questions, that
shall be for the advantage and happiness of Europe » (CBSG, p. 419).
[37]   « So far as Europe is concerned, a new order of things seems to be

to become more and more active in European political affairs so as to paralyse German ambitions.

Undoubtedly, the best appraisal of Strossmayer's conduct towards the Austrian Monarchy has been given by the Bitish historian R. Seton-Watson: « It was Strossmayer's misfortune that his faith in Austria was greater than the faith of those who controlled her destiny, and the bitter disillusionment of his political career would have amply excused an attitude of open hostitlity on his part. If he still hoped for a brighter future, this was due not to any signs of statesmanship in Vienna – for this the Magayars monopolized till the close of Strossmayer's long life – but solely to the unconquerable optimism of the Christian prelate »[38].

It would be wrong to say that the Bishop entertained any animosity toward the German nation, but, on the other hand, it is evident that he was fearful of what Germany might do in Europe and in the entire world. It is true that he did believe that every nation should unite and become its own master, but in the case of Germany he kept deploring the moment when Baravia would become totally germanized, or as he says: « Rejoyce, my dear Baravia, until it is time since once you are transformed into Germany, I do not believe that you will have any reason for rejoycing any more ». Small countries like Belgium, Switzerland, Holland, Sweden and Norway, in his opinion, experience a greater happiness than large countries since their appetites are curbed by the awareness of the limits of their power. None the less some small nations may go through agonies if they are forced to live in alliance with huge nations[39].

The Bishop's apprehension of the potential expansion of Germany, which might eventually cause conflagration in Europe, was based on his firm conviction that pagan instinct in a man often thriumphs, and this element to some extent appears even in a

---

in birth-throes. God has so placed England in Europe, that it is bound to it by a thousand ties, but at the same time by its insular position is set apart from Europe's petty passions and disputes, and is best qualified to play the part of arbiter in all difficult questions ». *Ibid.*, p. 423 (Strossmayer's letter to Gladstone of October 24, 1876).

[38]   R. SETON-WATSON, *The Southern Slav Question...*, *op. cit.*, 128.
[39]   TS, p. 359 (His « Travelogue »).

nation, too. This factor is emphasized in his correspondence with Lord Gladstone[40], in his « pro memoria » to the Russian government[41] and also in his « Travelog », written prior to the both documents in which his reflections are lucid and vivid upon the future possible adventures of Germany[42]. He admits that the Germans are extremely capable people in promoting culture and material prosperity, but at the same time he perceives a great peril in these abilities if they are not used for the advancement of justice. « There is a danger », he warns the Russian officials, « that the Germans -- due to their recent triumphs and never heard of successes – may become so puffed-up as to begin to think of their exclusive dominion over entire Europe; and there is every reason to believe that this might create in them another morbid and insane desire as to extend the boundaris of their realm all over the world ».

Two factors become evident from Strossmayer's said Document to the Russian leaders: first of all, that the aboriginal instinct in a man primarily tends to subjugate the other people to himself and that this primeval tendency was manifsted very often in the history of mankind as for instance in Alexander the Great, Napoleon Bonaparte, in the Romans, in the French and so on. Then hereafter he concludes: « If this irrational desire of the Germans is not checked by their great intelligence and prudence, they will precipitate entire Europe into ruins but in the final stage themselves. This aspiration of their (Germans) to bring under their dominion either the entire world or its various segments has God Himself for their adversary who had not only provided the eternal principles in the Gospel for the eternal salvation of mankind but He had supplied the human race with fundamental rules for the material prosperity – and God evidently intended – that all the nations should free themselves of their egotistical and tyrannical tendencies so that they may live togheter in harmony, sharing the truth, justice and charity... »[43].

---

[40] CBSG, pp. 437 and 442.
[41] KRS, II, 50, 51, 54 and passim, in « pro memoria ».
[42] TS, p. 332.
[43] KRS, II, 51-52. Cf. also TS, pp. 331-332. Strossamayer maintained that Bismarck was after conquering all of Europe. See KRS, III, 347.

3. - Russia and Strossmayer

Having in mind what has been said so far it should be easy for everybody to comprehend why Strossmayer so ardently endeavored to make Russia more interested in the European affairs and to strengthen the position of the Southern Slavs. It is not within our scope to place all his communications with the Russians in the chronological order, nor do we consider it necessary. In addition, Strossmayer had stated hundreds of times that Russia and the Southern Slavs were predestined by divine Providence to play the most important role in Europe and that there was no power on the earth to stop them or to prevent their marching on this chartered course. This idea he communicated in his « pro memoria » to Pope Pius IX in connection with the Eastern Question[44], and it seems that he had filled up the ears of the British distinguished clergyman, Canon Liddon, in Djakovo with this motto so that the Canon himself kept repeating it: « These Christian races of the Balkans are the predestined heirs of the future »[45].

In spite of Strossmayer's extreme idealism toward Russia and the Southern Slavs and their mission in Europe as « to rejuvenate the aging Europe with their faith and piety »[46], he was not so blinded as not to perceive the faults and inadequacies of the Russian leadership and also the petty rivalries among the South Slav nations. Princess Trubeckoi, Dr. Heesen, Vladimir Soloviev and his many other friends among the Russians kept informing him on the situation in the czarist Russia. Often he voiced his opinion to Fr. Rački and to his Russian friends that « the Russians are men of courage but their politics and diplomacy are immensely shallow and superficial. And this is the source of so many miseries »[47].

On the other hand, when V. Soloviev was extremely critical in his writings of the situation in Russia, of her government and its

---

[44] KRS, II, 113 and passim. See also Strossmayer's letter to Prince Nicholas of Montenegro. *Ibid.*, III, p. 310.

[45] R. Seton-Watson, *Disraeli, Gladstone...*, op. cit., 85.

[46] KRS, II, 113 (Strossmayer's « pro memoria » to Pope Pius IX, dated May 25, 1877).

[47] *Ibid.*, pp. 89-90 (Strossmayer's letter to F. Rački, dated February 22,

shortcomings and equally so of the Russian Church, Strossmayer
and Rački tried by all means to make him act more docile. Neither
Strossmayer nor Rački suspected the sincerity and openness of their
Russian friend, but they reasoned that in the situation like this it
would be more appropriate and fruitful if they would occasionally
flatter « the Russian vanity and ambitions as to persuade them to fulfill the mission (in Europe)... »[48]. Both Strossmayer and Rački were
well acquainted with the reality that the Russian intelligentsia were
religious and that the Russian people were willing to interefere in
the Balkans as to help the Christians on that peninsula to free them
from the Turkish slavery[49].

It appears that Soloviev, Rački and Strossmayer were correct
in appraising the intellectuals of the then Russia, their religiosity
and proneness to enter into the union with the Church of Rome,
but it is also evident that their knowledge in this respect or the
Russian general public and its feelings was almost nil. As a result,
Soloviev died completely disillusioned as far as his strivings for the
reunion of the Churches (Eastern and Westen) were concerned.
Strossmayer and Rački, on the other hand, died with the hope that
some day, as Strossmayer put it, « the task of the next century will
be to bring this idea into reality » and the Orthodox Church of
Russia would liberate herself from the State's fetters and thus afford
freedom to the Church of Rome[50].

At any rate, it is obvious that in the mind of the Bishop the
first step, which Russia must take in securing her political position

---

1877). « It seems to me to be the voice of God », he writes to Gladstone,
« which is speaking through those events, and at the same time warning
the Russians to put many things in order in their own house, if they wish
to remain worthy of the favour of the best European nations and able to
fulfill the goals of Providence in Europe and Asia alike ». CBSG, p. 432.

[48]   KRS, IV, 57 See also *ibid.,* pp. 3-4.

[49]   *Ibid.,* III, 145. Strossmayer is equally critical of the people in Petersburg (Leningrad) and in the Vatican for being slow and inefficacious in
solving current and pressing problems and for not being able ta grasp the
significance of the situation. In addition, the prelates in Rome were not
aware of the fact that the Russian intelligentsia would instantly enter into
union with the Church of Rome, if they were not afraid that the Church
of Russia would authomatically lose its autonomy with all her traditions
and customs which were so dear and indispensable to any intelligent Russian. Cf. also *ibid.,* p. 223 and passim.

[50]   KRS, III, 145, p. 287.

in Europe and which might eventually lead her into the union with the Church of Rome, was to establish a concordat with the Holy See. For this purpose he wrote « pro memoria » to the Russian government which bears the title « De momento et utilitate conventionis quam inclitum Russorum imperium cum Sancta Sede Apostolica stabilire opporteret ». (The Significance and Usefulness of the Concordat which the Glorious Russian Empire should Establish with the Holy Apostolic See). In reality, the convention by itself between the Holy See and Russia would usher her (Russia) *ipso facto* into the European family and her very presence would contribute greatly to the creation of political equilibrium. The Bishop felt it necessary to advise the Russian Dynasty and the Russian leaders to abandon Asia for the time and to focus her attention primarily upon European affairs. In the aforsaid Document he preoccupied himself with finding the cause of the existing prejudices against the Russians. This was accomplished by displaying the national traits and tendencies of each major European nation and what Russia was expected to do here and now. Here are some descriptions of the situation in Europe and some of his suggestions to the Russians:

1. Strossmayer was totally aware that Russia, while accomplishing her mission in Europe, would be confronted with numerous difficulties, but on the other hand he expressed his hope that the wisdom, courage and patience of the Russians will overcome them. He openly told the Russian government that all of Europe would be seized « by horror and fear » by the Russian presence. He also admitted that the fear of the European nations of the Russian interference in Europe is unfounded, but on the other hand Russia is expected to do her share in dispelling these baseless fears. He does mention some facts which greatly contributed to the above mentioned European opinion, namely, that the Russian tendency has been and still is to suffocate the freedom of religion and that of human conscience. What is more, Europe was under the impression that the Russian attitude is totally anti-Catholic. However, the Prelate holds responsible for this tragic situation not only the Russians themselves but the popes, too, who in their numerous allocutions

have attacked Russia and her policy. Many European Catholic newspapers and periodicals, especially French reviews, were fulminating against Russia. He finally came to the following conclusions: if you (Russians) enter into a pact with the Holy See, the popes will discontinue speaking against you. The Catholics of Europe attentively listen to the supreme pontiff, and once he stops speaking against you, he will be followed by the Catholic leaders and the various editors, especially by those who are at present most outspoken against you since « they have some exaggerated notions about the rights and the authority of the Holy See ».

2. It is known to everybody that the peoples of the Latin (Roman) race by their very nature are inconsistent and mobile. This trait accounts for the fact that they are sometimes in favor of entering into coalition with the Russian nation and again they are at times against it. This is the case even though they should promote this mutual harmony if for no other reason then for their own interests. History teaches us that whenever the French turned against the Russian people they never did it for their own interests but for the interests and benefits of someone else. At this time they are favoring the cause of the Turks more than of the Slavs. However, the French Catholics would follow or rather they will change the course of their politics towards the Slavs if they learned that the glorious Russian empire had entered into alliance with the Holy See. We should never forget that the French Catholics exercise a great influence upon the shaping of French foreign policy.

3. What has been said about the French goes equally for the Italians. The Italians will remain Catholics all the time. Don't let anybody be fooled by the present situation in Italy in which the Holy See is in crisis, and consequently think that the power and influence of it (Holy See) will disappear. Italians are quite aware of the prestige and moral influence of the Holy See, and they will utilize all possible means to keep it in their midst. What is more, the Holy See will come out of this struggle with the Italian government stronger and more fitted to fulfill its divine mission once it is freed from these temporal and wordly chains and powers. Our

Lord performed the greatest work on the cross when he had been abandoned by all and left to Himself. The Holy See will break these earthly shackles, and then it will perform more efficiently its divine mission entrusted to it. There is no doubt that the Russian nation will win to her side Italy if she enters into a pact with the Church of Rome. What has been written about the French and the Italians can be also applied to the Spaniards.

4. Before we say anything about the Poles, we deem it necessary to mention that it has been a well-known fact that both Rački and Strossmayer in their correspondence were extremely critical of the attitude and of the mentality of the Polish nation. The principal reason for this severe criticism of the Polish people lies in the fact that the Poles had always identified their politics with their Catholic faith and the Catholic Church. In the opinion of the two Croats every nation must elevate itself above its own religion if it wishes to work with and to cooperate with the other nations. Strossmayer in his « pro memoria » accuses the Poles of being blinded by hatred against the Russians and being willing to enter into an alliance with the devil himself as long as it is against the Russian nation. The Poles in their shallowness go so far as to subject the Ruthens to various tortures and thus they drive them away from the Church of Rome. According to the Bishop the animosity of the Poles toward the Russians was so intensive that they would neglect their own national interests just to be against the Russians. Besides, the Poles are constantly filling the ears of the Holy See with their complaints against the Russians as if they were constantly fighting against the Russians to preserve the freedom of their own country and religion. And finally he suggests that the Russians try to understand the Poles and sympathize with them by showing freedom of conscience and religion .

5. The Hungarians are the worst enemies of the Slavs: they utilize all the methods and the means to hold the Slav nations in slavery. On account of this they plot with the Germans against the Austrian Monarchy to divide the Slav nations between the Germans and themselves. What is more, the Hungarians are in favor of the Turkish tyranny over the Slavs in South East Europe; they

are genuinely turcophiles since they opine that the death of the
Slavs is a *conditio sine qua non* to their dominion. Russians, by
entering into a pact with the Church of Rome, will bring an end
to the Hungarian vilifications against Russia, and at the same time
they will endear themselves to the Austrian Dynasty which is sincerely devoted to the Holy See[51].

At the end of this lenthy Document the Bishop offers the following suggestions to the Russian government:

« As far as the concordat (with the Holy See) is concerned the
following questions can be put forth: 1st, is this pact feasible,
secondly, is the time opportune for it? I answer to the both questions with the definite yes. It is true that in solving any serious
problem some inner difficulties are encountered but, as the things
stand, men are given a sublime intellect and firm will as not to give
in to the obstacles, and by overcoming them all the prejudices and
animosities will be eliminated. God offers all the rewards to the
human labors. All the things are possible to the wise, patient, moderate and benevolent.

« And now what is the first step to be undertaken (in this matter)? In this concordat, first of all, the Holy See must offer a solemn and public guarantee to the glorious Russian government that
the Catholic religion will never be used under any pretext to diminish or to undermine the authority of the Russian Empire or
in any way to spread diffamations against it as far it often was the
case before either with the Poles, or the Hungarians and the other
enemies of Russia. The Holy See, the natural representative of the
supreme authority in the world, will be more than glad to offer
this since she (the Holy See) is aware that nothing is so detrimental to religion and to herself as the subversion of the natural order
which is intended by the great God for the benefit and the betterment of men; by the same token, the Holy See is predestined to
sustain and to make every just authority firm and stable, and she
considers every attempt impious and sacriligious which tends to cor-
rupt men and to undermine authority and discipline or to diffame
authority in any manner. This it the eternal and inviolable destiny of

---

[51] KRS, II, 51-58 (Strossmayer's « pro memoria »).

the Holy Apostolic See which she will gladly fulfill whenever she is given such an opportunity.

« Furthermore, in regard to this prospective concordat the imperial Russian government vice versa must offer publicly and solemnly the promise to the Holy See that its civil power and authority will never and nowhere be used as to be in its application detrimental and harmful to the Catholic religion. I have no doubt that the glorious imperial government is prompt and prepared to meet all the justified requirements of the Holy See in this respect; in addition, nothing is so noxious to the civil authority as to violate and to pervert the rights of human conscience since human conscience is the ultimate source of every reverence not only toward God and religion but also of every other authority. Everybody knows that God in some special way gets revenge upon those who dare use God and religion for the profane and unjust purposes.

« As I have learned, some special problems are at heart to the glorious Russian government as for instance: what language the (Russian) subjects – the Ruthenes – must use in conducting their liturgy and in what language divine law of the Gospel is to be explained? All similar and special problems like this one will be easily and promptly resolved as soon as the basic issues are properly solved. On the contrary, if the fundamental questions are left unanswered, then the secondary issues will become more and more complicated, and they will reach the point of unsolvency. As for instance, if the above mentioned question of the Ruthenes is left unsolved and in the present status, the Poles will constantly call to the Holy See: be careful, be careful, the snake is hiding in the grass; the Russian government wishes to destroy the last connection through which the Ruthenes are attached to the Catholic faith and to the Holy See. Once the agreement with the Holy See is accomplished, all these accusations will be weakened and almost will be totally deprived of any value.

« As far as the second question is concerned, namely, if the time is opportune to realize this concordat, my reply is positive: In Europe, as it looks to me now and as I have already indicated, it is evident that great things are about to take place. In our times it is expected that the Russian people and the entire Slav race – since their host of enemies are confused and made powerless – must gain for themselves the position in Europe and secure it for eternity in order to serve to the plans of God and to the interests of the entire mankind. Our times – this is obvious – are afflicted by birththroes. The old ideas are disappearing little by little while the new ones did not take on any concrete forms that they would be able to free mankind from fear and anxiety. It seems that the moment and the time have arrived for the Slavs... It looks to me that the most suitable thing to do for the glorious Russian Empire in this decisive and historical moment would be to procure the surest way through which you will overcome the prejudices of the world (against you) and at the same time to find more appropriate ways in meeting the extremely grave events which are about to occur.

« The Holy See cannot ignore the fact that the Slavs will perform a great influence upon the newly created situation in Europe. And this influence will be in favor of each authority and genuine religiosity and also in favor of that justice and equity which – after having eliminated every sort of egoism – will always give to everybody what rightly belongs to him; and what is more, through this mastery the best possible relationship among various nations will be reestablished and guaranteed. The Church, which is called the mother of all nations, cannot exclude from her maternal care and charity a nation (Russian) which is called upon to exercise higher and more divine missions in the world. The supreme pontiff, who is regarded the father of all nations, must desire to do instantly something about this that he may earn the glorious title of the father of the Slav race.

« Please, allow me to add one more observation to this dissertation of mine: the sacred law of the Gospel, which is divinely given to be a regulator to the entire human society, has today numerous and fierce enimies who are aiming with the axe at the root of this tree (the Gospel) with the open intention to exterminate the entire Christian religion and even to expel God – if it would be possible – from the human hearts and from the human society with their own laws. It is time that the two greatest and most glorious Churches, the long-time sisters, must put aside their mutual animosities and must come to the amicable agreement to work together in order to save the foundations of the Christian religion and of every human society, and in that manner the human race will be freed from the total destruction toward which the present irreligion – trying to undermine every kind of authority – is heading. It is time that the both Churches Eastern and Western – and of the former one the glorious Russian nation is the worthiest representative in the world – must become aware of the fact that there is only one point of division between them, and that is found in the governmental structure, and the rest they share in common: the same faith, the same sacrifice and the same apostolic priesthood, therefore they must pursue the same goals, by constantly retaining their individual liberty, and thus becoming more efficient than earlier in fulfilling their missions and by combatting their inner shortcomings with greater efficacy.

« The Author of this " pro memoria " has known a great number of men of all sorts of religious and philosophical persuasions and has observed that these most noble minds are obsessed by some inextinguishable desire for the unity of the entire human race of whichh the Lord had spoken in the parable of one shepherd and of one flock. As it was the case with the Roman Empire – spread all over the then known world – which had prepared the way for the spread of the Gospel, thus in the present circumstances the newly tremendous invented power of steamships and electricity will serve to achieve this holy unity (of mankind); and for this unity as the ultimate and the most noble goal the divine blood had been shed. Toward this design and destination of unity willingly or unwillingly the entire human race is moving, and this is being accomplished not only by way of virtues and merits but also by errors and hallucinations which God is using as a means in achieving higher goals. It must be of the ulmost interest that in accomplishing this goal of human solidarity these two oldest Churches (Eastern and Westen) take the initiative through the mutual harmony, and let these two Churches champion in the mutual love which will completely triumph at the end of the world. This is the most sublime goal toward which the prospective concordat must strive.

« The writer of these lines is in accordance with the above scope – of course in the confidential manner. (The Author) thinks that all this (concordat and the rest of it) is feasible – and more so since he is enjoying the friendship of a man who holds high position in Rome and whose influence in the Vatican offices is great.

« I beg your pardon for my having written this hastily and incoherently since I am overburdened with my daily duties. If these matters, of which I have written, prove a little, please, consider them insufficient, but on the other hand this is a sincere document of my admiration toward the illustrious Dynasty and the glorious Russian nation. I beg you, however, again and again not to reveal the identity of this Author since it might place me in a grave danger. I have written (this) on the Feast of the Nativity of the Bl. V. Mary (September 8) in the year of 1872 »[52].

Another portion of the document deals with South East Europe, that is, with the liberation of the Southern Slavs from the Turks; and it was one of the chief goals of the Russians – in Strossmayer's mind to accord freedom to the Christians in that corner of Europe. This topic will be treated in greater detail later on. Naturally, the Bishop himself wondered and was almost a bit apprehensive what impression his dissertation would make upon the Russian Dynasty and government. It also appears from Strossmayer and Rački's correspondence that at that time the South European problem would get priority by the Russian government to that of entering into concordat with the Holy See[53]. Judging by the subsequent events, it seems that their assumption was correct.

It is extremely difficult to follow all Strossmayer's vicissitudes in reaching the agreement between Russia and the Church of Rome. Through Cardinal Franchi he succeeded in stirring up the Rus-

---

[52] *Ibid.,* II pp. 61-64. At the bottom of the last page of his dissertation the following statement is found: « It will contribute a lot to the success of the discussed concordat if a Russian Catholic were sent to Rome to expedite this matter » *Ibid.,* p. 64.

[53] KRS, II, 68-73.

sians and the Vatican to initiate the preliminary talks in this regard.
(Strossmayer and Rački were acquainted with the secret negotiations between Russia and the Vatican). The preliminary discussions between the Russians and the Holy See commenced in Vienna, Austria, and they were conducted by the Papal Nuncio Mgr.
L. Jacobini and the Russian emmissary Ubril. The first pre-agree-
ments between the interested parties were reached on October
31, 1880. In the following year Czar Alevander II was assassina-
ted and was succeeded by his son Alexander III, who almost immediately wrote to pope Leo XIII expressing his desire for close
cooperation between the Churches and also among the States.
Pope Leo in his reply to the Csar expressed his solidarity with
his intentions. Most probably the exchange of the letters between
the Pontiff and the Csar accelerated the second stage of the agreement between Russia and the Vatican which was signed in Rome
on December 24, 1882[54].

The Vatican was greatly interested in assuring the freedom
for the Catholics in Russia. In the month of June, 1881, both
Strossmayer and Rački were in Rome, and the latter was offered
the position of a metropolitan for all Catholics in Russia. For
quite some time the Bishop of Djakovo kept pleading with Canon
Rački to accept the position since he viewed the presence of Rački
in Russia to be of « extreme importance in every aspect ». At the
beginning Rački seemed to be undecided but later on he refused
the offer[55], Strossmayer on the other hand regarded this offer to
Canon Rački so highly that he expressed his intention of taking
up the offered position had he been any younger[56]. Rački, with
his erudition and tact would have paved the way for the speedier
concordat and would have eliminated many misunderstandings between Russia and the Vatican.

In our opinion there was another reason, besides Rački's refusal to become a metropolitan of the Catholics in Russia, for the

---

[54] *Ibid.,* pp. 392-393. – Concordat between the Holy See and Russia
was signed in 1905.

[55] *Ibid.,* pp. 394-397 and 406-408.

[56] KRS, III, 69.

slow-moving process in reaching a pact between the Vatican and Russia, and that was the total preclusion of Strossmayer from actively participating in the talks. It seems that the Roman prelates were jealously guarding their « slow » moving discussion with Russian officials from any outside intrusion. This attitude of Rome would have occasionally irritated the Bishop of Djakovo[57], but it never discouraged him from looking for new either direct or indirect connections and avenues to speed up the reaching of the agreement. In order to accelerate the talks Vladimir Soloviev threw all the weight of his influence upon various Russian personalities who were close to the Csar[58], while Strossmayer in the meantime kept close contact with the Russian delegates, Butenev and Izvolski, in Rome[89]. In addition, the Croatian Prelate corresponded with his friend, Prince Nicholas of Montenegro, who was an intimate friend of the Russian Czar « by placing himself at the Prince's and Csar's disposal »[60].

4. - Lord W. Gladstone, Strossmayer, and the Southern Slav Question

Undoubtedly, one of the chief aims of the Bishop was the liberation of the South Slavs from the Turks in whose captivity they had spent over four centuries under most gruesome conditions. He threw himself unsparingly into awakening the conscience of Russia, Great Britain and the Holy See in order to come to the aid of these neglected and forgotten people. His activities in this regard reached their peak in 1870's. It is not easy to follow the

---

[57] « I advise those in Petersburg again and again », he writes to Rački, « to reconcile with the Vatican by all means. If those in the Vatican and in Petersburg were clever enough, they would appoint me as an intermediary, and I would eliminate all the existing difficulties. I am still corresponding with Princess Trubeckoi in Petersburg ». KRS, IV, 45-46 (Letter dated November 16, 1888).

[58] Ibid., p. 51. Soloviev was notified by his friends while he was in Zagreb that the Csar was still willing to sign an agreement with the Holy See. Ibid.

[59] KRS, III, 365.

[60] Ibid., p. 310.

chronological order of his undertakings in this respect. By the early 1870's the problem of liberation of the Southern Slavs was acute. Due to the uprising of the Christians against the Turkish dominion and the Turkish bloody reprisals and the almost helpless Christians in Bosnia, Herzegovina, Bulgaria in 1875, the whole problem assumed great dimensions; thus all European powers became preoccupied with this burning question. Since the Austrians and Hungarians (and especially Count J. Andrassy, Austrian Foreign Minister) were turcophils, Strossmayer was left no other alternative but to look for help somewhere else as Great Britain and Russia to put end to the Turkish atrocities in South East Europe.

Strossmayer wrote his first memorandum in regard to the situation in South East Europe to Cardinal Franchi (The Bishop of Djakovo gave personally this document to Franchi in Rome on January 8, 1876, and the copy of it is found in the archives of the diocese of Djakovo, dated April 20, 1876 under No. 397). In this memorandum he instructed the Cardinal and through him the Holy Father what steps and attitude they ought to take toward the uprising of the Christians in Bosnia and Herzegovina against the Turks. Strossmayer's action was motivated by the fact that the Sultan had asked the Holy See to exercise its influence at least upon the Catholics of the said two provinces as to make them remain quiet. The Prelate suggested to Franchi in the mentioned Document that if the Holy See did not consider it opportune to side with the rebels of Bosnia and Herzegovina, then at least the Vatican should refrain from giving either private or public opinion on the matter. He also instructed Cardinal Franchi that the promises of the Sultan to ammeliorate the conditions of the Christians in South East Europe were illusory and unworthy of any consideration. In addition, the Bishop expressed in this document his firm belief that the Christians in these regions would obtain their freedom in the nearest future with their own constitution[61].

---

[61] Cited by A. Spiletak, « Bishop J. G. Strossmayer and the Eastern Church », in BS, XXIII (1935), pp. 284-285. Strossmayer secretly sent 500 florins to the Montenegrian Metropolitan (Greek Orthodox) for the Herzegovinian refugees. *Ibid.*, p. 283.

Needless to say, this Document of Strossmayer to Cardinal Franchi bears a great similarity to his « pro memoria » to the Russian government, and in his letters to Lord Gladstone the same arguments are found word for word. In all these instances – especially in « pro memoria » and in this extensive letters to the British Statesman – he succintly analysed the Turkish policy and attitude toward the Christians by placing a factual emphasis upon the Turkish brutalities perpetrated upon the defensless Christians and upon Turkish unwillingnes to afford any freedom to them. In his correspondence with Gladstone and in his memorandum to the Russian government he most determinedly calls for their immediate action and intervention in South East Europe[62]. While he urges the Russians that « the glorious Russian Empire, among other things, is predestined to free South East Europe from this Turkish plague and to bring about the occasion when the Christian mysteries will be celebrated in the famous church (in Constantinople) of St. Sophia »[53], on the other hand he suggests to Gladstone what course Great Britain is expected to undertake in this regard: « It is my conviction, then », he writes to Gladstone, « that the preservation of peace and the attainment of the great aim which all friends of mankind have before their eyes, mainly depends upon England's attitude. But to this end England would have to lay aside all petty scruples, and support honestly and wholeheartedly the efforts of Russia »[64].

It is not our goal to offer a detailed picture of the events in solving the Eastern Question, since this has been done by many historians, but it is rather our purpose to present Strossmayer's role in these occurrences which are actually unknown and to point out how spiritually akin were the Prelate and Gladstone. Whoever happens to read their correspondence will instantly notice that both of them arose above the particular interests of their respective churches and devoted themselves to the common interests of Christ-

---

[62] CBSG, pp. 417-424 and passim. See also « pro memoria » in KRS, II, 59, and A. Spitelak, loc. cit, in BS, p. 284 (Memorandum to Cardinal Franchi).

[63] KRS, II, 60.

[64] CBSG, p. 421.

ianity; and what is more, they were in continuous search of making
Christianity and Christian nations to be of service to the less
fortunate non-Christian races and nations. Only under this perspective one can understand why Gladstone, after receiving Strossmayer's letter of October 1, 1876, had decided to abandon the
retirement that he was enjoying and to consider the problem of
the South European Christians « of the first rank »[65]. Strossmayer,
in the reply to Gladstone's heroic decision, said: « Your letter
greatly honoured, rejoiced and encouraged me. You have done
well », he wrote to Gladstone, « in leaving your retirement, for,
my dear friend, God has placed you on such a height, that even
the evening of your life belongs not to yourself, but to your
distinguished nation and to all mankind »[66].

In regard to the solution of the Southern Slavs Question several factors deserve to be brought out. First of all, Gladstone
desired by all means to publish Strossmayer's reports to him on
the situation in South East Europe in the British press. In his
opinion this would largely contribute to the arousing of the conscience of the British public, since the Bishop of Djakovo still
enjoyed a great popularity in Great Britain on account of the
writings of the British newspapers about him during the Vatican
Council. Unfortunately, Strossmayer was afraid to comply with
the wish of Gladstone because of the possible reprisals of the
Austrian-Hungarian governments against him »[67]. Gladstone was also very much aware that the number of the « Anglo-Turks » was
too great, and he begged Strossmayer for more information as
« to secure local autonomy in the provinces of Bosnia, Herzegovina and Bulgaria »[68].

---

[65] « I cannot tell you », he writes to Strossmayer, « how much I associate myself with the internal feeling of that letter. The question of the suffering provinces of Turkey is for me a question of the first rank. It has dragged me from my retirement, which to some extent I was beginning to enjoy, after forty-four years of continual struggle in English political life, and
after almost reaching the term of sixty-seven years of age. I can indeed assure you that in many respects it is for me a sacrifice, thus to change the
current of my ideas and of my daily work, and to trust myself once more
to a stormy sea » (CBSG, p. 424).
[66] Ibid., p. 420.
[67] Ibid., p. 424.
[68] Ibid., pp. 424-425.

It ought also to be added that Gladstone was well acquainted with the Turkish atrocities done against the Christians in South East Europe which he had exposed in his famous pamphlet « The Bulgarian Horrors and the Question of the East », published on September 5, 1876. It is equally true that the British Statesman threw the whole weight of his influence on the side of the Christians in the provinces of Turkey in Europe. It was also of great consolation to him that he was not isolated in championing the cause of the Southern Slavs. Both the Anglican and Catholic clergy were to great an extent sympathetic with Gladstone[69]. His most vociferous supporters, undoubtedly, were Canon Dr. Liddon[70] and Rev. Malcolm MacCall, especially after they had returned from Serbia and after having paid a visit to Strossmayer in Djakovo who had supplied them with the details on the gruesome incidents in Bosnia and Herzegovina. There was another public and distinguished figure in Great Britain, Edward A. Freeman, who had devoted all his intellectual abilities to presenting the horrible situation of the Southern Slavs in the Turkish European provinces for over twenty years in various British Reviews: *North British Review, Edinburgh Review, National Review, British Quaterly Review, Fortnightly Review, MacMillan's Magazine*[71].

All three of them, Gladsone, Freeman and Strossmayer, shared the same views on the Eastern Question. When one reads the works of Freeman, he actually feels that he is reading Strossmayer's « pro memoria » to the Russian government and his letters to Lord Gladstone. It was Strossmayer's firm persuasion that there was no other

---

[69] Cf. R. Seton-Watson, *Disraeli, Gladstone...*, *op. cit.*, 16-21 and especially 83-86.

[70] « As a rule », Canon Liddon said in his sermons, « it is undoubtedly better for us, the ministers of Christ, to avoid reference to topics connected with the public action of the country... But there are times when silence is impossible... Such a time is surely upon us now, when we as a nation are slowly awaking to a true estimate of recent events in Eastern Europe and of our involuntary share in them ». Quoted by. R. Seton-Watson, *ibid.*, pp. 84-85. Canon Liddon also wrote to Dr. Dale: « I cannot help saying to you how greatly the history of the Eastern Question has affected my feeling toward those who are not members of the Church in England ». *Ibid.* p. 568.

[71] Edward A. Freeman, *The Ottoman Power in Europe, its Nature, its Growth, and its Decline* (London, Macmillan and Co., 1877), pp. XXI XXII (Introduction).

solution to the Eastern Question, or as the Prelate writes to Gladstone: « Strengthen the Christian people in their autonomy and the
Turks in Europe are done for... Europe's problem simply consists
in making the Turks disappear from Europe, if possible without
bloodshed and great upheavals »[72].

Gladstone, as well as Strossmayer, did not believe that Turkey,
after so many diplomatic warnings, was capable of introducing and
willing to introduce new reforms for the betterment of the Christians;
therefore he agreed with the Bishop that all talks with the Turks
in regard to reforms « are null and indeed mere talks, but once
expelled, the Turks will never be able to return. After the expulsion,
there will be either autonomy or the intermediary and provisional
state of a foreign regime »[73]. E. A. Freeman is almost on the same
line with his countryman Gladstone and Strossmayer: « As long
as any Christian land remains under the Turks, there will be discon-
tents and disturbances and revolts and massacres... the standing
cause of discountent and revolt and massacre (is) the rule of the
Turks »[74].

Strossmayer's constant urgency and suggestion to Lord Gladstone that Great Britain should come into cordial and intimate
cooperation with the Russians indicates that he wanted to bring
these two powers into some kind of an agreement as to employ
threats against the Turks in order to force them to leave Europe
and to retire into the boundaries of their country of their own accord. Since this disire was never realized, and since on April 24,
1877, the Russian troops attacked Turkey, on Sepetember 3, 1877,
Strossmayer wrote to Gladstone that the Turks « are not worthy
of any consideration », and that it was a sacred duty of the European Christians to free their brothers in South East Europe[75]. This
was Strossmayer's constant refrain, expressed in his letters to Gladstone and to the Russian government, that the Christians should
get united in freeing the Southern Slavs. It is also evident that the

---

[72]   CBSG, p. 422.
[73]   *Ibid.*, p. 427.
[74]   E. A. FREEMAN, *op cit.*, p. X.
[75]   CBSG, p. 431. See more on the Russo-Turkish War by R. SETON-
WATSON, *Disraeli, Gladstone...*, *op. cit.*, 168-232.

Bishop kept continuously urging the British Statesman to use his influence so that Great Britain, in the case of conflict between Russia and Turkey, should remain, at least, neutral, so as not to hinder the noble intentions of the Russians in the Balkans. The British historian, E. A. Freeman, opined in the same manner as the Bishop did[76]. Strossmayer was quite frank with Gladstone in telling him that Russia had some of her own interests in the Balkan peninsula, but he urged him that in the case of possible cooperation between his country and Russia they would be in position to tell the Russians « thus far and no farther »[77].

Did Strossmayer contribute anything? or did he speed up in any sense the realization of the Russo-Turkish War? It is hard to say. However, it is evident from Strossmayer's correspondence that he continuously kept urging the Russian government to occupy Constantinople. This he communicated many a time to the Russian Dynasty and to the Russian political leaders through Princess L. Trubeckoi[78]. It is interesting to observe that the Czar himself highly favored and shared the same idea. As a matter of fact the Csar sent the instructions to the Grand Duke, his brother, who was in charge of military operations that he should arrange the occupation of Constantinople « with or without the agreement of the Turks ». In all probability this would have been realized, had not the Turkish intelligence intercepted the Csar's telegrams. Due to this incident the Gran Duke received them with quite some delay, and consequently he did not act according the wish of his brother[79]. Strossmayer even after the Treaty of San Stefano of March 3, 1878, did not abandon the idea that the Christians should expel the Turks from Constantinople. As late as on April 17, 1880, he wrote to Gladsone: « I can hardly tell you how happy I should be if I ever lived to see Christian worship celebrated in magnificent Aga Sofia »[80].

---

[76] « The deliverance of the subject nations (Slav nation and Greeks) ought to be, if possible, the work of all Europe. Failing that, it should be the work of Russia and England together », writes E. A. FREEMAN, *op cit.,* p. XII and also in the same work, pp. 166-250.

[77] CBSG, p. 421 and passim.

[78] KRS, II, 169 and passim.

[79] Cf. R. ŠETON-WATSON, *Disraeli, Gladstone...,* op. cit., 329-335.

[80] CBSG, p. 442.

Strossmayer's apprehension of the stand which the Holy See might take in case of the conflict between Russia and Turkey was not unfounded. And precisely on account of this reason he attempted to prepare the Vatican officials for this eventuality. This was done in his memorandum to Cardinal Franchi. Whether or not the Cardinal had instructed Pope Pius IX on the situation in the Balkans we do not know. However, it is a fact that the Pontiff on April 30, 1877, condemned the Russians with the following words addressed to the pilgrims of Savoy: « During these days – to be more precise at this very moment – the great schismatic power (Russia) is placing its mighty army with tremendous artillery on the battlefield with the sole purpose to punish the pagan power (Turkey) accusing it that it was unjustly ruling and exploiting its subjects who are professing the same schismatic faith. (The Pontiff is referring here to the Bulgarians, Rumanians, Serbs and Monte-negrins). The war has begun, and we do not know which of these powers is going to come out victorious. We know, however, very well that on the side of one of these powers, which calls itself Orthodox, and in reality it is schismatic, rests the hand of God's justice becaue of its fierce persecutions which it has inaugurated against the Catholics years ago, and these persecutions are still going on »[81].

Of course, the Bishop became exceedingly disturbed by the Pontiff's pronouncement against the Russians, and his first reaction to it was not to go to Rome for the golden celebration of Pius IX's bishopric. As he said « there is no place for me any more in Rome for the forthcoming celebration... The way it is said it looks as if the Pope is the protector of Islam against Christendom. What a lack of wisdom!... Oh, Rome, this is not the way to gather you squander »[82]. Finally, the Bishop changed his mind and went to Rome since the Pope himself expressed his wish to see him. While in Rome he wrote on May 25, 1877, a momorandum to the Pontiff on the situation in the Balkans and on the Pontiff's already cited statement. The Bishop made the following comment on the Pontiff's words:

---

[81] KRS, II, 105.
[82] *Ibid.*, p. 106 (His letter to F. Rački).

« Your Holiness was totally justified for reprimanding the Russian Empire for the committed iniquities against the Catholics, but on the other hand it is said very often – which nobody in good conscience can believe – that the intention of Your Holiness was – in this duel between the Turks and the Russians – to wish the victory to the Turks, who are the worst enemies to the Christian name, and to invoke the punishment upon the Russians. In this manner, Your Holiness, your words are interpreted in the public... I beg, Your Holiness », he continued to say, « if ever occasion would be offered, that you may deign to interpret your former allocution, and in what sense it ought to be understood »[83]

All these incidents indicate that Strossmayer wanted by all means to make the most favorable climate in Europe for the Russian undertakings in the Balkans. During his sojourn in Rome in May, 1877, he contacted the French Ambassador, Emmanuel de Noailles, in Rome and made serious attempts as to engage the French representative to influence his government in Paris to declare itself in favor of the Russian invasion into the Balkan peninsula. Unluckily, he did not receive any cooperation or understanding[84].

At the end it remains to us to allege how Strossmayer envisioned the Balkans to be organized once the Balkan nations were liberated from the Turks. It looks though that he took quite a few detours on this issue especially in regard to Bosnia and Herzegovina. Canon Liddon reported the views of the Bishop to Lord Gladstone, namely, that Strossmayer advocated that Bosnia and Herzegovina should be united with Serbia and Montenegro, and that this political combination would curb Russian ambitions in the Balkans[85]. In his first letter of October 1, 1876, to Gladstone Strossmayer proposed that Bosnia with its own government should be placed under the protection of the Serbs as a reward to them for their bravery against the Turks[86]. At the beginning of 1878 he wrote

---

[83] *Ibid.*, pp. 112-113.
[84] *Ibid.*, pp. 324-325.
[85] Cf. R. Seton-Watson, *Disraeli, Gladstone...*, *op. cit.*, 85.
[86] CBSG, p. 420.

to Gladstone that « in present conditions it would be impossible to entrust the administration of these countries (Bosnia and Herzegovina) to the hands of the Serbs, with reservation of the Turkish suzerainty – a course which I regard as the most practical; on the other hand, it is not easy to imagine any other suzerainty or influence on an international basis, without great confusion. There is then nothing left, in my opinion, but to make these countries quite autonomous and to retain Turkish suzerainty, perhaps defined by international law »[87].

One would be wrong in assuming that Strossmayer did not want Bosnia and Herzegovina to be united with Croatia. As a matter of fact, he was notified by Princess L. Trubeckoi that one of the plenipotentiaries at the Congress of Berlin (1878) had told her – while she was visiting with Prince Gorchakov in Berlin – that Bosnia and Herzegovina should be annexed to Croatia. Naturally, the Bishop encouraged her to work in this direction through her friends, even though he did not have much faith that the suggestion would ever become a reality[88]. In other words, the possibility of annexing Bosnia and Herzegovina to Croatia was totally eliminated by the Austrians and Hungarians, and therefore no other alternative was left to the Bishop in order to prevent the Hungarians from taking these provinces to themselves. He could only advocate the Serbian protectorate over Bosnia and Herzegovina or complete autonomy for them under Turkish suzerainty, as he had suggested to Gladstone.

According to the Treaty of San Stefano (March 3, 1878) Bosnia and Herzegovina had to become autonomous provinces under the suzerainty of Turkey, but this point of the said Treaty was reversed at the Congress of Berlin on the insistence of Count J. Andrassy (Austrian Foreign Minister) it was aligned again with the secret agreement of January 27, 1877, between Austria-Hungary and Russia – signed by the Russian Ambassador in Vienna, E. Novikov and J. Andrassy – in which (secret agreement) Russia had conceded to Austria-Hungary to occupy and annex Bosnia and Herzegovina as

---

[87] *Ibid.*, p. 435.
[88] KRS, II, 179.

a recompense for remaining neutral in the military conflict between Turkey and Russia.

Whether or not Strossmayer had any influence on the Treaty of San Stefano, in which his desire regarding Bosnia and Herzegovina was realized, we do not. However we do know that he kept urging Princess Trubeckoi to employ her influence upon the Grand Duke, Nicholas Nikolaievic, to throw the Turks out of Europe and to make Bosnia and Herzegovina autonomous under the Turkish suzerainty[89].

Strossmayer's plans in regard to Bosnia and Herzegovina had other obstacles, and these were of the utmost significance. His thesis did not have much popularity among the Croatians in the Croatia proper and much less among the populace of the two involved provinces, especially among the Catholics and a certain segment of the Mohammedans who were directly involved. The Franciscans, their faithful and some leading Mohammedans were strongly in favor of being occupied or rather liberated by the Austrian troups, led by one of the Croatian generals; and the latter was realized in the person of General Joseph Filipović who was shortly after the annexation removed from Bosnia on account of supposedly « his excessive croaticism »[90].

As it has earlier been remarked, it is not easy to comprehend Strossmayer, particularly on the matter of his stand on the question of Bosnia and Herzegovina; on the other hand, he wanted to see free all the Southern Slavs that they might map out their own future and eventually decide for themselves what they thought was best for them.

He was not only concerned with the interest of the Croatian nation, but also with the interests of the Serbs, Montenegrins and Bulgarians, He wrote to Gladstone: « ... I have to recommend to you the Serbs and Montenegrins. So far as the former are concerned, it would be very desirable that all Old Serbia should be

---

[89] Princess Trubeckoi wrote to Strossmayer on January 23, 1878 « pas paix avant la prise de Constantinople ». (Trubeckoi's correspondence with Strossmayer) AJA XI A/L. Trub. 19. Cf. also KRS, II, 141 and pp. 144-147.
[90] KRS, II, 36-37, 180-187 and especially 193-195.

handed over to them... The Montenegrins with their splendid and truly heroic prince, I hardly need to recommend to you. If any people deserve the world's admiration, it is this splendid Montenegrin people, which has taken up its abode like an eagle on a lofty and barren crag, in order to buy its freedom and independence by a thousand sacrifices and renunciations for centuries »[91]. « Bulgaians », he writes to Gladstone on another occasione, « are an extremely quiet, sensible and hardworking people, rich in domestic virtues. A moral and hardworking people is *ipso facto* fit for self-government. An independent administration, if it was granted to this fine Slavonian race, would set free forces that would soon do much for material and for moral civilization; and ecclesiastical self-government, partially introduced, would serve them as a school for political self-government »[92].

---

[91] CBSG, pp. 434-435.
[92] *Ibid.*, p. 419.

INDEX OF PERSONAL NAMES

TOPICAL INDEX

CONTENTS

DATE DUE

GAYLORD

PRINTED IN U.S.A.